H<u>ome</u> S<u>chool</u>:
Taking The First Step

H<u>ome</u> S<u>chool</u>:
Taking the First Step

a program planning handbook

by

Borg Hendrickson

Mountain Meadow Press

Home School: Taking the First Step

by Borg Hendrickson

Published by   Mountain Meadow Press
                 Box 447
                 Kooskia, Idaho 83539

First Printing 1989
Printed in the United States of America

Library of Congress Catalog Card Number 88-090625
ISBN 0-945519-08-7

Table of Contents

Note: All names used herein as examples are fictitious. Feminine and masculine references are intermixed with no bias intended. Interpretations of statutes are those of a layman and do not constitute legal advice.

Acknowledgment

Special thanks to the many
home educators throughout
the United States whose
survey and telephone interview
responses provided useful
information for this book.

Dedicated to
the public school children
who called me Ms. Borg
and who taught me
that children do not belong
in public schools.

Choice

Tall, hulky, but not athletic. A doughy sort of hulkiness. Andy wore gabardine pants with white tube socs and oxfords in an era of blue jeans and tennis shoes. He wore a brown corduroy jacket with a dingy, simulated fur collar, the hem and sleeves too short. Bulging out of his sleeves, his forearms dangled, exposed. He looked ignorant. His brown eyes hung expressionlessly under droopy lashes, and he stood or sat, silent, still, sometimes leaning slightly as if he might keel over. Yes, he looked ignorant, but his IQ? 140.

Andy was about to graduate from high school, a virtual nobody amongst his peers, his teachers, his community . . . an unaccomplished boy . . . his brilliance blackened by lack of notice, lack of individual attention to his talents and needs, lack of academic and emotional nurturing. No one had intended to turn Andy into a nobody; it was simply that he'd been run through the system, the complex, striving but struggling, misshapen system called "public school." While the system hadn't tried to fail Andy, it had failed him. He'd been crushed in the cogs, permanently crippled, endlessly unfulfilled.

Despite the good efforts of many skilled educators and even the meager effort of those not so skilled, the American public school system misses the mark all too often. Andy exists in multiple numbers — some of high intelligence, some of low, and even some of average intelligence, regardless of public education's egalitarian, middle-of-the-road attempts to teach to the average.

We don't need to lay blame. We don't need to rage with anger. We could attempt systemic reform, join the public school reform movement, but the system is truly not likely to be satisfactorily repaired . . . . . . and in the meantime your child is growing, becoming an older and older learner, until his time with "school" will be gone. Yes, you need to deal now with " in the meantime." Doing so requires choice.

How will you educate your child?

I am a former public school educator — a total of seventeen years, kindergarten through college, including teacher and teacher aide training. While I strove diligently to teach well myself, never during those seventeen years did I not question the efficacy of public schools. I continuously grappled with the mammoth, unwieldy system that public education is, became depressed at times with the stranglehold the system often administered to children's curiosity, creativity, thinking, and sense of well-being. I taught alongside many excellent teachers who managed in their own corners of the school building to fashion as many miracles as they could — despite the system. However, I also taught alongside several of the dregs of the teaching vocation. They outstayed me, incidentally, and are still there. Their perpetual presence and the overpowering dominance of the colossus that the education system has become drove me away from the public schools.

During most of my years as a public school educator, home school was a barely mentioned anomaly and the reality of home schooling as remote as a rhodora in an untouched wilderness. I had always home schooled my daughter, I realize now — evenings, weekends, summers — reading, writing, gardening, health, values, and so on, but I had not become aware of home schooling *per se.*

Then one year my brother and his family returned to Idaho to begin a ministry and to establish a Christian school. His small school was in many respects a home school. While I didn't agree with all of his teaching methods, I could see that he, his wife, and his three children supped on academic nourishment within a close and supportive family environment. The family was the educational setting. Because learning was so integral to family life, wherever the family went, along tagged learning.

I was impressed. I began to read about home schooling. Andy roamed through my thoughts as I read. Many Andys. Gradually, home schooling emerged in my mind as the best educational alternative for parents who truly intend to make a wise choice for their children's education. Thus were planted the seeds of this book. Home-school parents, I recognized, need to design educational programs that will provide a fine education for their children and also be acceptable to public school officials. I realized, too, that with my public school background I could help home schoolers design quality programs . . . without turning their home schools into public school clones. Providing that help is the intention of this book.

Home School: Taking the First Step is a book for parents who have elected to home school for many diverse reasons. My brother's reason was religious, a reason shared by a majority of home educators today. However, thousands of additional parents teach their children at home for other reasons. These parents also need guidance as they set out to establish effective learning environments at home.

Yes, the reasons are numerous. The benefits and rich rewards experienced by home-schooling families are likewise numerous and are noted throughout this book. But we must admit at the same time that difficulties don't entirely hide from home schoolers. Be fore-warned, for example, that home schooling isn't for the lazy. Also, at the beginning, personal uncertainty may tug at you. You may fear causing your children educational harm. Questions about legalities, materials, methods, and programs may fill your mind. You and your children may at first not feel entirely comfortable with each other as learners and teacher(s). Pressure from family and friends who think home schooling constitutes child neglect may nudge at your con-science. Almost inevitably you will have to deal with some of these difficulties. However, I believe the strength of your commitment to home schooling will grow as you read this book and other books about home schooling and as you talk with practicing home school-ers. *Home School: Taking the First Step*, for starters, is chock full of confidence-builders. It shows you explicitly how to proceed. As you do begin, however, there are a few key personal characteristics you should nurture within yourself.

First, naturalness. Home schooling, you'll discover, is a much more natural process than one may expect. Have you taught your toddlers to make a peanut butter sandwich? Have you taught your daughter to sew on a button? Read to your youngsters regularly? Gardened with them? Taught your son to ride a bike? Pointed out sights, sounds, fragrances, textures, and flavors in your children's world? All such interactions with your children just happen natural-ly, but they are home schooling. To officially home school you needn't propel your family into a lofty world of educational space. That, in fact, is one of the things you'll be avoiding — that other world, that world of school. Instead you can keep your children at home or bring them back home to their world, your world, and there you can avoid school-space, so you can truly, naturally teach and they learn.

Patience is a second key characteristic. Establishing a home school takes time. Learning takes time. Success takes time. Accumulating results takes time. Improved relationships with your children may take time. Caution yourself not to rush back to public school or point fingers of impatience at yourself before your home school has been carefully rooted, watered, and given ample time to flower.

Third, flexibility. Decisions won't light like butterflies onto your shoulder. You will have to study your options, argue the pros and cons of various possibilities, be open to various routes, be willing to alter your direction, listen to your children, and deal with your daily doses of home-schooling quandaries.

Fourth, participation. Heeding research which shows that parent involvement is vital to student success, public school personnel have lately invited parent participation. This is a positive step. However, in view of the research, we should recognize that to send children into the institution of public education in the first place is counteractive to that research. Parent participation is instantly diminished once the child walks out the front door to board the bus that will take him to school. Home school offers an extraordinary opportunity for parent participation in a child's education. And perhaps nothing could be more supportive of your child's learning efforts than your close and constant participation in those efforts.

Lastly, faith. You *can* home teach. Have faith in yourself. If you're feeling confused or burned out at any point, seek support and counsel — from your spouse, a fellow home schooler, a support group, a friend, God. You can home teach.

May I give you your first measure of support? Section One in this book will answer many of your initial questions and lead you to other resources for further answers. Sections Two and Three, the heart of this book, will show you how to plan your home school in a manner that will provide you with a sound beginning as a home teacher and that will most likely prove acceptable to public school officials. Sections Four, Five and Six offer information about legalities, support groups and services, and resources. The three appendices discuss teaching methods or approaches, effective teaching, and the lesson plan. Finally, a glossary defines a roster of educational terms you may need to understand.

I wish you and your family well . . . as you take your first step towards home schooling and throughout the duration of your joint educational journey.

Borg Hendrickson

✱✱✱

Home-Schooling Questions and Answers

Questions and Answers

Like most potential home schoolers, you no doubt have many questions about home schooling. Some of your questions will be answered by your state's laws or established procedures. Others will best be answered by already practicing home schoolers. Many will only be answered via the immersion process once you actually start home schooling. To begin, however, Home School: Taking the First Step provides many answers, much in the form of step-by-step procedures you can follow to become a home schooler. First, however, let's address a few broad-view questions, questions frequently asked by parents preparing to take the first step to home school.

1. Is Home Schooling Legal?

A. Courts and state legislatures have warranted the possibility of home schooling in all the individual states. While the states have been granted the right and responsibility to see to the education of their citizens, a number of court cases have established that states may not limit school attendance to public schools. Nevertheless, there is no question that the states do have the power to reasonably regulate, inspect, and supervise schools. Your home school may be one of those "schools." Your state's education officials flex the muscles of educational authority in their own fashion and to whatever degree your state's legislators have decreed. As you read through Section Four of this book, "State Regulations and Procedures," you will get a sense of the degree of legal rigidity or flexibility your state allows with respect to home schools. Then, once you send for a copy of your state's requirements and consult with other home schoolers in your area, you'll begin to understand how your state school officials, and even local school officials, operate in their dealings with home-schooling parents. You'll find that home schooling is an option, but that some requirements and/or limitations may exist.

B. All states have compulsory education laws which require parents to see that youngsters of designated ages are schooled. In a few states laws apply almost no restrictions and requirements to home schoolers, but before you *silently* home school your children, check on your state's laws and confer with practicing home schoolers. Know the consequences of ignoring compulsory education laws. You may decide to take the risk, but at least you will have made an informed choice.

C. As you study your state's home-school requirements and compulsory education laws, beginning with the legal information for your state provided in this book, look for the answers to questions such as the following:

1. How is *home school* defined by my state?

2. Who may home school in my state?

3. How old can my children be before I must submit their names as home-schooled children?

4. Who has jurisdiction over home schools in my state? Who supervises home schools in my state and school district?

5. How many hours and days must my home school be "in session" each year?

6. What courses must I teach?

7. Do I need a curriculum of my own? Do I need to write out lesson plans? Do I need a list of materials and resources that I plan to use?

8. Must my children take standardized achievement tests?

9. What records should I keep?

10. Is there a formal home-school approval process that I must follow in order to legally establish my home school? Are there deadlines related to that approval process?

For now, just let these questions serve as food for thought while you read on. Sections Two and Three in this book take you step-by-step through planning processes that enable you to find and use the answers to all the above ten questions and much more. Also, Section Four provides you with answers to many of your legal questions.

D. New legislation is enacted and new court cases are processed periodically which result in changes in the legal picture of home schooling in individual states. Home schoolers not only remain alert to these changes, many home schoolers choose to affect the direction and impact of those changes through their own monitoring of legislative activities and lobbying of legislators. In the planning stages, however, you will want to concentrate on accurately informing yourself with up-to-date legal information. Section Two describes means for doing so.

2. Must I deal with my local school board and school administrators? If so, how can I work successfully with them?

A. Although in a few states home schoolers submit documents directly to state boards and state departments of education, in most states home schoolers need to deal in some manner with local school boards and school administrators — in a few cases, even if the home-schooled students have become satellite students of private schools or religious schools or have enrolled in correspondence schools. In fact, in some states, all home school issues and proceedings will be handled locally. But don't be dismayed. Identify with whom you will need to interact; then find out as much as you can about them; ask established home schoolers in your school district for suggestions and support; know the education laws in your state; be exceptionally well prepared as per the procedures outlined in Sections Two and Three of this book; program yourself to be firmly, persistently, but calmly diplomatic; and forge ahead looking forward to your board's approval.

B. The more amicable your relationship with local school officials, the better, for you may wish to *use* your public school in various ways during your home-school year — science lab privileges, sports or other extracurricular activity participation by your children, use of audio visual materials and equipment, academic consultation with school staff, and so on — and you may need board approval to do so. In other words, realize the rewards to yourself and your children in maintaining from the outset the best possible relationship with your local school board and school personnel.

C. When dealing with your local school board and staff, remember that they are likely to know little or nothing about home schooling. This means that you must provide them with pertinent information. If you follow the planning procedure outlined in Section Two, you should have that pertinent information. You should be prepared, for example, to present your state's compulsory education laws and any home-schooling laws, plus rules and regulations that have been adopted for the "reasonable regulation" of home schools. Then, of course, you need to demonstrate that you are complying with the laws and regulations — as you will be if you complete your planning as outlined in Sections Two and Three with adaptations for your state's requirements.

D. Some school board members and superintendents may not only know little about statutes and procedures related to home schooling, they may harbor negative attitudes towards home schoolers based partly upon the board members' lack of knowledge. You may face school personnel who are initially hostile, or who consider you a threat to the institution they support with much time and energy, or who think you are a crazy person for being radical enough to home school. Realize, too, that school personnel power structures vary with respect to decision making. Often the superintendent's recommendations sway all decisions and he, therefore, may be the key person with whom you will deal. During exchanges with school personnel consistently present yourself calmly, diplomatically and knowledgeably. Present as thorough a home-school proposal as possible, making sure that it complies fully with your state's requirements. In other words, appear serious, sensible, and nonthreatening, yet confident in your knowledge of procedures and in the quality of your proposal and determined in your intention to home teach. The procedures outlined in this book will help you gain such confidence and determination.

E. You may wish to point out several of the research studies that have been conducted which show that home-schooled children fare very well in comparison with their public school peer group. The following are a few samplings and sources of such findings:

Hewitt Research Foundation — Stanford and Iowa Achievement Test scores from 75th percentile to 95th percentile achieved by several thousand home-schooled children across the country.

Weaver, Roy et. al., "Home Tutorials vs. Public Schools in Los Angeles," *Phi Delta Kappan*, December 1980, p. 254-255. — Home-tutored children scored higher on standardized achievement tests than did their peers in the Los Angeles public schools and also made significant gains in maturation and social growth.

Gordon, Edward, "Home Tutoring Programs Gain Respectability," *Phi Delta Kappan*, February 1983, p. 398-399. — A majority of 2000 home-schooled children from various backgrounds achieved notable academic, attitudinal, and motivational progress.

Living Heritage Academy — Achievement test scores averaging 72nd percentile (grade-equivalent gains of 1.4) during each home-school year were earned by several hundred home-schooled students in Texas.

Arizona Department of Education — Home-schooled children scored at above average levels on standardized achievement tests in the mid-1980's.

Alaska Department of Education — During the first half of the 1980's home-schooled children consistently outscored their public school peer groups on standardized achievement tests.

Duncan, Verne, Oregon Department of Education — 76.1% of Oregon's home-schooled students scored above average on achievement tests in 1986.

Wartes, John, Woodinville, Washington — A 1987 comparison of Western Washington home-schooled students' achievement test scores with national norms showed that, with the exception of grade 1 math scores at the 49th percentile, the home-schooled students at each grade level scored above the 50th percentile in all subjects.

Tennessee Department of Education — In 1986, home-schooled students in grades 2,3,6 and 8 outscored public school students consistently. In national comparisons, the home-schooled students scored in the top 3% in math, top 4% in spelling, top 1% in listening skills, and top 6% in environmental knowledge.

Washington Public Instruction Department — Documentation showing across the board higher performance by home-schooled students over public school students.

Additional research results are available. If you would like to study them in greater depth, you may wish to write to the Hewitt-Research Foundation for their "research packet," and send for the following three bibliographies: "The Evidence Continues to Grow, Parent Involvement Improves Student Achievement" from the National Committee for Citizens in Education; Thomas Hughes' "Home Education: A Bibliography" from the University of Colorado; and Brian Ray's "Home Centered Learning Annotated Bibliography" from Seattle Pacific University. You may further want to begin saving news clippings and notes regarding the many studies and test results that demonstrate the academic failings of public schools. Be cautious, however, of using the latter to launch an attack on public schools in general or on your local school district. Attacks typically do not result in cooperation, but rather in conflict.

F. If your initial investigations into the status of home schooling in your state suggest you may encounter opposition from school officials, you may choose to consult a lawyer or join the Home School Legal Defense Association before making any contact with school officials.

G. Once you have carefully informed yourself of the home-school laws in your state and made initial contact with school officials, you will want to remain available for communications with them. If their posture appears positive, feel free to openly communicate over the phone, in person, and by mail. If, on the other hand, you discover that their attitude is skeptical or negative, you may want to limit communications as much as possible to mail. Why? First, when you know antagonism exists, comfort comes with fewer face-to-face encounters. Second, offhand remarks are less likely to occur in writing. Third, strong emotional reactions on either side will be given time to mellow before responses are sent. And fourth, you will have written documentation of all exchanges, proposals, agreements, deadlines, and so on. If phone calls come, be unerringly polite, but insist that comments, promises, and requests be committed to writing and sent to you for your careful consideration and response. If face-to-face meetings are unavoidable, and if they take on negative tones, remain objective, rely on your own well-researched information, be *professional*, and amicably leave at a propitious moment. Visibly take notes while there, request just before you leave that the school personnel with whom you've been talking write out their statements and send them to you. If their doing so seems unlikely, summarize their comments by reading aloud to them your notes. Tell them you'll respond soon. Then calmly leave. To confirm your understanding of the exchange, you may wish to type your notes, date them, list persons present, and send a copy to each person who was present.

But do remain thereafter available for communication. Being evasive at this point may arouse suspicion and further ire. Retreat, consult with other home schoolers and a lawyer if need be, restudy the statutes and procedures, recognize the true legal limits of the school officials' authority to determine if they have overstepped their bounds, and prepare your response. Avoid responding with more than what is needed if antagonism is present. Just prepare what you are legally obligated to prepare in response. You may even choose to completely ignore other areas for which they request information or action. You want to avoid confrontations over issues that simply muddy the waters, that are not legally issues that school personnel in your district have a right to address. Politely acknowledge their concern over such issues, but avoid commenting in response.

H. Relax. Only a very small percentage of the home schoolers in our country are pushed by local school boards and administrators into court. Most issues can be and are resolved through persistent nonjudicial communication. Also, many school personnel today are becoming more and more open to, even favorable towards, home schoolers. One aim of Home School: Taking the First Step is to enable you to present so impressive a home-school plan that school personnel will not just be favorable, but highly agreeable and even highly cooperative.

3. What are my options if I'm not legally qualified to home teach?

A. In almost all states certification of home-school teachers is not mandatory. Check the "Basic Information Chart" in Section Four of this book for your state's specifications regarding certification.

B. If yours is one of the few states in which home-school teachers must be certified, consider other alternative schooling options: enrolling your child in a church school or other private school, correspondence school, or community alternative school; attaching your home school as a satellite to a private school; becoming a single-family private or religious school if allowed in your state; arranging for a certified person in your community to do the home teaching (for the most part); enrolling your child as an extension student with a public school; moving to a state which does not require that you be certified. Please note also that many states are quite liberal with religious-conflict exemptions from adherence to public school regulations, including certification requirements. (Ironic, isn't it, that in our country we are allowed conscientious objection to two institutions: war and the public schools.) If you feel particularly energetic, you may want to join with other parents to start your own multi-family private or church school. (Read Robert Love's *How to Start Your Own School*, a couple issues of the *National Coalition News* or a copy of the "National Directory of Alternative Schools" published by the National Coalition of Alternative Community Schools, or portions of Allen Graubard's *Free the Children*) Perhaps you or your spouse works for a company that would be willing to create a quality, private "company school" for the children of its employees. You might try the certified teacher-consultant-supervisor option, if it is allowed in your state. In any case, read carefully through the information sent to you by your state department — upon your request — to determine which option will be the most feasible in your state.

C. In every state you will find home-school support groups. Contact them to ask about alternatives for noncertified or legally nonqualified parent teachers. See Section Five for a list of home-school groups in your state or region.

D. Consider taking the National Teacher Exam or any teachers' exam given in your state in order to verify your literacy. Fear not . . . these exams test *basic* skills knowledge. Also, if you pass, check your state's statistics on the scores of persons in your state who have taken the test. You'll find failures! In some states, many failures. However, regardless of low scores, some of those who failed may be teaching in the public schools. In fact, certification is granted in some states to applicants who score at the 50th percentile. This information could provide good ammunition in a battle to prove your qualifications.

E. If even *you* doubt the effectiveness of home schoolers who are noncertified, consider the impressive results of the studies noted in question *2, e.* About 80 percent of the parents who home taught those children included in the studies were not certified and most did not have college degrees.

F. If yours is a state which requires certification or maintains other restrictive teacher qualification requirements, perhaps you and others would like to challenge those requirements in court. Read *Phi Delta Kappan,* June 1986, "Emergency Certificates, Misassignment of Teachers, and Other 'Dirty Little Secrets'" by Robert A. Roth for a stunning rundown of public school staffing practices that indirectly lends support to noncertified and nonqualified home educators. Locate and read home-school studies, such as those noted in answer *2, e* above. You may also wish to contact the Home School Legal Defense Association in Virginia before engaging in any interactions with officials. (Address under <u>Virginia</u> in Section Five.) Also, from time to time some of the home-school periodicals list lawyers friendly to home schooling.

G. As noted earlier, in response to certification and other qualification requirements, some parents opt to *silently* home teach their children. As a last resort — are you one of them?

4. Will my home-schooled children be too isolated? Don't they need socializing?

A. Since you are already concerned about your children's socialization, it is likely that you will see to it that they are not too isolated. And, yes, they do need socializing, but . . .

B. Who says socializing is the exclusive territory of peers? Children need various kinds of socializing: with relatives — young, old, and in-between; with neighbors and friends — young, old, and in-between; with your entire immediate family (perhaps most important, yet most neglected); and *sometimes* exclusively with peers. Public school children, who interact almost entirely with peers, become what has been termed "peer dependent," a state of dependency into which I doubt you want your children to sink — unless, of course, you'd like your children's choices of clothing, hairdos, readings, activities, values, behaviors, and more, dictated by their peer group.

C. According to *The Random House College Dictionary* (N.Y.: Random House, 1973), the term *socialize* means "make fit for life in companionship with others." Have you visited a public school playground lately or spent a day eavesdropping on public school children's conversations? My 20 years of on-the-scene observations confirm that children in public schools learn (every day, every year) that "companionship with others" involves bullying, gossiping, ostracizing, competing, fist-fighting, humiliating . . . how lengthy a list I could write (and some involve the teachers as well as the children). Then consider a few statistics: During the 1987-1988 school year 2000 weapons, 150 of them guns, were found on students in our public schools. And how many, we wonder, were not found? Every month over 250,000 students and 5000 teachers are assaulted by students on school premises, and approximately 2.4 million students are robbed. Drugs of various degrees of potency are routinely available in virtually every public school in the nation. You can imagine what happens *within* a child as he becomes "fit for life in companionship" with other public school children. How *fit* do you want *your* children to be?

D. Nonetheless, your child does need some socialization with other children. You can arrange for that and yet maintain more control over your child's socialization experiences than public school teachers are able to provide. Conflicts will surely arise even in carefully selected peer situations, and you won't want to overprotect, but for your home-schooled child you can at the least minimize the indoctrination effect. Arrange and/or encourage your child's involvement in youth group activities — and be involved yourself at times too. Sports activities, musical groups, church groups, nature clubs, arts and crafts workshops, Scouts, community drama groups, neighborhood kids' activities, kiddie parades, youth roller-skating or ice skating, children's reading clubs, storytime at the local library, and so on, are often potential socialization opportunities in even the smallest of American towns. If few are available, perhaps you and another parent or two could organize some. Many home-school parents and kids join each other for regular fun days, field trip days, or craft days. Taking your child to a public park at times when other children are typically there is another option. Also, public schools offer special kids' activities in which your child may be able to participate. As noted under question 2, if your relationship with your local school board and with school administrators is friendly, you may be able to use the local schools in this way. Explore possible participation for your child in school band or choir, science fairs, sports teams, etc., if you and your child are interested in such activities that the public school offers. Sometimes special classes are offered by local organizations, such as the YMCA or craft associations, or by local alternative schools, classes which may fit into a home-school student's schedule and bring him in contact with other learners.

E. Socialization can also take place within your child's learning community. You need not teach your child alone. Instead, develop for him a learning community — an elder who share-teaches a craft with him or shares stories of old with him, community service folks who involve your child in their service work, neighbors with whom he can exchange favors (such as errands or chores), team experiences with other children and with adults, pen pals, a librarian who accepts his volunteer help in a library, a younger child to whom he can read, customers who buy his small business products or services (such as a neighborhood kids' newspaper, vegetables for sale, a neighborhood yard-garbage clean-up service, or a vacation dog-watching service), a music instructor, a dance instructor and fellow dancers, an older person with whom he simply likes to visit a lot, an expert who visits your home to "teach" a day's lesson, a practitioner with whom he could be an apprentice, anyone with whom your child shares learning or from whom your child learns.

F. Read together and discuss together biographies of people who have contributed significantly to or exhibited sensitivity to the welfare of the community, of human society globally, and of the environment.

G. Play *cooperative* games with your children. You can turn many board games and outdoor games into activities in which players help each other reach a common goal. Begin by sending for a copy of the Animal Town Game Company catalog and the Family Pastimes catalog for good selections of cooperative games. (See addresses and details in Section Six materials list.) These catalogs may also stimulate your thinking so that you might develop cooperative games of your own. To help yourself along, you may wish to read the *Parents Magazine*, April 1988, article "Everybody Wins" which discusses and gives examples of cooperative games or one of the following books about cooperative games: *The Cooperative Sports and Games Book* or *The Second Cooperative Sports and Games Book* both by Terry Orlick; or *The New Games Book* edited by Andrew Fluegelman.

H. Contrary to the opinions of many public educators, your child's positive sense of self may improve in your home-school social setting, rather than diminish. During a 1986 study of 224 home-schooled children, John Wesley Taylor V found that home-schooled children scored at or above the 91st percentile mark on the Piers-Harris Children's Self-Concept Scale, a measure of self-esteem. Only 10 percent scored below the national average. According to another study, public school children lose their sense of self-worth dramatically as they progress through the grades — from 80% with a strong sense of self-worth at school entrance dropping to 20% by fifth grade and to 5% at twelfth grade. Several of Raymond Moore's publications elaborate on the significance of home schooling in the development of a sound self-concept. (Moore's publications are available from Hewitt-Moore Research Foundation of Washington State. See Section Five "Support Services" for the Hewitt-Moore address.)

I. If you are living in a physically remote location, you do have a more unique situation with regards to isolation and socialization. Activity may be the key; i.e., staying active with a wide variety of home projects. And you can be a model for your children as a person who enthusiastically pursues her own interests. Pen pals and phone pals is another possibility, or even CB or ham radio friendships. Also in this case, reading about others who have lived and worked in isolation may provide models for such a lifestyle. You might try stories of the lives of zoological researchers, archaeologists, anthropologists, and adventurers, for example. Lastly, if possible, you could invite visitors, perhaps other children, to stay with you to work on a particular week's project or arrange for a sibling exchange with a family who lives elsewhere. Your children could trade brothers and sisters with children from another family for a few day's time.

J. Finally, consider the results of a study done during the sixties by Dr. Harold G. McCurdy of the University of North Carolina. Dr. McCurdy sought information about the childhood lives of twenty historical geniuses in order to derive common factors in their upbringing. He discovered three such factors: 1) "a high degree of attention focused upon the child by parents and other adults, expressed in intensive educational measures, ... and usually abundant love;" 2) "isolation from other children, especially outside the family;" and 3) "a rich efflorescence of fantasy, as a reaction to the two preceding conditions." ("The Childhood Pattern of Genius." *Horizons*, May 1960) You need not have genius expectations for your child, and socialization with peers is without doubt beneficial to some extent; nevertheless, isolation or a lack of socialization for your home-schooled child can be dealt with and aspects of isolation combined with abundant attention and love from you may prove beneficial.

5. What if my child is "exceptional?"

A. Take heart. In many states, special exemptions from compulsory education laws are allowed for exceptional children. You may find the route *home* simpler with your exceptional learner. Write your state department for copies of the laws and regulations. Check information from home-school support groups.

B. Be wary of labels that public schools may have placed upon your child. *Learning disabled*, for example, has become overused (i.e., unjustifiably used in some cases), according to an abundance of research. There are even cases in which students identified as learning disabled were upon further study found to be intellectually gifted! There are, of course, learner labels based upon true individual learner characteristics and there are test results that do indeed establish exceptionality. A child's being severely mentally retarded, for example, may be unquestionable. Generally, however, be skeptical of labels applied to kids by educators. If you have a child labeled "learning disabled," you may wish to read Gerald Cole's *The Learning Mystique: A Critical Look at Learning Disabilities.*

C. If your child truly does learn slowly, according to your own observations as well as other information, then home teaching is almost without exception going to be highly beneficial to your child. You will be able to provide him with an approach that suits his pace, with loads of individual attention, with methods that are particularly matched to his learning style, with a noncompetitive setting, with much needed motivational feedback, and with desperately needed love and acceptance. If he has been attending public school, it is possible, even probable, that none of the above have been provided. Recent efforts to curb the numbers of students who attend special education classes in public schools and to place them instead in regular classrooms are not likely to alter this fact. Such a move may, in fact, exacerbate the problems of the slower child and provide all the more reason for you to remove your exceptional child from public school.

D. A 1986 study by the Appalachia Educational Laboratory and the Kentucky Education Association, involving public teacher responses to a survey covering methods of teaching marginal learners, resulted in several recommendations. Among the most frequently noted successful methods were 1) a reinforcing atmosphere, 2) wide use of community facilities and resource personnel, and 3) designing instruction for individual students. (From "Tips for Teaching Marginal Learners" published by the AEL and the KEA.) I think you'll agree that these tried and proven methods can much more satisfactorily and easily be practiced at home school than at public school.

E. If you have a special education child and you are interested in learning more about learning handicaps you may wish to contact the Council for Exceptional Children, the Association for Children and Adults with Learning Disabilities, and the National Committee for Citizens in Education, all of whom offer publications related to the education of children with learning handicaps. (Addresses in Section Five – PA, VA, MD.) You may also want to review copies of *The Exceptional Parent* magazine. (Address in Section Six.)

F. Studies have demonstrated that exceptional children on the lower end of the academic spectrum fare much better on tests when the administrator of the test is a familiar person. In view of this, do all that you can to insist that you, your spouse, or a certified-teacher friend of your child give your child achievement tests or other necessary tests, either before or after your child has been labeled "exceptional."

G. If your child is gifted or talented, sending him to public school may constitute, educationally, the metaphorical kiss of death. Home schooling may indeed save his most precious of assets: his exceptional ability and his love of learning. Home schooling may literally save the *life* of his thinking and creativity. Need I say more? (Also, see the National Association for Gifted Children, the Council for Exceptional Children and the *Gifted Child Quarterly* and *Gifted Child Today* magazine listings in Section Six.)

6. If I decide to home school, how can I find out more about child growth and development and its relationship to education?

A. Observe children. Watch your own children and others; take mental or written notes as you do so. Those older than your child may provide clues to the next stages in your child's growth. Watch for changing styles and attitudes involved in your children's interactions with other people, young and old. Especially watch for those areas of life on earth that interest and enthuse your children. You'll be gaining ideas for areas of study to include in future lessons for your children. Equally important clues can be gained from noting the length of your children's attention spans and the level of action in their activities. You'll discover, for example, that attention spans grow with age, and that typically a higher amount of action will be an important element in the lessons of the youngest of your children, or at least alternated periods of active and quiet activity. Using information such as this, you can develop home-school lessons and activities that will involve appropriate time spans and action levels.

B. Go to the public library and to nearby college libraries. You'll find both popular/informal and more technical books on the subject of child growth and development. Read enough to give yourself a feel for your child's upcoming growth stages and to derive ideas for home study methods and subjects that will appeal to your child at his current stage. Several of the available books about home schooling offer descriptions of young learners in action, providing readers with clues to childhood development. You may wish to read Raymond and Dorothy Moore's book *Home Grown Kids*, for example. (Also see "Readings" in Section Six.)

C. Read parents' magazines. *Children, Parents Magazine, Christian Parenting, Parenting* and *Mothering* are five possible choices. Likewise, read books on parenting, such as Wayne Dyer's *What Do You Really Want For Your Children?* and James Dobson's *Parenting Isn't For Cowards.*

D. Remember that children develop at individual paces according to organic time clocks and that at home school you'll want not to interrupt or try to reprogram your children's natural paces. Doing so is a serious public school flaw. For the sake of egalitarianism, public schools attempt to corral the varying developmental time clocks of children into single, age-mandated learning rates. Studying information about child growth and development will help you understand generally your children's stages, but always rely on your own observations to determine how your children individually fit into your findings.

E. Raymond Moore, a well-known home-school proponent, has written extensively about school readiness and unreadiness, as did John Holt, David Elkind, and several others. Moore points out that many studies, often ignored by public schools, indicate that we place youngsters in formal learning situations far too early and that home is the best environment for learning and socializing until a child is between 8 to 10 years old. If you are interested in learning more about school readiness, you may want to read Raymond Moore's *School Can Wait* and *Better Late than Early.* David Elkind's *Miseducation* also provides insights regarding child development and school readiness. These writers and others confirm for us what we may have suspected all along — forced learning is unhealthy and can result in deep frustration, lethargy, rebelliousness, and a lifelong aversion to schooling and to learning.

F. Check a college bookstore for books about human growth and development, books which are typically the texts for courses the college offers. Also check Christian and other bookstores.

G. If feasible, attend parenting workshops and/or participate in parent support groups. Check regional newspapers for possible announcements listing topics, times, and places. Check area college catalogs for parenting courses. Some home-school support organizations also offer parenting courses and workshops.

H. If you have serious concerns about your child's growth and development, make an appointment to see a pediatrician or youth counselor to discuss your concerns. Public school counselors or school psychologists may be helpful or lead you to other help. And often pastors and priests can offer suggestions for professional help. Don't wait. Frequently in public school classrooms serious concerns are dealt with through traditional and ongoing methods of maintaining control rather than through sincere, active attempts to *help* the child *now.* Avoid relying on such public school disciplinary means of dealing with serious behavioral problems. Remember, as you and I know, public school may be the *cause* of a child's developmental problems!

7. If I decide to home teach, how can I find out more about teaching methods that are supported by current research?

A. Go to a university library near you to find journals for educators in the specific fields of your interest. Although the presumption is that the readers of most of these journals are public school classroom teachers, usually the methods can easily be applied to teaching just one or two or three children at home. Also you can usually trust that the methods offered in these journals are based on up-to-date educational research, research which has become more and more reliable.

You'll find many, such as *The Reading Teacher* for elementary grade teachers of reading, *School Arts* and *Arts and Activities* for art and craft instruction, *Learning* and *Instructor* which include teaching ideas in varied subject areas, *The Computing Teacher* for computer activities and software reviews, *Journal of Reading* for secondary reading methods, and several others.

B. At university libraries and bookstores you'll also find dozens of books — many easily used by nonprofessionals — about teaching methods for virtually every subject. Look for the most comprehensive ones. You may find, for example, James Moffett and Betty Jane Wagner's book *Student-Centered Language Arts and Reading, K-13: A Handbook for Teachers*, a guide to the design of a language arts and reading curriculum.

C. Write to organizations, such as The National Wildlife Federation (address in Section Six), your local fish and game department, arts councils, health and safety organizations, literary groups, and so on, many of which frequently publish materials for use in teaching — materials typically more than sound with respect to teaching methodology.

D. Search for other books about home schooling; you'll find several revealing and wonderful depictions of fine teaching methods. For a beginning, try these:

> Nancy Wallace's *Better than School*, a well-written, insightful record of a family's home-schooling experiences beginning with their initial decision to home school and their proposal to the local school board.
>
> John Holt's *Teach Your Own*, home-school philosophies and how-tos; *What Do I Do Monday?* - philosophies, how-tos and math and reading sections.

21

Howard S. Rowland's *No More School*, an account of an American family's year of home schooling in Spain.

Theodore E. Wade's *The Home School Manual*, includes subject area teaching suggestions.

Mario Pagnoni's *The Complete Home Educator*, computer education methods.

Raymond and Dorothy Moore's *Home-Style Teaching*, home education in action.

Paul Copperman's *Taking Books to Heart; How to Develop a Love of Reading in Your Child*, a guide to reading sessions at home for parents of children 2 to 9.

Micki and David Colfax's *Homeschooling for Excellence*, home-schooling philosophies, experiences and methods of the Colfaxes whose sons were accepted by Harvard, Yale, and Princeton after being almost exclusively schooled at home.

E. Confer with experienced home schoolers regarding methods they have found successful. Those with whom I've spoken give foremost emphasis to the need for flexibility and to the importance of not copying public schools. You'll find many suggestions for teaching methods from other home schoolers in *Home Education Magazine*, *Growing Without Schooling*, *The Teaching Home*, *The Parent Educator and Family Report*, and other home school publications. (Addresses in Section Six.)

F. Make friends with a public school instructor who is an excellent teacher. (Avoid consulting other public school teachers.) The excellent teacher probably reads current research literature, takes courses in the application of that research, and practices applying that research in his classroom. Ask him for recommended readings or even a course you might take and perhaps for permission to observe him in action. One caution: watch and draw from the subject matter teaching methods, not the from the public school system in action. Inculcating yourself with public school classroom processes will likely lead to stifled teaching and learning at home. You won't want to duplicate public school methods *en masse*, just borrow a few subject area methods that work.

G. Read Appendix A, "Teaching Methods/Approaches" and Appendix B, "Effective Teaching" at the end of this book.

H. Do not ignore what your children themselves silently or verbally tell you about effective teaching methods. *Teaching methods* should not imply *imposition*. Children often know for themselves their own effective learning methods, and teaching methods should primarily be means by which parent teachers encourage and stimulate learning methods that work for children. Listen to your children's *methods*.

8. How can I be sure my children will be motivated to learn at home? I don't want to have to force them.

A. If your children have already attended public school, they may need a period of weaning from forced learning. Children are sometimes unmotivated to learn (or to be in any way productive)*because of* the methods used in public schools to make them learn and produce. While many attempts to motivate public school students involve enthusiasm and the genuine interests of children, others are negative in nature. Think about some of those negative methods: surveillance, coercion, regimentation, forced conformity, competitive pressure, punishments, and extrinsic rewards (letter grades, stickers, awards, privileges, parties, etc., external to the act of learning itself). Children first of all can become stressed by such methods. Also, they'll likely conclude that learning is supposed to be done, not because of their fascination with the world of knowledge nor because of their innate love of learning, but because some other person pressures them to learn and threatens punishments otherwise or because a reward is offered as the result of carrying out the act of learning. Pressures, punishments and extrinsic rewards — for something one just naturally loved to do as a toddler — often results in sadness, in a sense that something is askew, and in a lack of genuine self-motivation — even amongst the brightest of children. Many of the brightest just tolerate school while following their deepest learning passions outside of the classroom. Or they learn to vegetate. To tune out. Or to rebel. In fact, education researchers estimate that between 10 and 30 percent of all high school dropouts are intellectually gifted.

Research demonstrates that if the rewards are removed, the *extrinsic* ones, motivation will begin to emerge. Deep within, your children already naturally, organically love to learn. Let them *intrinsically* — inside themselves — feel the joy and excitement, because therein lay the true, natural, most highly motivating reward — and the most highly effective learning. Once you and they are able to rekindle that joy they were born with, motivation and learning for them will never cease. And you will have given them an exquisite lifelong gift.

B. You can in fact urge and feed that inner joy. Your children do seek your acknowledgement and approval of their learning efforts, and you can provide it in several ways. The most important way perhaps is offering your companionship in their efforts. Be close, be supportive, be facilitative, be physically and mentally involved with them as they learn. Take them and their efforts seriously. Respect those efforts. Encourage them to freely question. Help them find answers. Your involvement will demonstrate to your children that a love of learning is one of your values and joys. You will be modeling. You will be nurturing.

C. There are also verbal means to encourage motivation. Acknowledgement, for example, can be extended verbally. For instance, you should frequently comment on specifically what it is you like in the work your children do. Not, "That's a nice story," but "I love that funny, clever clown in your story! His antics are described in such fine detail." Or more objectively, "You were trying to draw a pattern for your new toy box. But you fear the pieces still don't fit quite right. Do you want to remeasure and adjust them?" Such acknowledgement statements confirm the learner's efforts. They don't steal away the learner's intrinsic motivation to continue. Train yourself to use them.

Also, let your child own his own achievements. Not, "I'm so proud of how colorful your picture is." Instead, "You must feel mighty proud of how colorful your picture is." Or, "You sure can feel satisfied with the towers on your sand castle." Or, "I'll bet your tummy's growling for those vegies you're growing so well in your garden." Comments like these let the pride rest where it belongs, inside your child. And there it will lead to self-evaluation, self-motivation, and trust in oneself as a learner-doer.

D. Again, I urge you to read books like those already noted above that depict and describe home schooling. You'll see learner motivation at work. Also, confer with experienced home schoolers. This is always possible at least by telephone if you get in touch with a support group. (See Section Five.)

E. Finally, have faith in and patience with both you and your children. Especially if your children have previously attended public school, the motivation issue may be a problem during the days of transition to home schooling. Struggle with it, work with it, trust your intuitions. Read and reread items b. - d. above until they become ingrained aspects of your involvement in your children's learning. And look for ways of enmeshing more home and environment into your children's schooling, and less of *school* into their schooling.

9. Where will I find the materials I will need to teach my children at home?

A. All around you! One major deficiency of public school is that the environment in which we live and the *real* world of the child are most often left out. At home the world around you can provide you with a plethora of educational material. Life itself can become your children's educational medium. In public school the system is the medium and, as we well know, problems result.

How can you bring the real world into your home-school lessons? A few examples: To introduce a unit of study on simple machines to a group of fourth graders, I once hung on the wall for visual and tactile exploration common household and woodworking tools — a nail clipper, a curling iron (fulcrums and levers), a screw, a door wedge (inclined plane), etc. In this case real-life objects that were just lying about the house and garage were used to stir interest and lead into structured lessons. To enhance a unit of study on the life cycle of plants, you might help your children dig up and plant seedlings from your lilac hedge, or let your children plant your tulip bulbs, or root cuttings from a houseplant in a glass of water, or grow sprouts, or take *learning* tours through a local park or forest, or press and dry plants harvested from the outdoors at different stages in their growth. To study rural life versus town or city life, take *learning* trips to a farm, to a small town, to a metropolis. Work these items and places into your plans for each unit of study, so you have clearly in mind your children's learning goals as you guide them into and through the world around them. In fact, each time you begin to plan a unit of study, ask yourself what and how many real objects and places are available that you can work into your plans.

B. There are hundreds of materials suppliers throughout the U.S. Their names and addresses are listed in various home-schooling books and in the many home-school newsletters and periodicals. You'll discover many that supply materials for general use, others for specific subject areas only, others for particular educational philosophies or approaches, such as Bible-based education. Hundreds are both listed and annotated in three large resource books, Mary Pride's *The Big Book of Home Learning* and *The Next Book of Home Learning* and Donn Reed's *The First Home School Catalogue*. In addition, resources are often noted or reviewed in the major home-school magazines. To get started, however, look through the teaching materials portion of Section Six in this book where numerous and varied suppliers are listed.

Remember, too, that you needn't look at all available materials to get started; that would take weeks. But don't accept the first batch of materials that comes to your attention. Do look through enough to find those that suit your children's learning levels and learning styles, that offer potential for learning in gradually greater degrees of difficulty; each new body of knowledge and skills based upon earlier gained knowledge and skills, that will help you make learning fun and stimulating for your children, and, very importantly, that suit your teaching style. You want to find materials that not only include information you want to teach (your curriculum) but that feel right to you as a teacher — this will get easier once you've taught a bit and know how you like to teach. Be adventuresome; be flexible. If, for example, you are more comfortable with and more stimulated by teaching with manipulatives, realia, environmental items, etc., then look for manuals and texts that allow for the inclusion of lots of those items. A couple of good examples of teaching aids along these lines are the *Naturescope* teacher's manuals for science (National Wildlife Federation), and a couple of books with self-explanatory titles, *Art From Found Materials* by Mary Lou Stribling and *The Backyard Scientist* by Jane Hoffman. Also, consider journal writing based on outdoor experiences, teaching math with manipulatives (try Mary Baratta-Lorton's *Math Their Way*), creating real-life historical dramas, or building the Mayflower from a textbook picture (instead of just looking at the picture). If you are a teacher who feels most comfortable teaching with aids and texts such as these, you will feel stymied, frustrated, trapped, and bored with a prepackaged full-curriculum program that follows a similar method in all subject areas and/or that keeps you and your children sitting in your learning chairs all day. On the other hand, perhaps a blend of methods and materials is best for you.

At any rate, as you begin to look for teaching texts and manuals and aids, listen to your intuitions about those you could comfortably and enthusiastically use to teach and those that, in turn, would make learning most interesting to your children. Among the many teachers whom I have observed throughout the years, those who have been the most creative in selecting and inventing materials that suit their teaching styles and the most creative in designing lessons that use those materials . . . have without exception been the best teachers. You can be creative too.

C. Many Christian, alternative and other private schools offer materials to home schoolers, as do other cooperative services. Several such schools are listed in Section Six.

D. Your local school is also a potential source of materials. If you've established a friendly relationship with a local principal, ask him about the possibility of borrowing materials. Many of the public school teachers' manuals allow for flexibility, even encourage using the accompanying texts only as supplements, but few public school teachers actually do use texts selectively or do go much beyond the texts. Instead, the texts dominate and control most classroom activities. At home, you can go beyond . . . so public school texts aren't to be feared, just used selectively and creatively.

E. In several states curriculum guides and materials lists are available (usually for a fee) from the state department of education. Check the summary for your state in Section Four for the availability of guides and other materials. Curriculum guides are skeletons of the knowledge and skills a student will attempt to gain as he works through any course of study. Methods of teaching and materials used for teaching are sometimes recommended or suggested in guides, but usually not mandated. You can use some, reject some, add some, alter some. But, you may find a state curriculum guide helpful as a reference, especially if you feel unsure about designing an entire curriculum yourself in a particular subject area and in selecting materials all on your own.

F. University bookstores often shelve teaching materials useful to home schoolers, and Christian and other bookstores not only may have teaching materials and books full of teaching ideas, but may be able to order many for you if you supply the names of the titles you want. In large towns and cities you may be able to find a school supply store where all sorts of teaching supplies, from glue to textbooks, are available. And if you're looking for computer software, most large towns have computer stores. As you browse through the software offered by those stores, you might jot down names and addresses of the companies who make the software and write to ask for catalogs. In the company catalogs you are likely to find numerous programs unavailable locally. Also, software distributors from whom you can order at wholesale prices advertise in computer magazines. There are numerous software suppliers in the United States now and thousands of educational programs for computer use.

G. For materials in special interest areas, such as art, music, rock collecting, wild game biology, bird-watching, dancing, etc., ask local adults involved in those fields for recommendations and check with organizations related to those subjects.

H. Some of the organizations included in the support list in Section Five of this book offer instructional materials, and there are many other organizations that do so as well. Check with your local, regional and state home-school support organizations for suggestions. If you enroll your children as home-school satellite students of a Christian or other private school, you will probably be provided materials as well as full curriculums. Look them over carefully ahead of time to be sure they project your educational philosophies and suit your teaching style and your child's learning style. Also, be sure they allow the degree of flexibility you seek.

10. Having been home schooled for a period of months or years, will my child be able to enter or return to public education smoothly should I elect to send her?

A. Studies have shown that home-schooled children typically perform above national averages on achievement tests, as previously noted in question 2, e. In view of these studies, you probably needn't fear that your child won't compare well academically with public school children.

B. Your child may be required to take placement exams and her coursework may be reviewed for course verification by public school personnel as part of her admission into an accredited public school. If school personnel hesitate to acknowledge your child's home-school achievement and attempt to place your child below her academic level in public school, you may need to insist that placement exams be given. In any case, you will want to oversee this process yourself and give input regarding her placement. Have faith that you can have an influence in this matter. In fact, be determined to have an influence. Dr. Linwood Laughy's *The Interactive Parent: How to Help Your Child Survive and Succeed in the Public Schools* provides step-by-step guidance on how to remain in control of your child's education in public school. To learn how to thoroughly introduce yourself to your child's public school, you may wish to read the article "A,B,C, or F; Test Your Child's School," which appeared in *Parents Magazine*, November 1987 issue. Also, you may wish to contact the National Committee for Citizens in Education for information regarding parental rights and involvement in public schools.

C. Be sure you keep full and accurate records of your child's home-school attendance, work, materials, tests, etc., as delineated in Section Three. These records will provide evidence to a public school staff of the sequence and levels of your child's lessons and of her achievement.

D. Be aware that in public school your home-schooled child may stand out as unique in some ways from other children, perhaps especially in learning style and thinking capacity. Support these uniquenesses. They are not deficiencies; they are assets. They are in fact the stuff of which true learners are made. They are exactly those assets your home-schooling efforts can lovingly set out to nurture.

E. If you have socialized your child according to the suggestions given in question 4 above and in other ways you and she devise, she will likely socialize herself comfortably when she returns to public school. She will already have acquaintances among public school children and, perhaps, teachers, and may already be involved in activities with them. She will probably have interacted frequently with a variety of adults and will have gained skills that enable smooth, rewarding relationships with teachers as persons and as new members of her learning community. In addition, she will have acquired at home a strong set of values and views that will enable her to socialize at public school without loosing the *self* you have so lovingly helped her develop.

However, do keep tabs on this issue. As earlier acknowledged, public schools are not typically pleasant or particularly healthy places with regards to socialization. During your home-school years with your child, the two of you will have developed a close, trusting relationship; maintain that relationship when she enrolls in public school. You can learn to periodically check in with her emotional/psychological/social frame of mind and discuss with her any problems that evolve out of her public school social interactions.

F. Also, do be prepared for initial change anxiety. As anyone might, your child could experience a period of anxiety due to the process of change. You can attempt to ease the anxiety by introducing her ahead of time to the public school building and personnel or by becoming an observer or volunteer in her public school classroom. If you do enroll her in public school, frequently be a presence there, at least for the first few weeks.

G. Don't be surprised to find that the pace, regimen, crowding, and other organizational factors at public school cause the greatest anxiety and stress for your child when she enrolls. To ease her into the routine, explain and discuss with her ahead of time the pattern of public school days, the numbers of students in classrooms, the lessening of freedom and friendliness she may experience, and other such factors that you are aware of that are peculiar to the public school she will attend. Let her vent her frustrations with any of this and express her views and thoughts about how she can deal with these factors. A visit to the classroom and with the new teacher may help. Ask the teacher to describe the daily routine and to provide a small tour of the facility explaining how various locations in the building will relate to your child's daily life at public school.

H. Continue to provide opportunities for your child to interact with her home-school learning community even after she returns to public school. In this way, she will be comforted by the integration of the old into the new and not as likely develop a sense of estrangement. At this time, remember, too, that you, as her home-school teacher, should continue to be a part of her expanded learning community. Find hours to spend with her in the fashion that you and she spent them in home school.

11. If my child completes twelfth grade at our home school, will he be issued a diploma by the local school board or by the state board of education?

A. No. In a few states, *maybe.*

B. Before his senior year, encourage him to think about college choices if he is planning to attend college. Most colleges don't require a high school diploma; they are more concerned with SAT* or ACT* scores. However, if his college choice is one of those that does require a diploma, you probably will want to contact the college about obtaining a waiver to that entrance requirement, particularly if his SAT and/or ACT scores are high. A slight trend away from the use of SAT and ACT scores seems to be underway in some of the nation's colleges. However, those schools do look for hard evidence of other sorts — high school records, achievement test results, extracurricular projects and endeavors, and the like. With deliberateness, you can maintain and provide such written evidence of your child's home-school years. Otherwise you might consider having him attend the final semester of public school or accredited private school, provided all of his coursework is accepted, so that he can get a diploma from an accredited school. Along these lines, you might consider enrolling him as a satellite or correspondence student for his senior year with an accredited school. In this way he could earn a diploma, but remain at home for school. Another option for him at 18 years, or earlier upon local school recommendation, is the GED** exam. Check your state's regulations regarding when and under what circumstances the GED can be taken. If you've been able to establish good rapport with your school district personnel, you could ask the superintendent for a letter stating that your home-schooled child has completed the equivalent of a K-12 education, as a recommendation for taking the GED early. Enrolling in a community college would be another option since community colleges typically have only one entrance requirement: that the student be eighteen years of age. Then his community college credits could be transferred to a four-year institution should he elect to

---

*SAT and ACT are the Scholastic Aptitude Test and the American College Testing Service aptitude test, which are taken by many high school students nationwide as a prerequisite to college entrance. The tests measure verbal and mathematical skills and are considered predictive of college academic success.

**The GED exam is the General Education Development exam taken by nonmatriculated secondary students or adults who hope to earn a high enough score on the exam to be awarded a high school diploma by the state department of education.

transfer, and the effects of no high school diploma would be eliminated. Also, do check your state's home-schooling procedures; yours may be one of the few states that makes a diploma available.

C. You may have the same concerns regarding job applications if your child does not plan to attend college. Again, check your state's home-school diploma position. Please realize, too, that nothing stops you from giving him a diploma from home school. On job applications, in this case, he may state that yes he did graduate after twelve years of schooling — his school? — home school. He would want to be prepared to explain the depth of his home schooling and the skills he possesses, particularly those applicable to the job for which he is applying. Many employers, in fact, have begun to distrust the credibility of a public school diploma and look for actual *evidence* of academic ability. On the other hand, your child may wish to consider the GED exam. Be aware, however, that some employers will hesitate to hire a GED graduate, because the employer may suspect that the graduate was a high school dropout, and "dropout" has uncomplimentary associations for many employers. A small job experience record from your child's teen years and an impressive academic record will help. In any case, having no diploma is not an insurmountable obstacle and may turn out to be no obstacle at all. There are many many highly successful adults in our nation who entered the world of occupations and careers with no public school diploma.

D. When applying for college or a job, your young adult should be coached to interview well. Often, just letting the interviewer know who he is, what he has accomplished, what his goals are, how he feels about work, and so on, will open avenues. He can also have available to hand to the interviewer an outline of courses completed and projects undertaken during his secondary level home-school years; perhaps portfolios of polished home-school project samples; and letters of recommendation from former employers, customers (if he's run a small business), resource people with whom he's studied or worked. The problem, you see, for an employer or a college admissions officer is not that an applicant has been home schooled, but that the routine school documents aren't available. So what then should the officer or employer ask to see? Upon what evidence of competence should he base his decision about the applicant? The home-schooled job or college applicant needs to supply the answer to these questions — without being asked.

12. I wonder what my friends and relatives will say about our home schooling. How can I deal with social pressures from people who disapprove?

A. Smile. Yes, smile; then back that smile up with knowledge about the accomplishments and the frame of mind of home-schooled kids. Your own home-schooled children will eventually be your live evidence, but, as cited above, documented research results are available, too. Know those results. Use them. Shying away from doubters and doomsayers may only prolong the home-school mystery for them. Help them hear about home schooling and become acquainted with you as a home schooler.

B. Read regional and national home-school newsletters and magazines. Many times readers write in to share their responses to the nay-sayers in their lives, responses that may work for you too. Home schoolers have learned to be ready to point out that their children choose home education; that their children like having a loving parent who helps with math, reading, science, and other subjects; that their children benefit from not having to wait their turn in a class of twenty-five. They also help their children learn to respond to questions about home schooling.

C. Be convinced before you start home schooling that it is the best route to learning for your children. Make a list of your own complaints about your children's experiences in public schools, their reactions emotionally to public schools, and just about public schools in general. Read about the flaws of public schools, teachers, and administrators. You can read about them in dozens of books and articles and other publications. *Our Nation at Risk*, the first chapter of Holt's *Teach Your Own*, the first half of Laughy's *The Interactive Parent*, and any large town's daily newspaper are starters. Then look again to confirmation of home-schooling successes — in books noted earlier and in the research studies noted in question 2, *e.* By the time you've read just a few items, the deep seeds of becoming convinced will be planted. Once convinced, you will feel so sure about the fact that you are doing the best thing for your children by home schooling them that comments from other adults won't deter you. In fact, you may feel guilty at the thought of not home schooling them. You can convey that feeling to friends and relatives who question you, and you can tell them what you've read about public schools.

D. Establish your statement of reasons and rights as explained in Section Two ("Statement of Intent" item 5) and your educational philosophies and learning goals for your children as explained in Section Three ("Curriculum and Materials"). Recalling the great importance of your reasons, rights, philosophies, and goals may help you convey your convictions to others with calm confidence.

13. OK, I do want to take the first step towards home schooling — I want to plan my home school — but how do I truly know if I have what it takes to be a home-school teacher for my children?

A. Do you thoroughly enjoy being with your children, engaging in a variety of activities with them, working with them, teaching them crafts or hobbies or how to do household jobs, discussing many topics with them - topics of interest to them? Do you value your children's ideas? Are you generally patient with your children? Can you let your children find their own way without too much interference from you? Can you assist your children, rather than lead or push them? Do your children enjoy being with you? Are you and your children friends — or would you like to be friends? Do you have a desire to help your children grow in a truly supportive, friendly, peaceful atmosphere? Do you like the idea of one-on-one (or one-on-two or three) teaching for your children? If you can answer *yes* to most of these questions, you have reached first base in your assets for home teaching.

B. Are you a literate person? (A college degree is definitely not a necessity.) Do you enjoy learning? Do you like to think, question, analyze, and function independently? Are you competent; that is, are you able to take hold of new projects, follow them through persistently and accurately and thoroughly, and complete them? Do you enjoy books? Do you pursue knowledge in those areas that interest you? Do you enjoy sharing knowledge? Do you like hands-on and explorative learning as well as book learning? Mostly *yes* responses to this set of questions tell you you've reached second base.

C. Are you willing to learn more about home schooling by researching your state's school laws (not as difficult as you may think); reading a few books about home schooling; talking with established home schoolers; searching for home teaching/learning materials (fear not, as noted above, lots of help is available); and by planning well, very well, and yet allowing for flexibility for your home school? Yeses? Base three!

D. Are you determined? Are you willing to prepare your home-schooling plan or proposal so well that you will feel confident and determined when you approach school officials and/or when you start home teaching? (Preparing the proposal and facing school officials, if required, will probably be the most trying and the least joyful part of your entire home-schooling experience. After that, work, but joy!) Will your determination even extend into the area of demeanor when you face school officials; that is, can you be calmly diplomatic? And finally, are you willing to go to court if you must? This last is not necessarily a prerequisite to proceeding towards your home-school goal, but you may need to answer it for yourself at some point — you need to be aware of how far you are willing to go. Ask yourself, "How deep is my sadness about what has been or will be happening to my children in public school? How much do I value them and their education?" Are you determined to take them home for school? Have you reached **home** base?!

Congratulations if you did reach home base! Take a break, smile to yourself over the wonderful educational freedom you and your children will experience, read sections Two through Six ahead, and then begin work on your plan. *Bon voyage* !

If you didn't reach home base, read through the sets of questions again. Not every question needs a *yes* response, just most. (Home-school parents are fallible.) Look carefully at the questions to which you answered *no*. Have you underrated yourself? Or are there ways of reversing the answers through effort or endeavor on your part? Should you investigate the world of home schooling a bit further and then try the questions again? Perhaps, for example, by contacting a home-school support group in your area you could discuss issues that concern you with someone who is already home schooling. Maybe you could even visit a family during the act of home schooling. Locate books or magazine and news stories concerning home schooling, read them, and let them give you more of a feel for the experience. (Nancy Wallace's book *Better Than Schooling*, Howard Rowland's *No More School*, and an issue of *Growing Without Schooling*, *The Teaching Home* or *Home Education Magazine* would be fine first choices.) Perhaps you'll wish to consider the other options noted in question *3, e* above. However, if you found yourself short of home base, but still burning to home teach your children, I suspect you do have what it takes. I suspect you simply need to explore the matter further in order to discover that you can do it.

The above sets of questions and answers may make home teaching sound formidable. However, it truly is not. **Hundreds of thousands** of parents across our nation are happily home teaching. In fact, Alfie Kohn in the April 1988 issue of the *Atlantic Monthly* estimated that the number of home-schooled children in the United

States has grown to between 200,000 to 300,000 today, while Dr. Raymond Moore has estimated the figure is in excess of 500,000! Such figures suggest an obvious conclusion: home schooling is effective and pleasurable. Nevertheless, home schooling is not always easy. Effort and determination are required, and you do need the basics of your own literacy, the ability and willingness to learn, and a pleasurable relationship with your children.

Once you feel fairly convinced that home schooling is best for your children and you, read Section Two, "Your Home School Plan." There you'll find examples of the kinds of plans you *may* be required to complete. It includes most of the various requirements that are included in the fifty sets of state regulations and procedures for home schoolers throughout our country. Section Two could be subtitled "Choices and Requirements" because you may be required to complete almost all, just some, or almost none of the included possible plan ingredients. The other ingredients are presented for your choice — yay or nay. Each type of planning procedure is included in at least a few states' requirements and some in most states. The intent of Section Two is not to inundate you with a multitude of plans to complete, but to enable you to complete both those required and those you elect to complete. Section Two is a handbook for parents who want to plan a home school, and should first be read entirely through and then be used as a menu from which to select and as a practical guide to your home-school planning process. Following your reading of Section Two, you will want to read Section Three for in-detail coverage of four important components of your home-school preparation — evaluation, curriculum, lesson plans, and records.

Now that you have a general map of our upcoming route, let's embark on your home-school journey. Take along all of your concerns for your children's education. Wear comfortable, sturdy walking shoes for our trek through the planning stages. And remember to pack a suitcase full of anticipation for the freedom and the control that you and your children have the capacity to achieve when you arrive at our destination: home school.

✳✳

Your Home-School Plan

Why Plan?

Are you interested in bringing your child's school home or are you interested in integrating home into your child's schooling? True home education results from the latter. Were you to attempt the former, to bring school home, the process would be relatively mechanical. You could copy! Copy school, that is. Public school. But what we're interested in here is home education, and that process may not be so easy. Worth it? Emphatically, yes! — according to tens of thousands of home-schooling families throughout the United States today. Why? Because those family members enjoy close, reciprocal relationships; because social and values guidance evolves from within rather than from without those families; because learning for them is commensurate with patience and love; because their lessons are as explorative, creative, and flexible as family members wish; because home-school time is their friend, not their constraint; because their school building is comfortable and intimate; and because their school doors can be freely opened to the larger world outside. Yes, home schooling is worth it and wonderful, but it is not as routine as copying.

While the home-school route is much simpler in some states than others, most states require various documents and procedures for initial and continued approval of home schools and for the maintenance of schooling records for every child. Also, as you will see here, there are reasons that you yourself might want to prepare and maintain certain items. The aim of this section of *Home School: Taking the First Step* is to offer you all the preparatory options — both those that may be required and those you may select — and to show you how to accomplish them. What is included in this section, then, represents your choices. Explicit explanations throughout the section and samples at the end of the section will enable you to successfully complete those planning options you choose.

Some of the documents described in this and the next section may appear annoyingly schoolish to you. Rest assured that such appearance is purposeful and intentional. A major aim of these two segments is to enable you to create paperwork whose appearance is unquestionably schoolish.While you'll want to avoid duplicating public schooling as an overall process, you can advance your progress towards the establishment of a home school by designing plans and paperwork that imitate those of public schools. Public school officials, who may have the power to accept or challenge your home-school program or proposal, would be hard-pressed to question documents that appear in all or most respects similar to the public school documents they have accepted for years. These paper landscapes will provide the official picture — the crucial picture — of your home school, for school officials will seldom if ever see your home school in action. There will not likely ever be an approval or denial of the *actual*, only of the paper work you present. Therefore, let's make your paperwork as schoolish as we can in order to free your children from a schoolish education.

In the interest of supplying all the information and explanation you will need and of encouraging thoroughness in your planning, I have included many possibilities and much detail in this section and also the next. Please take a moment now to look briefly at the samples at the end of this section. Referring to them frequently as you read this section will help you recognize that none of the tasks described here are formidable. Let's consider, then, the possible home-school planning tasks and the reasons one might want or need to complete these tasks.

First of all, you need to home school legally (unless you're willing to go underground and to deal with the potential discomfort of having to hide or to face the possible legal consequences). Second, you need to plan your home school thoroughly. Thorough planning is essential for two reasons:

1. Many states require or expect such planning before approving a home school.

2. In order to begin and carry out your child's home education effectively, *you* need a solid plan.

Now you may be one of those who bristles upon reading in number one above the phrase *states require* and other regulatory-sounding terms you will encounter in your attempt to home school — such as *officials, official procedures, case law, regulations, statutes, codes, laws, mandates, state's rights, state's responsibilities, education department requirements*, or the simple phrase *you must*. If such a heavy dose of these words all at once here leaves you feeling as if you've been riddled by bullets, I suggest that you may need to desensitize yourself to their effects in order to remain rational, to plan efficiently and fully, and to face (let's state it gently) the folks you may need to depend upon for approval of your home-school plan if you live in an "approval state." In truth, they're not all bad folks imposing oppressive regulations. In many school districts, they're quite open, receptive, and helpful — and yet do need to carry out their responsibilities. Remember, too, you may find them and their school facilities useful in any variety of ways once you begin home schooling. In other words, good relationships with these folks could prove beneficial in the long run. More importantly, though, remember why you want to home school and for whom. Try to remember that following the required procedures is not a squelching of your need for freedom, but rather is a route to freedom. Biting your tongue, remaining calm, and trying to follow the expected procedures may be the only way you will be able to bring your children *home* for school.

We need to recognize, too, as stated in reason number two above, in order to begin and carry out your child's home education effectively, *you* need a solid plan. In fact, having a solid plan can actually provide you with the flexibility you no doubt are seeking for your home school. How can a solid plan provide flexibility? First, once you have the legal path properly laid and the mechanics of a record-keeping system ready to use, you'll be freer to concentrate on designing creative, stimulating lessons. Then, having also planned well enough to know your youngster's learning goals and tasks, and your teaching materials and resources, you will have on paper and in your mind, as you teach, the core direction of your child's lessons. You can then encourage your child to move, to explore, to expand, and to achieve within and around and branching out from that core direction. Letting your learner wander aimlessly, and letting your child's teacher — you — wander aimlessly, most of the time and with no perimeters, may lead to aimless ends or no ends. You want, I know, to give your child what the public schools don't give him: the right to follow his interests and fascinations, to learn because he loves to learn, to stretch the sinews of his thinking. Great! But he still needs focus, goals, and a sense of task direction, even if he is the designer of those directions. Also, there should be a basic body of knowledge that he aims to acquire. A kind of age-appropriate literacy embellished with philosophies and passions of your own and his own. Thorough planning will ensure that your home-school lessons encompass that basic body of knowledge, plus self-initiated embellishments, and that your lessons are delivered within what is for you a comfortable, workable balance somewhere between structure and disorder.

To begin the home-school planning process, we will look first at the legalities — a pocketful of indisputables if you wish to legally home school, and another pocketful of guidelines telling you how states expect home schoolers to proceed. Then, we'll look at the design of a home-school program proposal in eleven workable segments. In Section Three we'll take a closer look at four of those segments. When we're done, you'll be ready to prepare your proposal for presentation to school officials for approval and/or to begin home schooling. But first, let's consider one final note.

State requirements for setting up and/or continuing home schools obviously vary, although every state permits home schooling in some form. Your state may have few guidelines, few regulations, few requirements, or it may have many. If it has many, they may be liberal, open-ended, and cooperative, or they may be rigid and restrictive. However, common denominators do exist among most of the fifty states' home-school requirements, and it is to those typically stated requirements that the following procedure is addressed. Although the form for presentation to officials may need to be altered in some cases, were you to follow this entire procedure it would allow you to initially approach, or to responsively present an argument to, the education officials of any of the fifty states with an exceptionally complete home-school proposal. In the "Basic Information Chart" and in the "Summary of State Requirements and Procedures" in Section Four of this book you will find, in overview, the requirements for your state. However, although your state's requirements may not include all elements of the procedure below and although the choices are fully yours, I recommend that you follow the procedure as closely as possible — at least the major segments of it. By doing so, you'll be providing yourself with that solid plan spoken of above. Please realize, too, that the procedure is an initial one — a laying of the groundwork — after which maintenance tasks can be accomplished with little consumption of time while you concentrate on enjoying and teaching your children. Also, if you live in one of the many states that require you to deal with your local school board, you may be questioned and even challenged beyond the stated requirements and well into your school year or even during later years. By carrying out the following procedure you will not find yourself scrambling last minute to come up with information with which to respond. Instead, you will be prepared. Then the freedom of home teaching and home learning can be fully enjoyed by you and your children.

Learning Your State's Home-Schooling Guidelines

Begin with whatever statutes, regulations, requirements, procedures . . . in general, the guidelines . . . that your state has adopted with respect to home schools. If home-school program approval is required in your state, you should consider yourself responsible for informing local school officials of those guidelines. Although these officials may be generally cognizant of state compulsory school attendance statutes, they may know little or nothing about the statutes' application to home schooling (according to the law, the courts, or accepted practice) or about other adopted procedures for approving home schools in your state. They may be completely unaware of the scope of their own role in a home-school approval process and, likewise, of your rights as a potential home-school parent. However, at the outset, *before* you have contacted the local officials in any way, you'll need to inform yourself.

To begin that self-informing process, look to Section Four of this book. There, in quick-reference format, the "Basic Information Chart" tells you your state's compulsory attendance ages, whether or not you need to be certified to home teach, whether or not you must teach a state-required core curriculum, and the minimum number of hours and days per year that your home school must be in session. Following the chart, in narrative format, the "Summary of State Regulations and Procedures" advises you of numerous, specific guidelines that are particular to your state. In some cases, for example, you'll discover that forms must be completed, deadlines must be met, meetings must be held, or that you will need to declare your home a private school, or that you must allow for official supervision of your home school, or that you will need to arrange for the administration of achievement tests for your children, and so on.

After reading your state's summary in Section Four, you should compose a brief letter to your state's department of education requesting a copy of all laws, regulations, and other procedural information related to home schooling in your state. Ask for compulsory education and truancy laws; regulations relating to religious and other private schools and home schools; and other requirements or procedures related to home-school approval and programs. (See state department addresses at the end of Section Four.) As an alternative, you may find your state's education laws in a university law library or perhaps in a large public library or in the library of a friendly lawyer, if available. You may still need to request any special procedures or regulations that have been adopted by your state department of education in response to state statutes or to public need. In many states, guidelines exist that stem from the statutes or go beyond the statutes, and you will be expected to know those guidelines and to follow them. However, you'll want to discuss any such extraneous procedures, since they extend beyond laws, with practicing home schoolers in your state. You'll need to determine whether or not they are indeed mandatory or might instead be safely bypassed by you. You may at this point be thinking you'll need a lawyer. But, at least for now, you truly aren't likely to need one. Reading the statutes and other published guidelines is not an overwhelming task. I found my reading of them to be relatively easy, although I discovered that two or three readings drew out the most information and enabled the greatest understanding. Typically, the applicable laws are not lengthy. Besides, *you* need to know what you are doing . . . and why, and how the law backs up what you are doing. You need to be knowledgeable enough about the law yourself to proceed wisely and knowingly and to respond to questions that are asked of you throughout an approval process or program review.

Local, regional or state home-school support groups may be able to provide you with the necessary legal and procedural information and further hints about how to begin. Thus, to supplement your request to the state department, you would be wise to contact a support group or two; they are typically more than willing to be informative and helpful. (See Section Five for groups.) However, please do remember that the surest knowledge you can gain of the legalities is firsthand knowledge. Moreover, you will want to have copies of applicable statutes, regulations and other documents in hand. You should establish, in fact, a file of such legal and procedural information to which you can refer as you develop your home-school plan, as you deal with school officials, and as you begin to implement your plan.

In an article in the January/February 1984 issue of the *Mother Earth News*, home-school proponent John Holt recommended that potential home-school parents contact their elected legislators in order to secure pertinent information. Holt's contention here was that the state department of education will be impressed with and attentive to the fact that national or state legislators have taken an interest in your requests and needs and, therefore, state officials will respond fully and quickly to you. Holt further suggested that talking personally with state department officials could benefit you, especially if you suspect that local officials might be uncooperative. In other words, the assistance of state officials may bring to bear either silent or vocal pressure upon your local school board — in your favor, if such is necessary. As I requested, during the research stages of this book, education statutes and home-school guidelines from the fifty state departments, I received full and quick response from forty of them. Another six responded slowly, a few not too fully. Only four needed further prodding. In view of the good response I received, I suggest that *if* your first attempt to secure information from your state department of education fails, consider contacting a state legislator. Also, *if* your first impressions of your local school board's attitude uncovers negativity, consider personally contacting one or two top state education officials. Support group home schoolers may be able to suggest the names of cooperative or sympathetic officials. In such situations, Holt's recommendations may prove useful. I hesitate to endorse them wholesale, however, because several of the comments I've received from home schoolers throughout the nation indicate, first, that cuing in or stirring up influential folks before you have fully informed yourself can backfire on you, and second, that functioning beyond the level of a whisper during the planning stages can be risky in some states. You may eventually even decide to continue at a whisper — to silently home school. However, a simple letter requesting compulsory attendance laws and other information from your state department is probably not too risky. So I suggest you start with that, and make other contacts with officials only as elapsed time or unsatisfactory response makes such contacts appropriate, wise, or necessary.

As noted, most of my queries to the state departments provided plenty of information, willingly given. It is possible, however, that the individual who responds to your letter will attempt to brush you off with a preemptive remark regarding your state's practice of not recognizing home schooling as a legitimate alternative to public education. Or perhaps his remarks will indicate that your state maintains a hands-off policy. While this latter remark may sound negative; it may be in fact positive. "Hands-off" may mean that your state doesn't regulate home schoolers at all! The former remark regarding nonrecognition of home schooling probably is not true. It may mean that your state department of education discourages home schooling as much as possible, and the responder has just made the department's first attempt at discouraging you. Perhaps your state doesn't recognize home schools, but does recognize private schools, and in your state a home school can operate as a private school. On the other hand, the individual may appear to comment cooperatively in her written response to you, but only attach your state's teacher certification requirements to that response — as a not-so-subtle hint or delay. At any rate, don't let negative remarks and responses stand unquestioned as truths or guidelines. Remember, every state allows for home schooling in some fashion. Call upon your determination, continue your independent search for information, write again asking for more detailed information (specify: compulsory attendance laws, etc.), consider trying John Holt's recommendations, and, as outlined below, continue working on your plans to home school.

Then, once your have secured the pertinent legal information, read it carefully, take notes, check dates to determine if one document (or clause within a document) supersedes another (home-school procedures in your state may be undergoing change), compare documents if obtained from various sources, reread, and reread again. Make special note of items that apply to unique situations, such as home schooling a handicapped child, or a child living in a remote location, or a conscientious/religious objection to public schooling. Then using the documents and Section Four of this book, write out:

1) Your own checklist of items that will apply directly to you as you work through the approval process — procedures you should follow, forms for which you should send, records you should set up, curriculum specifications you'll need to consider, deadline dates, and so on. Procedural Worksheet #1 follows here to help you get started.

2) Another checklist which includes specific clauses in the law, and the duties, rights, regulations, requirements, privileges, etc., that constitute the legal underpinnings of home schooling in your state. If legal case histories involving home schools are available to you and of interest to you, you might also take note of their results. (Check with regional home-schooling organizations for case reports or check public court records.) See Procedural Worksheet #2 for help.

After spending one or two sessions studying legal information in the manner noted above, you will have a fairly full picture of how you stand as a potential home schooler in your state. For instance, you will know how well you are legally qualified to home teach, how many and what kinds of requirements you will have to fulfill in order to legally home school, and how much local school district involvement in your home school you may have to tolerate. As I mentioned earlier, you should set up a file in which to keep the legal information, your two checklists, and from here on any further information and all communications regarding legal matters.

At this point, you will have accomplished one of the two tasks we set out to accomplish at the beginning of this portion of this book: You will have informed yourself. Now, using the above two checklists, begin to prepare a written *legalities* overview that you can later use to inform local school officials if you find it necessary. Again, you needn't be a lawyer to write a basic overview. Write your overview in a fashion you feel comfortable writing and that you feel is appropriate for your circumstance — for example, a list, a chart, a narrative, a letter, notes for oral presentation — including quotations from the statutes as appropriate. Case reviews and court decisions that you presume would be apropos to your situation could also be cited. Then, particularly if your overview will eventually be submitted on paper to local school officials, be sure to edit and revise and polish your writing. Keep in mind as you write that school officials are your likely audience and your purpose is to inform — objectively, accurately. Also remember that you want your overview, and every other written or oral item you submit, to represent you as a literate, competent person — literate and competent enough to home teach.

The comfort that comes with knowledge should by now be settling into your mind. You have informed yourself of the legal basis of your home-schooling effort and fully prepared yourself to inform others (even to inform a lawyer, with no fee for *his* searching the laws, if you should at any time later need a lawyer). Tuck your written overview safely into your file. It will wait for you there while you proceed, as outlined below, with your home-school plan.

Procedural Worksheet #1

My state _____

Ages of compulsory education _____

Daily/weekly hours home schools must be in session _____
_____

Number of days required for a home-school year _____

    yes / no   School officials can legally inspect my home school.
                How often? _____

    yes / no   My children must take standardized achievement
                tests. Which children? _____
                Who can give the tests? _____
                Where can they be given? _____
                To whom must the results be provided?
                _____

    yes / no   I must have my home-school plan/proposal officially
                approved by the following school officials:
                _____

Deadline dates I must meet and documents I must provide in writing before my school year begins:

_____   _____
_____   _____
_____   _____
_____   _____

Other documents I must provide during my school year:

_____   _____
_____   _____
_____   _____

The above documents must be submitted to:

            _____
            _____

Deadlines school officials must meet and actions they must take in response to my submittals:

_____   _____
_____   _____
_____   _____

Home-teacher qualifications in my state:

yes / no   I must be certified as a teacher.
yes / no   I must work with a certified consultant.
yes / no   I must have a college degree.
yes / no   I must have a high school diploma or GED.

Other home teacher qualification requirements or options:

_____
_____
_____

My children's
Names   Age/Grade   Courses I must teach

_____   ___/_____   _____
                                 _____
                                 _____
                                 _____
_____   ___/_____   _____
                                 _____
                                 _____
                                 _____
_____   ___/_____   _____
                                 _____
                                 _____
                                 _____

Records I must maintain:

_____
_____
_____
_____
_____

Other procedural items I should note:

_____
_____
_____
_____
_____

Procedural Worksheet #2

My state _____

My state's definition of a home school: _____
_____
_____
_____

My home school can be operated as (circle all that apply):

    a home school   a private school   a satellite school

    other: _____

Terms, phrases, sentences that seem especially significant from state laws:
_____
_____
_____
_____
_____
_____
_____

Other legal/procedural items I should note:
_____
_____
_____
_____
_____
_____

Things I have learned from other home schoolers about procedures/laws in my state:
_____
_____
_____
_____
_____
_____
_____

Statement of Intent

Many states require that you prepare what is commonly called a "statement of intent" or "notice of intent" — in other words, a home-school program proposal. Statement of intent requirements vary in form from state to state. The statement typically includes items such as basic personal information about your enrollees, a notification that you will be home schooling those enrollees, confirmation and often explanation or demonstration of your compliance with all regulations and required procedures, and a thorough description of your home-school educational program. In your state the statement of intent requirements may be more complicated, simpler, or nonexistent. Some states specify formats for the statement of intent, some supply standard forms to be used, and others ask for both form completion and a description of all aspects of your program. In any case, preparing your statement of intent in full is your next task. Later, you can adapt the statement to the exact format required by your state for submittal to school officials. For the time being, you should think of the statement of intent as a document you are preparing for yourself, because you are the one who will benefit most from having completed it. You will have begun thinking through your home-school design well enough to convince yourself of its efficacy, well enough to feel secure as you begin to implement your program with your children, and, if necessary, well enough to effectively argue for your program. Your statement of intent, along with subsequent planning, will provide you with the concrete foundation of your home school. And concrete is hard to crack.

Let's look then to your statement of intent. First, several states delineate very specifically the contents and deadline dates and, as noted above, sometimes the form of your overall statement or the forms of its several parts, so be sure to obtain whatever written requirements and instructions your state's department of education provides to prospective home schoolers. By carefully reading those requirements and instructions you can make doubly sure you miss nothing. In the meantime, however, you can proceed as proposed here.

While studying the fifty sets of state home-school laws and procedures, I found that from the statement-of-intent requirements we could distill eleven possible statement segments:

1. Basic Personal Information — Enrollees.

2. Basic Home-School Building Information.

3. Evidence of Home-Teacher Qualifications.

4. Certificated Home-School Consultant.

5. Statement of Positive Reasons and Rights.

6. Plans for an Annual Evaluation.

7. Curriculums and Materials.

8. Lesson Plan Samples.

9. Plans for Ongoing Student Progress Assessment.

10. Schedules and Calendars.

11. Plans for Keeping Records.

Wisdom suggests that of the eleven you complete at least the major segments — for the sake of your own efficiency and effectiveness as a teacher, for the sake of consistency and quality in your child's education, and to begin to establish a trail of evidence that you have been doing a fine job of home teaching. State laws indicate exactly which segments you must complete if you wish to home teach legally. In the final account, however, the choices are yours.

Although you don't want to become so bogged down in paperwork (often the bane of public school teachers) that you lose your enthusiasm for home teaching, you should study the statement of intent segments outlined below and then complete those you find essential. An effort has been made to present them simply and graphically for ease of completion, and, as noted earlier, you'll find a sample of each segment at the end of this section. Keep in mind as you work that in almost all states you will only need to complete these items, as earlier noted, once at the beginning of each home-school year. In some states they are submitted in full only the first year and followed by notices of continuation each subsequent year. You would, of course, continue the record keeping and lesson planning and some scheduling throughout the year, but once you have developed a system for carrying out these tasks, they will not be too time-consuming.

Let's examine in detail, then, the eleven possible segments of a statement of intent or home-school proposal and the samples. Then you will be in a position to select those you will complete. Incidentally, when you begin to actually work through the following segments and accumulating papers-in-progress, establish a second home-school file, a statement of intent file, in which to store these papers. When (or if) you eventually submit them to school officials, be sure to keep copies of all documents in your file.

1. Basic Personal Information — Enrollees

In an effort to exercise their responsibility to see that the citizenry is educated, the states gather certain kinds of data on students within each school district. Typically this data is submitted by the parents to the local school office where it is kept as "permanent records," updated throughout the students' schooling years, and stored thereafter for reference purposes. Usually the information is quite basic and innocuous, with grades and achievement test scores added along the way. If a child has special needs, is an "exceptional" child, or such, information relating to testing and services provided with respect to those needs will be kept in separate files, usually in the special education department. In any case, the records provide documentation that your child, one of your state's citizens, is being educated.

If your children currently are or were previously enrolled in a public school, their permanent records already exist. If you have recently moved to the school district within which you now reside, you will need to give permission for the records to be sent to the new district from the district previously attended by your children.

Now, as you plan to *enroll* your children in home school, in almost all states you will be expected to supply the school district in which you reside with personal information regarding your children. The district will file this information in your children's permanent record files as continued documentation that they are being educated. Check your state's summary in Section Four and the information from your state department of education to determine if and when the personal information must be submitted. The basic personal information requested of you may include any combination of the following:

Your children's names, ages, sex, race, birthdates, address. Birth certificates may be requested.

Their parents'/guardians' names, address(es), phone number(s).

Your children's current grade levels, and names and addresses of the last public, parochial, or private school they attended, if any.

Notation of any identified special needs of any of your children, such as a need for physical therapy, speech therapy, education for the hearing-impaired or the blind, gifted/ talented education, or other forms of special education.

Complete immunization records and special health information (diabetes, asthma, epilepsy, etc.) for each of your children. If their immunizations are not up-to-date, you may be asked to update them.

Write out this information accurately and simply; then file it in your second, newly created file. (See Sample One, a Home-School Enrollment Sheet, on page 78 at the end of this section.) Later you will either submit your enrollment sheet as written or transfer the information to a prepared, standard form if your state supplies one. By checking your state's summary in Section Four of this book, you can quickly find out if a form is available. If so, you will need to obtain that form. If not, you will eventually submit the original (and keep a copy for yourself). Again, remember, each written document you submit represents you; each is a demonstration of your literacy and competence.

2. Basic Home-School Building Information

The states claim the right to reasonably regulate, inspect, and supervise all schools. That right may extend beyond the academic aspects of the schools and may include the physical nature of school buildings. As a home school, your home is a school building and perhaps subject to regulation, inspection, and supervision by public school officials. However, in many states actual physical inspections aren't carried out. Instead, you may be asked to provide information regarding your "school building" as a part of your statement of intent. In a very few states, you will have to demonstrate compliance with local fire, safety, and health ordinances that apply to all school buildings. In several states, a once-a-year visit is scheduled by a local school administrator to review your entire home-school program, and he will probably note your physical school setup during his visit.

If your home school is visited, the official will note some or all of the following factors, which are also those items you may be asked about or may just wish to include in the building information segment of your statement of intent:

Your building's address/location.

Names of all persons who reside in your home; i.e., if your home is going to be your home-school building. This is quite an intrusive request, and, fortunately, atypical.

The degree of physical safety and health your children will work under as you home school them. Consider fire escape routes and practices, smoke alarms, overall cleanliness, wash and waste facilities, etc. Check your state's regulations to see if you need formal compliance with ordinances.

The safety of your student records. Are they being kept in a moisture-free and fireproof area or are duplicates kept in a separate area so the records will not be lost?

The degree to which your home schoolroom is conducive to learning. Is it quiet enough, spacious enough, neat enough? Is it nondistractive? Does it include study desks or tables, chairs, lamps, project work surfaces, and so on? This may apply to your kitchen, if it is your "schoolroom," or perhaps you'll use more than one room for "school."

The overall atmosphere of your schoolroom. Is it pleasant, comfortable, cheery, peaceful, stimulating?

The presence of textbooks and other materials, such as children's magazines, a globe or other maps, art supplies, science supplies, an atlas, an encyclopedia set, musical equipment and materials, etc. You won't need all of these items immediately, but should consider gradually accumulating those you can afford, first because they are useful additions to your children's learning environment, and second, because they will be noted should a school official inspect your school.

The inclusion of a family-size library or at least the beginnings of one.

The availability of special equipment or environments. For example, do you have a computer and software, a tree arbor or nursery, a garden, a spotting scope, a microscope, a piano, bee hives, or other potentially educational items? These items are not essential, of course, but if you have them, do mention them on your home-school building report.

Compile a descriptive list of all of the above items that apply in your case. Then fashion your list into a written report, if required, for later presentation to officials or transference to a form if one is provided for this purpose by your state department of education or local school district. (See Sample Two, Home-School Building Report, on page 79.)

You may also take this opportunity to itemize potential educational facilities within walking or driving distance of your home-school building that are available to you and your children. You might list such places as a museum, art gallery, fish hatchery, print shop, gymnasium, science center, stage theatre, wildlife refuge, zoo, community education center, craft workshop, marina, and others. Also consider facilities that may be particularly related to subjects you will cover during your home-school year. Examples might be a post office, fire station, police station, and public library for primary grade studies of cities; local grocery markets and area farms for an intermediate grade unit on human food production; a factory, mechanical shop, or woodshop for secondary vocational studies. After working through the segment on curriculum below, you will develop more ideas to include here. Feel free to note briefly how these places will relate to your children's studies; then you can reemphasize and expand upon them later in the curriculum segment.

File your home-school building report with your home-school enrollment sheet as the first two completed segments of your statement of intent. At this stage you'll probably find yourself buoyed by the generation of ideas for facilities that you can include in your children's educational activities. You can smile in the knowledge that were your children public school students they would not visit and experience many, if any, of those real life places which can so easily enliven lessons. Feel confident, too, in the fact that educational research has demonstrated the tremendous effectiveness of the hands-on, multi-sensory activities that such places can offer to your children as they learn.

3. Evidence of Home-Teacher Qualifications

Having completed the first two segments of your statement of intent in a literate and competent fashion, you will have already begun to establish evidence of your qualifications to home teach. Of course, if yours is one of the few states that mandates that you be certified, and you're not certified, you'll have to consider other alternatives regardless of your literacy and competence, or consider going to court. (See question 3 in Section One for alternatives.) If you are certified for the grade levels and subjects you will teach, your qualifications shouldn't be questioned. You will simply need to attach a copy of your certificate to your statement of intent and skip to the next segment here. But in most states and most cases, your qualifications will be judged in part on your ability to present a coherent, polished home-school plan. In other words, the impression you first give to school officials is likely to be a paper impression. Make it a good one!

Among the pieces of paper you may need to submit is one that accounts for your actual qualifications to teach your children. First of all, however, you may need to convince yourself of your qualifications. Let me help: You may be interested to know that most private schools, even (or especially) the exclusive, exemplary ones, in the United States hire noncertified teachers. Other alternative schools, too, may hire certified teachers, but at the same time do not hesitate to hire noncertified ones within some fields of expertise. Even public schools, at least the better ones, bring in resource persons in various fields, such as craftsmanship, health science, or environmental science, to teach a lesson or two, a course or two, from time to time. Further, the number of full-time, regular teachers — without certification — teaching in our public schools each year is in the 80,000 range. And yet another segment of our public school teaching population holds only emergency certificates, granted due to local teacher shortages and for which there may be few qualifications. I might add, too, that a significant percentage of the approximate 230,000 certified teachers in our nation's public high schools are teaching some courses not in the fields for which they are certified and in many cases not even in which they are knowledgeable. The resource persons brought in intermittently to teach in public schools are typically competent in the specific subjects they teach. However, as for the thousands of uncertified, emergency, or out-of-their-teaching-field teachers in our public schools . . . well, it is difficult to estimate their degrees of competence or literacy or their success rates.

Potential home teachers need recognize that a high school diploma or equivalency, a college education or part of one, vocational education and occupational experience beyond high school, and special talents in any area are useful to one's teaching. Any background experiences along these lines that you can list for yourself will be given consideration as school officials attempt to determine your qualifications to home teach. However, we should all understand that a teaching certificate is not, in and of itself, a qualification that would ensure anyone's ability to teach.

In other words, aside from regulations, most parents are able to teach without certification. In fact, having discovered through the results of home teaching over the years that parents can successfully teach, most states now maintain provisions for home teaching by noncertified parents. Indeed, you may not only be an effective teacher for your children, you may be the best teacher for them. So let's take a look at your qualifications:

> First, what are your children's grade levels in the various subject areas, especially the core areas of reading and math? Now what's your hypothetical grade or skill level in those areas? Make a comparison. How far ahead of your children are you? Herein, we hope, is your first item of qualification to teach your children.

> Next, jot down your educational experiences, K-12, vocational, college, community courses, . . . all of them. Now you have your second set of items that qualify you to teach. You will want to secure copies of applicable diplomas, degrees, and transcripts to attach to your statement of intent if required or if you think doing so would be beneficial and appropriate.

> Go on to your job experiences. Have you become particularly talented in a job-related area that could apply to your teaching? Write out a description of those experiences and you'll have set three of your qualification statements. If you feel a job-related recommendation from an employer for

whom you've worked would attest to your competence, obtain one and attach it to your qualifications sheet.

How about hobbies or avocations or nonacademic skills and talents? Are you a pianist? That talent would be especially useful in teaching elementary grade children. Are you a naturalist or environmentalist? Useful in science instruction. Are you a seamstress? Useful in home economics instruction. Are you versatile in a foreign language that you plan to teach to your children? List those skills and talents that relate to the grade levels and subjects you will be teaching. Stretch your imagination; look for all the ways that your special talents could be useful as you teach your children. Then list those talents.

Have you been involved in educational or service groups, particularly any through which you have demonstrated competence and/or leadership ability? Have you been a toastmistress? A Chamber of Commerce officer? A scout leader? A Sunday School teacher? Have you earned special recognition through your involvement in such groups? Add these to your list and you have your fifth set of qualification items.

Do you have abilities to meet your children's individual learning needs that public school teachers don't have or that teachers aren't able to exercise in the public school classroom setting?

Have you considered taking the National Teacher Exam or a state teachers' exam if available in your state? A good score could add to your qualifications to home teach.

When you have completed this segment, you should have the makings of written evidence of your home-teacher qualifications that you can use to prepare a written statement, if necessary, or to fill in a required form on your qualifications. (See Sample Three on page 80.) The date for submitting your qualifications information is probably the same as the date for your enrollee and building information. Check your regulations.

You may wish to include a list, too, of other persons, such as your spouse, who will play roles in your children's education, along with the other persons' special qualifications and a brief explanation of how they will fit in with your children's lessons. See question 4, e in Section One of this book for the kinds of individuals who might make up your child's learning community. Educational research emphatically supports bringing such resource persons into the schoolroom; i.e., into the learning lives of your children.

In addition, throughout your home-school year, keep written records of any home-teacher education and improvement efforts that you undertake. If you take courses, attend workshops, seminars, or conferences in order to improve your skills as a home-school teacher, keep a record of those activities. Include transcripts when available. Further include any studies you've engaged in independently on teaching methods. Even a list of books or journals you've read about teaching could be included.

Any accumulation of educational experiences that will enhance your home teaching will benefit you and your children. But, in addition to that, you may at some time be able to use a record of those experiences to impress upon school officials your seriousness, earnestness, and knowledge as a home teacher.

4. Certificated Home-School Consultant

A few states exercise their right to supervise schools within their jurisdiction by requiring or offering an option for noncertificated home-school teachers to secure the assistance of a certificated educator. For example, the regulations or guidelines might indicate that you need to demonstrate that you have a certificated supervisor available to you. Or you may be requested more specifically to provide evidence that you have available to you a certified teacher consultant for planning, development of your curriculum, program implementation, or for consultation related to your child's learning exceptionality. In addition, the certified consultant may be required for monthly, quarterly, semester, or yearly progress or program evaluations. Progress evaluations might include actual testing by the consultant, a review of tests you've given, a review of your child's home-school work, a discussion with your child, or other means of determining progress. In any case, certified consultants or supervisors may be involved in a variety of ways. The terms *consultant* and *supervisor* as used here, incidentally, are not necessarily formal labels, but more or less descriptors of a role a certificated teacher would be asked to fulfill intermittently. By checking the summary for your state in Section Four of this book, you can quickly see whether or not you are required to have such a consultant. If one is required in your state, the summary will suggest the extent to which you will need to utilize the services of a consultant. You should also check for further details in the information you request from your state department of education.

Perhaps you find yourself resisting the idea of working with a certificated consultant. You may, for example, feel so negative about public education that you do not want a public educator involved in any aspect of your home school. Or you may fear that a lack of freedom might result from having a *supervisor.* Or you may presume such a consultant would attempt to dictate your curriculum. Perhaps you're just adamant about your right to function independently.

May I interject here, however, a statement made early in this section: ". . . home schooling is worth it and wonderful, but is is not . . . routine . . ." Now those legislators and state education officials who designed their respective statutes and other regulations to include a consultant requirement may have had any number of reasons for doing so. But the quote noted above implies a potential reason of your own for locating a consultant: You may simply need help.

In view of this possibility, I recommend that you consider securing the assistance of a certified educator whether or not your state requires one. You see, especially when you are first getting started, you may find it worthwhile, even necessary, to make use of a local educator's knowledge. As a means of suggesting areas in which you might benefit from help, let's look at the kinds of knowledge a certified educator may be able to share with you:

1. Knowledge of formats that schools typically use for records, curriculum designs, lesson plans, schedules, and calendars, and that are the expected formats for most information that you might submit. Also, the educator would know the appropriate formats for the records that you'll keep at home while your home-school program is in progress.

2. Familiarity with curriculums and course syllabi, particularly those used locally and which you may be expected or required to emulate as you design your curriculum.

3. Knowledge of the many means of routine student progress assessments.

4. Experience with achievement tests and their contents — especially useful if the consultant you choose has taught in your school district for a few years or more and has administered the locally given test at your child's grade level.

5. Acquaintances with and connections to public school staff members whose assistance also may be needed by you, such as a physical therapist, speech therapist, school psychologist, school librarian, art instructor, drama coach and others.

6. Knowledge of the uses of your child's permanent records kept at the local school and access to them. (You have legal access to those records, too, but there may be times when you would rather personally avoid the public school scene and yet obtain information from your child's permanent file.)

7. Awareness of special and extracurricular public school activities in which your child may wish to participate.

8. Familiarity with materials and resources appropriate for various age/grade/ability levels and subjects and means of securing them.

9. Awareness of audio visual and other equipment on hand at your local school that might be available for your use.

10. Perceptions regarding the personalities and philosophies of school administrators and school board members with whom you may have to deal.

11. Awareness of upcoming workshops and courses available to teachers that may be open to enrollment by home teachers in your area.

No doubt a local certified educator will have other knowledge as well that could be of use to you. Very likely the issue for you is maintaining full control of your home-school program yourself, even while seeking the assistance of a certified educator. If you work through much of your statement of intent on your own so that you have your ideas down on paper and then decide precisely what it is you want from a certified consultant, you are likely to get just what you want from that person and not what you don't want. In other words, by looking at your own information, you can come up with questions and areas needing further input, areas where state requirements indicate you must consult a certificated educator, or areas in which you just may want additional ideas. Then, when you meet with the educator whom you've chosen and who has agreed to cooperate, you can steer the discussion and control this outsider's input, handle the consultation sessions in a friendly, compatible fashion, and gain needed benefits.

If your state is one that requires a consultant, don't feel that you must ask your local school superintendent or another official for a recommended or assigned educator. Instead, feel free to investigate the possible candidates yourself. Look for a topnotch teacher who works with the grade level range and the subject areas with which you will work as a home teacher. Then, seeking cooperation, approach that person. Once her assistance is assured, add your consultant's name, address, degree held, certificate held, the teaching endorsements for which she is certified, transcripts if required, her current teaching assignment and school, if employed, and perhaps the reasons you chose her, to your proposal, to your statement of intent, or to any forms that require your consultant's name.

If yours is a state that does not require a consultant, your independent inclusion of one in your proposal is likely to impress positively the local officials responsible for reviewing and/or approving your proposal. Be sure to note the ways in which the consultant will be helpful to you, the ways in which your program may benefit from this assistance, and how your consultant's experiences as an educator relate to your home-school situation — grade levels, subjects to be taught, appropriate materials recommendations, and so on.

We don't want to ignore the possibility that you won't find a satisfactory local certificated educator to serve as your consultant or that you simply resist working with one, but still do want a consultant. In that case, you'll need to look elsewhere. You may, for instance, establish affiliations with a Christian or other private school that would result in the services of a consultant. There are numerous so-called "umbrella schools" in operation throughout the United States to which you might look for assistance. I should warn, however, that sometimes these schools delineate their own consultative role, which means that you may have less control over their input. There may be a certified teacher in your area who is not currently employed by a school district or is on a leave of absence and would agree to help you. Thousands of teachers leave the field of education each year (often the brightest of our teachers), to work for higher pay and greater prestige in other jobs. You could attempt to locate one who might provide evening or weekend consultations intermittently. Some home teachers have placed want ads in newspapers, newsletters, and magazines in search of a certified consultant. Should you take this route, be sure you ask for proof of valid certification and for references. You might check a few issues of Holt Associates' *Growing Without Schooling* where cooperative certified teachers are sometimes listed. In some states the state department of education may be a source of recommendations for potential consultants. Also, if your state requires every home-school educator to have a consultant, other home schoolers that you locate are probably in contact with at least one consultant and may be able to suggest someone for you. In the Seattle area home schoolers can call upon a cadre of certified teachers who are willing to help them. You and a local or regional support group may be able to organize such a group of certified helpers. In addition, if you have acquaintances among parents of other school districts in your area, one of those parents may be able to offer a name or two of good teachers in his district who might be willing to be your consultant.

Whichever process you use, take your time. Also, explore as much as possible the teaching background and talents of your candidates. To find out about them, ask others who know them or who have had children in their classes. As noted above, before contacting the person you choose, outline carefully for yourself the services you seek so you'll be able to present them in an organized manner for him. When you meet, he will probably be more inclined towards working with you if he sees that you are prepared, competent, and fully aware of what your home-school program is all about and of exactly what help you're seeking. Be specific and objective, but also pleasant and undemanding. If you're married, I suggest that you and your spouse together visit with him, at least for this initial meeting. I also recommend that you not take any of your children to this first meeting. You're asking initially for programmatic assistance, not, typically, for help in dealing with or working directly with your children.

Once you've reached an agreement with a certificated consultant, cooperatively itemize the consultant's responsibilities. Will there be reports to complete? Will he work in conjunction with a local school official as well as with you? Will he be responsible for reviewing test results or for arranging and administering achievement tests? Considering his role, do the two of you think he should meet your children? Try to set dates for further meetings and for consultative or supervisory activities for which he will need specific times. Take notes which can later be turned into a written report of your agreement. Attach a copy to his personal and qualifications information sheet in your file and deliver one to him. Then, when and if appropriate, submit one along with your other proposal segments to school officials.

Usually a consultant's involvement with a home school is not too time-consuming in the scope of an entire school year, but you may wish or need to consider offering some form of remuneration for the consultant's assistance. Finding a volunteer is often possible, and in some cases the local school district is obligated to provide a staff member to work with you.

We might note here also that once you begin working with your curriculum you may wish to establish a working relationship with more than one consultant, certified or noncertified. Perhaps you'd like to confer with a local science instructor regarding your home-school science lessons, and likewise a teacher of literature regarding creative reading lists and activities, and yet a third teacher who helps you with lesson planning and scheduling. Perhaps, too, you will find persons active or employed in specific fields, such as biology or music, who are not certified teachers, but who could serve as consultants as you develop curriculums in science and music. Also, don't ignore your fellow home schoolers. An experienced and successful home teacher, already established in your area, could be a beneficial consultant too. Remember, of course, the names of noncertificated consultants should not be used to indicate fulfillment of a requirement that you obtain the assistance of a certificated educator.

To complete, then, this fourth segment of your statement of intent, you will file for later reference or submission a personal and qualifications information sheet on your certified consultant with any appropriate attachments and a written report describing the extent of your agreement with the consultant. (See Sample Four on page 81.) Double check to make sure the latter reflects any and all state requirements related to your use of a consultant.

5. Statement of Positive Reasons and Rights

You may wish, or in a few cases be required, to preface or supplement your statement of intent with the reasons and rights you feel justify your decision to home school your children. Parenting responsibilities that stem from religious convictions are the most commonly expressed reasons and rights of home schoolers in the United States, and religious exemptions from compulsory education are the most commonly granted exemptions. But other justifications may be offered. Here are a few possibilities:

Special problems and/or needs of your children:

physical handicaps

learning handicaps

serious health deficiencies

severe hyperactivity or lethargy

rebellious behavior

evidence of a significant gap between a
child's intelligence and his achievement

intellectual giftedness

unusual talent in a specific area

maladjustment to school

academic failure

a fading joy in learning

a withering curiosity

Special issues of your own:

values conflicts with public schools

convictions of the conscience

dismay over the public school social milieu

unavailability of a good, local public school
teacher at your child's grade level

knowledge of the studies that show that
home schools work

knowledge of the studies that show that
public schools don't work

knowledge of research that shows that
children are sent to school too early

a burning desire to offer your children an
excellent and exciting education

a desire to feed your children's natural
love of learning (and to avoid standing
by while public schools squelch it)

Please recognize that I'm not making a wholesale recommendation here that you submit to officials a formal statement of your reasons and rights regarding home schooling, nor that officials would unquestioningly accept your reasons if you did submit them. I am suggesting, however, that you may want to create such a statement for one or more of several possible purposes:

Perhaps a statement of reasons and rights is required by your state in order for you to win approval for your home school. Check your state's summary in Section Four and your state laws and procedures.

You'll probably feel more focused as a home schooler if you write out your reasons **for yourself**. You may think of the statement of reasons as a means of confirming your child-related goals as a home-school parent. As time passes, you may use the statement as a guide and reminder of why you and your children became home schoolers.

You and **your spouse** as joint parents of your children may wish to compare and clarify together your reasons — as a means of screening their validity while you consider the serious issue of whether or not to home school.

You, your spouse, and **your children**, as a team, may benefit from bringing together your individual thoughts and feelings about why you'd like to home school. From such teamwork you may derive a strong sense of unity and purpose to bolster you during the approval process, the initial implementation process, and the weeks beyond.

You may feel that your reasons and rights are your most convincing pieces of evidence that you and your children should, or must, home school. Perhaps nothing would be more persuasive as you seek official approval.

Writing your statement of reasons and rights may be the most meaningful way to declare the strength of your convictions regarding the tremendous importance of your children and their learning.

Your statement of rights may afford you an opportunity to crystallize in your own mind your true, exact, legal rights as a home schooler.

You'll have worked out solid answers for friends and neighbors who frown as they ask, "Why are your children not going to school?"

Your statement of intent may appear to be incomplete without a statement of your reasons. Your plans may lack the force that a clear statement of purpose can give them.

Whatever the basis of your statement or list of reasons and rights, when you compose it, avoid vagueness. Your focus will become clearer with increasing specificity. Also, if you plan to submit your statement of reasons and rights as part of your statement of intent to school officials, you will want it to be explicit enough to not offer bait for debate. Offering officials what they may perceive to be a can of worms will only invite their opening it. So hone your wording and your ideas down to their most specific form. (See Sample Five on page 82.) Also, make no statement that would suggest that your purpose is to counter compulsory school attendance statutes. Doing so would be the equivalent of publicly stating, "My purpose is to break the law."

Begin at this point to use your statement of reasons and rights as your declaration of conviction, of determination, as well as of focus. File it, but refer to it frequently, particularly if your determination wavers, and keep it in mind as you plan your curriculum and lessons. In other words, know why you are doing what you are doing. Let the why of your home-schooling effort sink deep within you and become an integral part of your program.

6. Plans for Annual Evaluation

Most states require home schoolers to undergo some form of end-of-the-year evaluation of the home-school students' progress and also, in some cases, of the home-school program. Achievement tests are an evaluative requirement in many states, but other forms of progress assessment are allowed for in other states. Several states also require an overall review of the home-school program, including all files and records kept throughout the home-school year. This, of course, is one good reason for developing and keeping all plans, documents, and daily school records as you home school.

Your state guidelines may indicate that you can carry out the evaluative process yourself or that it must be carried out by a certificated consultant, or a neutral educator, or a school official. By checking the summary for your state in Section Four of this book you can find out if an annual evaluation is required, who should conduct your evaluation if required, and in what form it will need to be completed. Then you should **carefully read "Annual Evaluation" in Section Three** for a detailed discussion of evaluation procedures. Following that reading, you should write out a simple plan for how you will carry out any required annual evaluation. At this point the plan's purpose is to let school officials know that you are aware of the requirement and that you have a plan to complete it. This plan should be filed in you statement of intent file for later submittal to officials and, of course, for implementation at the end of your home-school year. (See Sample Six on page 83.)

In a few states the evaluation will occur not only at the year's end but also quarterly or at the end of each semester. If yours is one of these states, be sure your plan reflects the quarterly or semester evaluation requirement.

7. Curriculums and Materials

Many states require home schoolers to provide curriculums similar to public school curriculums for children the same ages as the home-schooled children. Usually this requirement is stated as "equivalent curriculum," suggesting that no less than the public school curriculum should be provided. Typically, however, "equivalent curriculum" actually refers to a basic or core curriculum rather than to the entire scope of a public school curriculum. Also, embellishments of your own and your children's are allowed. In other words, you can alter or create your own course syllabi for any particular course as long as the basics are covered and you can add subject areas or courses to the required curriculum.

Broadly, a curriculum is an aggregate of courses of study that a school offers to children at any one grade level. For a primary grade student, for example, the basic curriculum would include reading and math. It may also include science, social studies, language arts, music, art, physical education, and so on. The concept of a curriculum is simple: courses of study. The writing out of a curriculum is less simple: a list of specific learning goals to be achieved within each course of study.

You needn't feel as if your curriculum design needs to come out of thin air. Help is available in various forms. First, to write out your home-school curriculum you will need to find out which courses of study are required by your state. Check Section Four. Then **read "Curriculum and Materials" in Section Three** where you will find a step-by-step process by which you can design your curriculum. (Also see Sample Seven on page 84 at the end of this section.) Following that process, you can arrive at a satisfactory written curriculum for submittal to school officials, if required, or for maintenance in your files as evidence that you are providing required courses of study or simply that you are providing a sound curriculum.

Once you have established your curriculum, you will need to decide how to teach the curriculum and which materials to use. Sometimes your materials as well as your curriculum will need official approval. Whether they require approval or not, you will need to undergo an initial search for materials to use and to note how they correlate with your curriculum. To understand the materials search procedure read the materials portion of "Curriculum and Materials" in Section Three. Then write out a basic list of materials you plan to use to teach your curriculum. Please realize that this will be a basic list only, one from which you may deviate as the year progresses and one to which you may add other materials as you become aware of them. Your materials list may be integrated into your written curriculum as in Sample Seven.

After reading Section Three, complete and file your curriculum and materials list, perhaps bound in a notebook, in your statement of intent file to await submittal or later use. Even if you are never required to submit a curriculum or materials list, you will probably find yourself secure in the knowledge that you do have a solid, well-planned curriculum from which to work. Also, of course, if ever challenged in later months or years, you'll have proof of the quality of your children's home-school curriculum.

8. Lesson Plan Samples

Lesson plan samples are required during the approval process in only a few states. Some require lesson plans not during the approval process, but throughout the home-school year. In several states, in fact, lesson plans must be maintained for inspection by school officials. If your state upholds lesson plan requirements, please **read "Lesson Planning" in Section Three.** If yours does not require plans, you may wish to read "Lesson Planning" anyway and to consider regularly writing brief lesson plans. Again, maintaining lesson plans is another opportunity to accumulate evidence that your are providing your children with a sound education.

To find out if lesson plans are required, check your state's summary in Section Four and check information received from your state's department of education. In Section Three I have provided you with a lesson-planning procedure that should be acceptable to school officials. You may wish to plan in some other fashion, but if you need approval of your plans, I urge you to follow the procedure described in Section Three, "Lesson Planning."

If your state or local education officials request that sample plans be included in your statement of intent or home-school proposal, select a portion of each child's curriculum for which you can write out plans. If you select portions from the beginning of a course of study for each child, you'll be able to use the plans you design right away as you begin home teaching. Perhaps plans for one week, the first week of home school, would be sufficient to satisfy the officials that you are able and willing to plan your children's lessons. When completed, file those plans in your statement of intent file, but also keep copies in a plan book or notebook in which you will continue writing lesson plans, week-by-week, as you home teach. (See Sample Eight on page 85.)

9. Plans for Ongoing Student Progress Assessment

Assessing the results of your teaching in an ongoing fashion, if required or desired, means that you will utilize either activities or tests to measure your children's academic growth and you will do so frequently throughout your home-school year. Ongoing assessment can enable you to keep tabs on what your children have learned during any one lesson, what reteaching is needed, and which lesson to teach next.

Assessments take many forms. For example, if you and your children had just finished a lesson on the body parts of reptiles, you might ask your children to complete a worksheet on which they must label the body parts of a turtle pictured on the worksheet. By independently completing the identification and labeling of the turtle body parts and their functions your students would be, in effect, undergoing an assessment. You and they would find out what they had learned and had not yet learned. The assessment might have taken other forms. For instance, you might have constructed a matching quiz in which your children would have to match the names of the turtle body parts with their functions. You might have used a test that appears in the science textbook teacher's manual. At the primary level the student might have been asked to respond orally rather than on paper. He may even have been asked to pretend he was a turtle and to tell you about himself as a turtle. He could respond manipulatively, like shifting the pieces of a puzzle. Or you could take your child of any grade level into the field to respond orally with a live turtle in view. You could ask him to create a turtle in clay and label the body parts with tiny flags glued to toothpicks poked into the clay. Another possibility is asking him to write a letter to a friend explaining all he has learned about turtles and to let you read the letter before it is mailed. You could design a culminating project that would allow assessment. With your help, for example, your child might obtain, set up a home for, and care for a turtle. His ability to include an appropriate environment, suitable food, water, and so on, will demonstrate a knowledge of turtles. To accompany this project you might urge your child to keep a daily observation diary of the turtle's behaviors, daily patterns, food preferences, mode of locomotion, eye movement, and numerous other such observations.

Simple, routine parent-teacher observations of a child at work can serve as assessments, too. Sometimes progress is evident in a child's daily learning behavior and response. If someone asks you, for example, if and how well your toddler has learned to walk, you can easily tell them based upon your observations. A test or culminating demonstration of your toddler's walking ability is certainly not necessary. The key factors to remember regarding ongoing assessment are 1) that you as teacher see some demonstration of your student's knowledge and skills, and 2) that you assess frequently enough to adjust your instruction in order to help your child fill in the gaps and move ahead to greater knowledge and more advanced skills. You can be as creative as you wish in designing your assessments. Formal tests are not always required nor are they necessarily desirable.

Sometimes assessments are built into a particular teaching approach. Mastery learning, for example, includes an itemized accounting of the achievement of each learning objective, as per test results, before a student goes on to the next objective or set of objectives. In other words, objectives for a series of learning activities would be established, the student would carry out the activities, then take a test. If a high score (not necessarily a perfect score) indicates that the student has mastered the objectives, he moves ahead to the next group of objectives and activities. If he does not achieve a sufficient score to indicate mastery, he repeats the activities or completes alternate activities and then tries the test again (or alternate test). Ongoing assessment is obviously built into this approach.

Another approach with built in assessments is known as "diagnostic/prescriptive" teaching. This approach involves assessing or testing first; i.e., diagnosing. Then based upon gaps in the student's demonstrated knowledge or skills, activities are assigned; i.e., prescribed. The activities will, if successful, help the student fill in the gaps. Then he is retested.

You can check Appendix A, "Teaching Approaches," at the end of this book for other teaching approaches into which assessment procedures might be built. Whichever methods you use, for the sake of your statement of intent or home-school proposal, you may be required to account for the means by which you plan to assess student progress in an ongoing fashion and by which you plan to keep records of ongoing assessments. For the sake of maintaining evidence of your child's achievement, you will need to design means of recording the results of your assessments. Please refer to "Keeping Records" in Section Three for ideas about how to record those results. Once you have planned a procedure for assessment and for recording assessments, perhaps even several procedures for varying subject areas, write a brief description of your plans and insert it into your statement of intent file. There it will wait for submittal to officials and/or for you to implement once you begin home teaching. (See Sample Nine on page 86.)

Just as lesson planning and ongoing assessment are correlated with your curriculums, our next segment is also based loosely upon your curriculums. We'll look now at schedules and calendars.

10. Schedules and Calendars

Many home schoolers are required to submit schedules and/or calendars as segments of their statement of intent or home-school program proposal. School officials want to be sure that your schedules and calendars show that you are planning for all required subjects, that you will proceed in an organized fashion, that you include the number of required hours per day (if minimums have been set), and that your children will be "in school" the required number of days in the home-school year.

If required in your state, you should design a daily/weekly schedule for each child's home schooling. The schedules should reflect your lesson plans. In other words, the schedules should show the days of the week and the hours of each day during which home-school subjects will be taught. Although lesson plans and schedules are typically written for a week at a time, a schedule for one day in a public school might look like the sample below:

Monday

9:00	science
9:30	math
10:00	English
10:30	recess
10:45	reading
11:30	creative writing
12:00	lunch
12:45	story telling
1:15	social studies
2:00	recess
2:15	music
3:00	physical education

Your schedule may be more loosely drawn than this one, but remember that in part you are trying to achieve a paper impression. A daily home-school schedule similar to this one should satisfy school officials who want to see that you are in compliance with requirements. However, such a schedule should be considered by you only as a basic routine for daily home-school sessions. Stick to your schedule relatively consistently if you wish, but manipulate it freely as often as you need to in order to allow for field trips, academic presentations by resource persons, library trips, activity days with other home schoolers, lessons away from home (e.g.: music), learning projects, the diverse academic interests of your children, and also to allow for changes to a better routine that you later find useful.

Quite possibly you will find that a condensed version works fine, one in which less time is needed and therefore less time is allotted for some subject areas. During the typical public school day (from which required home-school hours are derived), much time is wasted on nonacademic time. At home, you can make concentrated use of the instructional hours and engage in enrichment activities the remainder of the day, if you wish. On the other hand, you could easily take advantage of the *extra* hours by moving ahead at an accelerated pace as the weeks go by.

A schedule change may be needed once you get started if you discover that your home-schooling schedule doesn't mesh well with your family-life schedule. Also, if you teach more than one child at more than one academic level, schedules may need shuffling before you settle on timing arrangements that work best.

If you alter the schedule significantly, sketch out a new one to keep on file. You may wish to create an official schedule for the file and separately maintain your own schedule. The official schedule should demonstrate that you are meeting state requirements regarding the number of schooling hours and subjects to be taught and should look similar to the above sample. Your unofficial schedule may be more flexible while you and your children in actuality still meet the hours requirement, but less formally and less rigidly.

While schedules show each day's routine, calendars for home schools (and public schools) show the entire school year and demonstrate that the required minimum number of days is included. You should either write out a calendar showing all the days your home school will officially be in session or buy a one-page, year's calendar and simply circle the days you'll be in session. School officials should be content to see that you are in compliance, and again, you can deviate from your calendar as long as you *officially* make up days missed. (See Sample 10 on page 87.)

If your state does not require you to submit schedules and calendars, you would be wise to rough them out anyway so you can assure yourself that you will meet hourly and daily requirements. Also, if you keep your schedules and calendars on hand, you'll have ready evidence that you are in compliance with required time frames.

11. Plans for Keeping Records

Maintaining complete records consistently could be vital to the continued existence of your home school. They may be necessary initially for approval of your home school, necessary later for proof of compliance with requirements or as evidence that you are providing your children with a sound and *equivalent* education. In the planning stages, however, you first need to become aware of the kinds of records you should keep or may choose to keep and of the forms in which to keep those records. Some we have already mentioned:

A file of legal information.

A statement of intent (program proposal) file, including all pertinent documents for each of the eleven segments of the statement that you choose to complete.

Ongoing records of home-teacher education and improvement efforts undertaken by you.

Ongoing log of certificated home-school consultant activities.

Ongoing lesson plans.

Ongoing progress assessment records.

In the "Keeping Records" portion of Section Three of this book you will learn about other home-school records that you may want or need to keep. At this point, however, you should design a plan for keeping whatever records are required or desirable. School officials will probably be most interested in records related to certain segments of your statement of intent, such as curriculum and annual evaluation, assessment records and attendance records, schedules and calendars. Check the summary for your state in Section Four and the information you receive from your state department of education for specifications regarding records to keep. **Then read Section Three before completing your written plan for keeping records.** Following that reading, briefly write out a description of how you plan to maintain records that are required or that seem important to you. Place that description in your statement of intent file for later submission to officials. If you are not responsible for explaining your record keeping procedures to officials, you will not need to write such a description. You should, nevertheless, design methods for convenient record keeping and then use those methods as you begin to plan and to teach.

With this we complete our walk through the components of a home-school plan or proposal, called here a "statement of intent." Samples of each of the eleven segments of the statement of intent follow in this section of the book. To further help you get started with your home-school plan, I offer the following checklist. After reviewing each segment of the statement of intent in this section, consider whether or not each segment is required, is important to you, or is neither required nor important to you. Then check those that you will want to complete because they are required or important.

Statement of Intent Checklist

I am required to complete this segment.	I feel this segment is important enough to complete.	Statement of Intent Segments
		1. Basic Personal Info – Enrollees
		2. Basic Building Info
		3. Home-Teacher Qualifications
		4. Certificated Consultant Info
		5. Statement of Reasons & Rights
		6. Plans for Annual Evaluation
		7. Curriculum and Materials
		8. Lesson Plan Samples
		9. Plans for Assessment
		10. Schedules and Calendars
		11. Plans for Keeping Records

Deadlines and other information related to the above checked segments of my Statement of Intent:

_____

_____

_____

_____

_____

_____

_____

_____

_____

Still in the offing, now, is working through each of the components of the statement of intent that you elect to complete, preparing those you must for presentation to officials, and then seeking approval if needed. The upcoming sections of this book are intended to help you carry out each of these tasks. First, Section Three takes you in greater detail into four home-school plan components: annual evaluation, curriculum and materials, lesson planning, and keeping records. You will need to read Section Three carefully before completing the related segments of your statement of intent.

Then, as you work on your statement or proposal, refer to Sections Four through Six of this book as necessary. In Section Four you'll find a chart and summaries delineating all fifty state and District of Columbia regulations and procedures and state department of education addresses. Home-school support organizations are listed in Section Five. In Section Six you'll find reading, resource, and curriculum source lists and finally a glossary of terms used in this book and/or used by the public school officials with whom you may interact.

Let's take a look now at the statement of intent segment samples and then move on to Section Three. You may feel yourself in the midst of much information that is new to you and, therefore, a bit overwhelming. Please realize, however, that although there may be several components to your home-school plan, not any one of those components is too difficult for you to complete — whether you are a certified teacher, a college graduate, or neither. You can successfully complete each component. Your planning will take some time, but the samples, explanations and aids in this book should carry you through the process.

Statement of Intent Segment Samples

The following samples include suggested formats and content of the statement of intent or program proposal documents. If forms are provided by your state's department of education or by the local school district, use those forms as you plan or transfer information to those forms later. The required content should be similar to that already described in this section or included in the samples. Adjust content as necessary. Of course, there will be as many variations in the actual wording of these documents as there are people who read this book. All samples are only samples.

Note that in brackets [ ] on the sample pages are comments directed at you. The items within brackets are to be read by you, but are not included as part of the sample format.

For Quick Reference

Explanations for the samples which follow here appear on the pages listed.

Sample One: Basic Personal Information - Enrollees

Home-School Enrollment Sheet

Mary Miller F born 8/1/76 (13) Box 171, Lee Lane, Sky, OK
Suzie Miller F born 6/6/78 (10) Box 171, Lee Lane, Sky, OK
Tom Miller M born 7/3/80 (8) Box 171, Lee Lane, Sky, OK
Billy Miller M born 4/2/82 (7) Box 171, Lee Lane, Sky, OK

[Note: Attach copies of birth certificates if required.]

Parents: Mark and Mazie Miller
Box 171 Lee Lane, Sky, OK 00001
phone: 111-2233

Students' current grade levels and previous schools attended:

Mary grade seven Fiddle Middle School, Sky, OK

Suzie grade five Intermediate Grade School, Sky, OK

Tom grade three Little People's School, Sky, OK

Billy grade one (not previously enrolled in school)

Immunization records: A copy of the immunization records for each child is attached. All are up-to-date.

Previously identified special needs:

Mary – none
Suzie – none At Intermediate Grade School in Sky, OK, Suzie participated twice weekly in a speech therapy program. At year's end she was exited from the program.

[Note: If Suzie still needs speech therapy, you would need to secure the services of a speech therapist, preferably the local school's speech therapist.]

Tom – none
Billy – Arrangements have been made for Billy to complete the usual school entrance, screening procedures administered to all incoming kindergartners and first graders in Oklahoma School District #4444.

date _____ signed: _____
(parent)

date _____ signed: _____
(parent)

Sample Two: Home-School Building Information

Home-School Building Report

Address of home school: Box 24, Pine, Idaho 50009;
located three miles NW of Pine
via Highway 12

Condition of home-school: Our home-school building meets county building codes and has established fire escape routes from all rooms. Our children have participated in building safety discussions and in fire escape practices. [Note: If required, attached a statement from fire and safety inspectors attesting to the quality of your home-school building.]

Safety of student records: [Include this item if required.] Student records will be kept in a moisture-proof area in a cardboard file box. Duplicates of attendance records and ongoing assessment records will be kept in a separate building. Records of annual evaluations will be kept in School District #555 safe as well as in our file box. [Note: The school district may require that you submit other records as well. If so, make note here of the safekeeping of those records.]

Home-school "classroom" environment: We have designated a small room in our home as our home-school library and workroom. Our kitchen table will serve as a desk during sit-down lessons. Thus far, we have a collection of children's books, textbooks, a dictionary and an atlas, totaling forty-four volumes, that constitute our home library. We also have access to our local public library's collection of 15,000 volumes, including encyclopedia sets appropriate for children. In our workroom, we also have a globe; United States, Idaho and Pine maps; a small aquarium; a terrarium; a piano; a work table; and miscellaneous math, music, art, and science supplies and equipment. We have access to a computer and educational software at the local public library. Our home school is surrounded by a natural world of creek, meadow, bushes, trees, and animal life which will allow in-the-field science studies. A mile-and-a-half down the road, within walking or driving or biking distance, is the Pine Historical Museum, the Pine Regional Bird Preserve, and the town of Pine, all of which will aid us in science and social studies.

[Note: If required and if your home is to be your home-school building, list names of all persons who reside in your home.]

Sample Three: Evidence of Home-Teacher Qualifications

Home-Teacher Qualifications

<u>Home teacher</u>: Mitzi Peters, mother

<u>Educational background:</u>

grades K-8   — East Elementary School
                        Salisbury, OR
grades 9-12 — East High School
                        Salisbury, OR
high school graduation — 1974
college   — two years at City Community College,
                        Salisbury, OR
music   — four years of private piano instruction
art   — participation in various, intermittent,
                        community education oil painting
                        and pottery workshops

<u>Occupational experience:</u>

1966   — youth host, Salisbury Historical
                        Museum
1974 —'77   — teacher's aide, Lincoln Primary School,
                        Stone, OR
1978 —'84   — assistant librarian, Stone Public Library
1985 —'88   — home-preschool teacher for two of our
                        children and three others

<u>Talents:</u>

piano; pottery; oil painting; storytelling; natural foods
cooking; and wild plant identification, collection,
preservation

[Note: If your spouse or other adults will assist you as a
home teacher, write a similar account of their education,
occupations, and talents, particularly those that pertain to
your children's home-school curriculum.]

Sample Four: Certificated Home-School Consultant

Certificated Home-School Consultant

We have secured the assistance of a certificated consultant.

<u>Certificated consultant:</u> Mason Sellers
     address: 1410 Doddridge Avenue, Blueville, KS 00001
     phone: 111- 4455

<u>Degree:</u>   Bachelor of Science
     1979, University of Oregon
     Elementary Education Major
     Library Science Minor

<u>Certificate:</u> Kansas Standard Elementary Certificate
     endorsements: elementary education & K-6
     librarian

<u>Current employment:</u> Sigwald Grade School, Blueville, KS

<u>Current teaching assignment</u>: fifth grade teacher

<u>Agreement:</u> Mr. Mason Sellers has agreed to assist in the development of our home-school curriculum and the selection of appropriate teaching materials. He has also agreed to meet with us twice each semester to informally evaluate our home-school program and to offer recommendations. Since three of our home-school children will be elementary level students and one a seventh grader, Mr. Seller's experience as an educator at the elementary level should prove most helpful.

[Since a certificated consultant is not required in Kansas and you would simply be volunteering this information, you would not need to attach copies of Mr. Seller's university transcripts and certificate.]

Sample Five: Statement of Positive Reasons and Rights

Statement of Positive Reasons and Rights

We the parents of Henry, Lisa, Corey, and Carlene Cellers wish to educate our children at home for the following reasons:

[List your reasons in clear, specific sentences. If appropriate, your compliance with the home-schooling statutes of your state should be noted.]

_____

George Cellers

_____

Tillie Cellers

Sample Six: Plans for Annual Evaluation

<u>Annual Evaluation</u>

We have arranged with Arizona School District #1000 for the purchase of copies of the Comprehensive Test of Basic Skills at appropriate levels for our two children, Tad and Jeff. The tests will be given to Tad and Jeff in our home by the certified head teacher of the Good Samaritan Private School here in Mars, Arizona, on April 14th. We will file copies of the achievement test results with the county superintendent and also maintain copies at our home school.

_____

Marvin Jones

_____

Mary Jones

Sample Seven: Curriculums and Materials

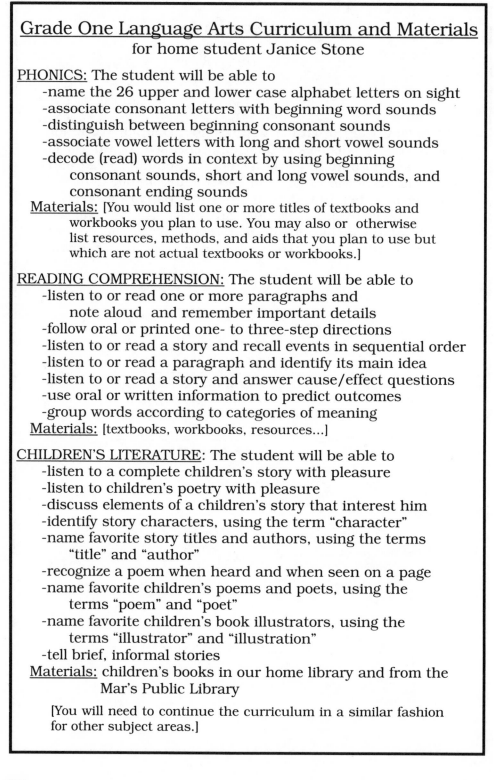

Grade One Language Arts Curriculum and Materials
for home student Janice Stone

PHONICS: The student will be able to
-name the 26 upper and lower case alphabet letters on sight
-associate consonant letters with beginning word sounds
-distinguish between beginning consonant sounds
-associate vowel letters with long and short vowel sounds
-decode (read) words in context by using beginning
    consonant sounds, short and long vowel sounds, and
    consonant ending sounds
Materials: [You would list one or more titles of textbooks and
    workbooks you plan to use. You may also or otherwise
    list resources, methods, and aids that you plan to use but
    which are not actual textbooks or workbooks.]

READING COMPREHENSION: The student will be able to
-listen to or read one or more paragraphs and
    note aloud and remember important details
-follow oral or printed one- to three-step directions
-listen to or read a story and recall events in sequential order
-listen to or read a paragraph and identify its main idea
-listen to or read a story and answer cause/effect questions
-use oral or written information to predict outcomes
-group words according to categories of meaning
Materials: [textbooks, workbooks, resources...]

CHILDREN'S LITERATURE: The student will be able to
-listen to a complete children's story with pleasure
-listen to children's poetry with pleasure
-discuss elements of a children's story that interest him
-identify story characters, using the term "character"
-name favorite story titles and authors, using the terms
    "title" and "author"
-recognize a poem when heard and when seen on a page
-name favorite children's poems and poets, using the
    terms "poem" and "poet"
-name favorite children's book illustrators, using the
    terms "illustrator" and "illustration"
-tell brief, informal stories
Materials: children's books in our home library and from the
        Mar's Public Library

[You will need to continue the curriculum in a similar fashion
for other subject areas.]

Sample Eight: Lesson Plans

Brief Lesson Plan

Subject Area: <u>SCIENCE</u>   Dates _____

Focus: <u>turtles as representative of reptiles</u>

Learning Objective: <u>Students will be able to identify body parts of the turtle and their functions, explain the turtle life cycle and needs, food, dangers, reptilian characteristics, and habitat</u>

Monday
Observe turtle. Open-ended questions.
Record observations on chart.
Build terrarium.

Tuesday
Biologist Kelly Green
Observe turtle.
Review, summarize, and add items to chart.
Organize chart items.
Determine what information we still need.

Wednesday
Further observations and library research.
Students identify and label turtle body parts and functions on turtle drawing on butcher paper and begin a mural showing habitat, food, etc.

Thursday
Orally quiz individual students.
Finish mural.

Friday
Individually complete turtle worksheets.
Give immediate feedback with butcher paper drawing.

[Note: In Appendix C explanation is give of each of the five lesson steps — anticipatory set, instruction, guided practice, closure, and independent practice.]

Sample Nine: Plans for Ongoing Progress Assessment

Home-School Student Progress Assessment

For both of our sons, Henry and James Sultan, we plan to engage in various, ongoing progress-assessment procedures and to maintain permanent portfolios of their work and of any written tests or quizzes for all subject areas.

Means of Assessment

phonics

worksheets
checktests
application in
  oral reading

math

worksheets
checktests
unit tests
applications

social studies

worksheets
unit tests
projects

science

worksheets
unit tests
projects
experiments
field work

reading/lit.

oral discussion
comprehension
  activities

language

worksheets
unit tests
observations of
  oral & written
  use of language

piano

observations
recital

computer

observations
application
  projects

library

observations
projects

Sample Ten: Schedules and Calendars

Weekly Home-School Schedule
for Susie & Tim Bayson, grades 1 and 2 respectively

Time	Monday	Tuesday	Wednesday	Thursday	Friday
8:00	phonics/reading/literature – – – – – – – – – – – – –				
8:45	math	computer	math	math	computer
9:15	social studies– – – – – – – – – – – – – – – – – – – –				
9:40	language skills– – –	piano		language skills	
10-12	science & field work	piano		science & field work	
12:00	lunch– –				
1:00	art & special interest activities– – – – – –– library work				

[Note that the above lesson schedule includes a required core curriculum plus piano lessons, art, and library. Other curricular or extracurricular activities may be included in your schedule. There is a possibility that you and your children are among the many home schoolers who gather with other home schoolers one day each week for field trips or activity days. Such days can also be included in your schedule. Just make sure that on the remaining days, the at-home days, your schedule includes the curricular areas and the number of hours required by law in your state.]

Monthly Home-School Calendar

November 88						
		①1	②2	③3	④4	5
6	⑦7	⑧8	⑨9	⑩10	⑪11	12
13	⑭14	⑮15	⑯16	⑰17	⑱18	19
20	㉑21	㉒22	㉓23	24	25	26
27	㉘28	㉙29	㉚30			

Sample Eleven: Plans for Keeping Records

Home-School Records

Means of keeping records for Shane & Kay Tuttle:

portfolios of work in all subject areas
portfolios of tests, quizzes, and other assessments
observation log to be kept by home teacher
social activities log
permanent files — report card
     test and quiz score records
     achievement test results
     previous grade report cards
     immunization records
     other health & dental records
attendance register
speech therapy records for Kay

[You may be expected to secure the permanent files in as fire-proof and moisture-proof a fashion as possible.]

Teacher-related records that will be kept:

lesson plan book
consultant activity file
weekly lesson schedule
yearly calendar

[You may not need to include all of the above items in your record-keeping plans. On the other hand, you may wish to add others. See "Keeping Records" in Section Three for a complete list of possibilities.]

Section **3**

Key
Components

Why Some Segments Become Key Components

As we walked through the eleven possible segments of your statement of intent in Section Two, it became clear that not all eleven segments are necessarily required by your state, or desired by you, or even essential to home schooling. But for reasons pertinent to your home-schooling situation and your state's procedures and laws, some segments will emerge as key components of your program plan. The four components covered in this section are among those that often surface as most important or most necessary, and they require more than the introductory explanations offered in Section Two. Therefore, in this section you'll find detailed discussions of annual evaluation, curriculum and materials, lesson planning, and record keeping.

Many home schoolers consider annual evaluations to be unnecessary and annoying. Nevertheless, evaluation procedures are included in many states as a requirement and therefore essential for legal home schooling in those states. Curriculums and accompanying materials lists are also usually required. Whether required or not, a written curriculum can serve as a critical map and compass for your children's academic journeys. Lesson planning may be considered by some to be nonessential, but in many instances is required and may be useful particularly for the beginning home teacher. Lesson plans can serve as the daily and weekly mini-map — a cutout, as it were, from the larger curriculum map. Perhaps most important of all components of your home-school plan and ongoing program is record keeping. As you'll see in the "Keeping Records" portion of this section, certain types of records are almost always required — attendance, immunizations, schedules and calendars, for example. Others may be required. However, you'll need to consider not just requirements when you decide which records are essential for you to keep. You may find that maintaining permanent evidence of the soundness of your children's home-school program is a key factor necessitating thorough record keeping.

Planning for and completing annual evaluations, curriculum outlines, and lesson plans, as well as maintaining good records, involves more thought and time than some of the other home-school program components. Read slowly and carefully through this section of the book. Study each element, use the worksheets that are provided, get assistance when needed . . . and have faith in your ability to successfully complete each component.

Annual Evaluation

Potentially useful and required by many states is some form of end-of-the-year evaluation of each home-schooled child's progress and/or learning program. You may be asked to account for your plans regarding annual evaluation in your statement of intent and to have those plans officially approved along with the other segments of your home-school program proposal. At the appropriate time, of course, you would then need to conduct your proposed evaluation. If not required, you may want to conduct a personal evaluation of your children's home-schooling accomplishments and of your teaching program in order to make decisions about your children's next school year.

The process and composition of annual home-school evaluations vary widely. The person responsible for the evaluation may be you or a certificated educator, and sometimes on-site reviews are carried out by school officials. In some states evaluation items must be submitted and "accepted" following their completion. Any of the following annual evaluation elements, singly or in combination, may be required in your state.

Standardized achievement tests.

Local or state-designed competency tests.

Review of and/or submittal of student portfolios.

Review of and/or submittal of curriculums, lesson plans, report cards.

Narrative reports on student progress in each subject area.

Narrative reports on student social progress.

Schedules and calendars.

Review of and a summary of quarterly evaluations.

A discussion between your child and a consultant.

Diaries, journals, or logs.

An inspection/supervision visit by public school officials.

Evaluation elements selected by you or by you and a consultant.

Official objectives for requiring an annual evaluation may be threefold: (1) to ensure that each of your children is indeed being educated; (2) to initiate means by which to improve student progress should it be lagging; and (3) to actuate improvement efforts for you as a home teacher if appropriate.

Standardized Achievement Tests

The most commonly required form of evaluation is the standardized achievement test. It is also one of the most controversial, even among non-home schoolers. Racial or religious bias, misuse or disuse of results, lack of correlation with local curriculum content, misinterpretation of results, inflated scores due to invalid or inaccurate norms, and similar issues are often cited as problems with the tests. Also, of course, for many home schoolers the *imposition* of tests is an issue.

Usually, however, if standardized achievement tests are a legal requirement, there is no way to escape that imposition. Sometimes participation in a satellite or correspondence program is used as a means to evade the tests. However, usually home educators required to arrange for the administration of achievement tests simply do their best to prepare their children for them. We should recognize, too, that the results of these tests have offered, and we hope will continue to offer, important and impressive statistical information for use in increasing public awareness of the benefits of home schooling. Your children's scores can be entered into those statistics, indirectly enabling you and them to further the home-school cause in our nation.

The requirements you must follow pertaining to your children's testing circumstances may be restrictive. Perhaps, for example, your children must appear at the local school at a specific time on a specific day to take the test with public school children of the same grade levels. You may try to have the circumstances altered, but often your control over the circumstances is limited.

Try to ease your children into the tests with explanatory discussions ahead of time. Usually standardized test teacher's manuals include practice tests which all teachers may use to prepare their students for taking the tests. You should be able to get a copy of the practice test and the teacher's directions for giving the practice test from a local school principal or superintendent. There is no official reason the practice test cannot be shared with you. Typically, too, school principals have copies of a test management guide or manual, sometimes called "class management guide." In such a guide may be found suggestions for student activities that would prepare students for the test content and item-by-item formats that appear in the test, as well as actual samples of test item formats. A principal is free to share this information with any or all teachers, including you.

Therefore, along with a request for a practice test, you may wish to ask about the availability of test management guide information of the sort noted here. Resistance locally to supplying you with any test information might be followed up by you with a call to your state department of education. You can explain your problem, request assistance, or request a copy of the practice test and other information from your state department.

Another source of test information is your certificated consultant, if you have one, or another teacher who has given the locally used achievement test at the grade levels of your children. The teacher will probably have taken mental or written notes of the content areas covered in the test and can also explain formats that appear in the test. She may even supply you with a copy of the practice test and directions. Although teachers do try to include test content within their year's instruction, oftentimes it is not the content but the formats in the tests that confuse students. Because the formats are not usually used at any other time during a school year, they are totally new on the day of the test. This is the major reason for giving practice tests. Noteworthy, too, is the fact that teachers are free to use the formats for regular assignments and activities throughout the school year and would certainly be wise to do so, as would you.

If you are able to secure a practice test, try to set up a mock test environment similar to the upcoming actual test situation. Follow the practice instructions carefully so your child can rehearse listening to and following them. After the practice test has been completed, correct it and then discuss with your child her answers and her reasons for her answers — in other words, her thinking processes. Her thinking may fully explain the logic of a wrong answer. Then tell her *what the test expected*, even though her answer was logical. Try to help her realize, too, that although the test experience is somewhat strange and scary, it is just another learning activity. Help her understand that it's an exercise in how well she can take a test or play the test game, if you will, rather than simply in how knowledgeable she is. Also, try not to add pressure by elaborating on the danger of a low score to your home-schooling status. Discussing typical testing time frames may further be useful. You can explain that some parts of the test may be timed and that this means she shouldn't dawdle with those portions of the test game. Tell her to relax, to enjoy the test items, but to move along. Incidentally, if a child finishes a test section before the time is up, she will have to silently wait. She might take a book along to read during the waiting periods. Before the testing begins, let the test administrator know your child has a book to read during spare time.

If you have not been able to secure information on formats or content before your children take their first achievement test, ask your children to tell you immediately afterwards about the content and formats. Take notes and save them for the following year. The specific content will change from year to year but be similar generally. For example, word attack sections in primary grade tests will cover similar content — phonics, deriving meaning from context, etc. — but the specific items will be different and slightly more advanced with each test level. However, the formats will be pretty much the same. So once your children describe to you the formats, you can use those formats for test preparation each year. You can also use them on activities during the year and even type your own practice tests using those formats.

Also, no doubt your fellow home schoolers will be able to tell you about the achievement test used in the local school. They may offer ideas about how to make the test-taking experience as comfortable as possible for your children. They may mention, for example, that if you can choose the person who will give the test, choose a person familiar to your child or acquaint your child with the person well before test day. Studies show that relaxed test-takers score higher and that positive familiarization between test-taker and test-giver also results in higher scores. Furthermore, a stranger who gives your child the test has no means of adapting his behavior and presentation in any manner that is sensitive to your child's personality, fears, or background. In other words, it is helpful for the test administrator to know your child. You may also want to familiarize your child with the room where she will take the test. You might even volunteer to be a test monitor in the testing room during the time your child takes the test. When public school teachers give achievement tests, they often welcome help with pencils, erasers, papers, and student questions. If you can't be a monitor, you might ask to sit at the back of the room as a silent observer at least the first day of the test. Be certain first, however, that your presence will not in this case distract your child.

Testing Conditions

If you suspect beforehand that the testing situation or conditions will be especially stressful for your children as well as any other attending home-schooled children, there are steps you can take to attempt to improve the situation. First, you should understand what happens when public schools plan for and administer standardized achievement tests. Typically the test company designates a two week testing period throughout the nation, and schools often elect to reserve the second week for make-up tests. During the first week, test subsections are administered in varying blocks of time over a three-to-five day period depending on the test levels and lengths. While sometimes public school teaching staffs agree generally upon testing hours, teachers are usually free to schedule their individual class test sessions as they see fit and they are encouraged to schedule the sessions when testing conditions are optimal for good student performance. Almost universally those conditions include hours when the teachers know students are most alert and yet most able to remain composed and quiet, when the classroom is cool and comfortable, when testing time blocks and breaks can be flexibly arranged, when any potentially disruptive students can be removed from the regular classroom, and when no outside interruptions will occur. The teacher administering the test is almost always the one who has worked throughout the year with the group of students he tests and is therefore the in-school adult with whom the students are most familiar. In many elementary schools, teachers' aides, office workers, or parent volunteers are on hand in each classroom to provide assistance with pencils and test papers, questions, unexpected disruptions, opening a window, offering whispered reassurances to nervous or weary students, and so on. Special-needs students are given their tests in individual or small group situations away from regular classrooms and by familiar adults.

Any child who takes a standardized achievement test, including a home-schooled child, has a right to such considerations for his test-taking situation. And so does any teacher! One key reason the test conditions are so important to public school personnel is that they want the test results to reflect well upon the teachers and administrators.

To arrange reasonable achievement test conditions for your children, I recommend that you visit with the principal or other person in charge of scheduling and/or conducting the achievement tests. Ask about the test site. Is it well ventilated (during warm months) or well heated (during cold months)? Is it roomy enough for the number of students who will be present? Will your children have comfortable chairs and desks or tables on which to work? If your child will take the test in a regular classroom with public school students, has the teacher been made aware that your child will attend the test session? Will he have an extra desk and chair brought in ahead of time? Is lighting adequate? Ask to see the site. Ask to meet the person who will administer the test. Then discuss timing. Sometimes public school administrators will schedule home schoolers' test sessions all in one day in order to make driving to the test convenient for the home-school parents. However, in the case of tests, the children's needs must take precedence if you hope for good results. Completing an entire achievement test in one day would be a tremendous strain, particularly for elementary-age children. I suggest that you do all that you can to arrange for a three-to-five day testing period and also to ensure that adequate breaks will be taken between subtests. Also, you as the teacher of your children know those times of the day when your children are best able to do sit-down work. Recommend to the test arranger that the test be administered during those times if in any way possible.

If the test arranger is reluctant to alter the proposed test situation in order to improve it, question him regarding the conditions under which the students in his school take the test. Ask him to describe those conditions in detail. If he is truthful, you and he will recognize that he is describing optimal conditions. Then suggest that the home-schooled children be given the same considerations. If a number of home-schooled children are being scheduled for the same test, you might offer the assistance of a committee of home-school parents to arrange the test sessions and situation and even to function as volunteer test monitors. Do realize that your requesting the same optimal test conditions that the teachers in the local public school maintain is certainly reasonable.

Test Selection

What of the tests themselves? In many states or school districts one test is specified as the one home-schooled children, as well as public school children, must take. Some states, on the other hand, require home schoolers to select their own standardized achievement tests and to then arrange for the administration of those tests. You may be specifically required, as part of your statement of intent, to complete and submit what is known as a "notice of test selection." This means the state or local school district will not mandate that you utilize the standardized test that they use, but that your children are required to take such a test and that you must submit a form or statement indicating that you are in compliance with the requirement.

In this situation, you'll need to shop for a test. The information you have received from your state department may suggest certain tests or provide you with a list of tests which have already been approved and from which you can choose. Otherwise, you will need to locate possible tests and select one on your own. If you have established a good working relationship with a local public school principal or superintendent, she may be able and willing to supply you with the locally used test. If you are affiliated with private or religious school administrators, one of them may be able to supply a test. You could also contact the state testing division of your state department of education, as mentioned above, or an area university's educational testing, research, or public instruction department. Then too, of course, state or national public education or home-school service organizations, such as the Hewitt Research Foundation in the Northwest, the Southeastern Educational Association in the Southeast, or the Bureau of Educational Measurement in the Southwest may be able to help you obtain test information and/or tests. (Addresses in Section Five.)

If you are totally on your own, remember that in order for the test you select to be approved or acceptable to school officials, it must be a standardized, normed achievement test. To be standardized uniform testing procedures must be used throughout the country. To be normed a test must have undergone a norming procedure during which a representative sample group of students was given the test. Then those students' scores become the standard by which all other scores are weighed until a subsequent norming procedure is undertaken. Incidentally, you will most likely want to secure the most recent edition of the test you select. Also, realize that no two tests cover exactly the same content. For instance, one may include participles in the language usage segment of the test and others not. One may include coins in the primary math segment and others not. Take advantage of any opportunities to preview test content — firsthand, or secondhand by visiting with others who have used the tests you are considering. This information can help you select a test that is well correlated with the academic areas your children have covered in their home-school lessons. Here are some generally accepted tests from which you might choose:

> California Achievement Test (CAT)
> Cooperative General Achievement Tests
> Comprehensive Test of Basic Skills (CTBS)
> Essential High School Content Battery
> Iowa Tests of Achievement and Proficiency
> Iowa Tests of Basic Skills
> Metropolitan Achievement Battery
> Sequential Tests of Educational Progress
> SRA Achievement Battery
> Stanford Achievement Test Battery

Test Interpretation

Although local school officials (and even teachers) seldom give great attention to individual student achievement test results, and in some cases don't understand the results, they will probably use your home-schooled children's test results to determine indeed if your children are being properly schooled. In actuality the test results for any one year are not highly significant. Only when you compile an ongoing chart of year-by-year achievement test results can you begin to see trends in your children's areas of academic strengths and weaknesses. This ongoing information can be significant. However, the officials may use single-year test results for your children to evaluate your children's progress and the effectiveness of your teaching.

In view of this, I provide here a brief explanation of test interpretation. Interpreting achievement test scores can be confusing and complicated, and it is essential that you have a basic understanding of the scores yourself. Equipped with such understanding, you will be able to exercise some control over the possible application of the standardized achievement test results to your home-school evaluation and to spot any misinterpretations by school personnel.

Realize first that all standardized test scores leave room for a margin of error. Test publishers call this the "standard error of measurement." Thus all achievement test scores should be considered as estimates. We know that a true score exists for each child who takes a test, but the actual score he receives only falls within a band or range within which his true score would fall. We can't be sure what that true score is. In other words, a percentile rank of 70 is an estimated score which indicates that his true score may be 65 or 68 or 75 or some other score within a certain range. Also, the range is broader closer to the 50th percentile point and narrower towards the 0 and 100 percentiles. Thus a percentile rank of 50, compared to a previous year's rank of 40 on the same test, does not indicate as much actual change as if the score had gone from the 85th percentile to the 95th percentile or from the 5th percentile to the 10th percentile. In fact, depending upon the value of the standard error of measurement, such scores may not indicate any change at all.

Let's look at some of the types of scores provided on achievement test score reports:

> **a. Raw score.** This score tells you the total number of items in any one category of an achievement test that your child answered correctly. All of the below-noted types of scores are derived from it.

The raw score is not typically accorded much importance. In fact, you may notice what appears to be little relationship between raw scores and other scores. It's relationship to the percentile scores in subtest categories, for example, will vary from subtest to subtest. To explain this variability, let's consider the percentile score.

> **b. Percentile score.** This score tells you how your child fared in comparison to all other children who took the same test. That is, the percentile figure tells you what percentage of those children scored below your child. For example, if your child's percentile score is 70, then you know that 69 out of every 100 children in the norm group of children who took the test achieved a score below that of your child.

A perfect, all-answers-correct raw score does not necessarily result in a percentile score of 100. Since the percentile score reflects how many students scored lower than your child, perhaps a perfect raw score in one category will yield a percentile score in the mid-nineties, not 100. In another category it may produce a percentile in the high-nineties, depending on the number of students who answered every item correctly. Thus, the percentile score allows comparison among students, whereas the raw score does not.

The percentile is frequently the score utilized for discussion by school personnel, although it is at times misinterpreted to mean a percentage of items answered correctly. If this misinterpretation occurs, look for any explanations of the scores that appear on the score sheet itself, typically on the back. These explanations will verify the correct interpretation — for both you and school personnel.

When interpreting the percentile score, remember this important factor: If the percentile score for one year in one test category is approximately the same as that score on the past year's test, your child has gained one full year's academic growth in that category. In other words, if your child scores at the 70th percentile this year and he scored at the 70th percentile (or thereabouts) last year, he has gained one full year's growth. The level of the test he has taken, you see, increased in difficulty by one year.

Therefore, if your child maintains a percentile rank of 70 (or any other single rank) from year-to-year, he is gaining a year's academic growth each year. If his score dips about ten or more percentile points during a single year or over a period of a few years, he may not be maintaining that rate of academic growth. If his score increases about ten or more percentile points, he is making progress greater than one year's academic growth. Further, note that if your child's score dips or rises dramatically just one year while the scores for all years before and after remain relatively the same, you can conclude that the off-year scores are probably invalid.

> **c. Grade equivalent score.** This score identifies the grade level at which the median test score is the same as that achieved by your child. (A median score is the score in a distribution which has one half of the remaining scores above it and the other half below it.)

Some test publishers are phasing out the grade equivalent score, and teachers are today not referring to it as often as in the past. People have a tendency to suggest that a high grade equivalent score indicates that a student should skip a grade or two and enter the grade identified by the grade equivalent score. While a high score indicates that the child who earned it performed above average among his grade level peers on his own grade level test content, it does not necessarily mean that he would do as well with content above his own grade level. A low grade equivalent score indicates that the child performed below average among his peers on his own grade level test content, but does not mandate that he should be put back a grade level or be retained, although it may be one consideration in making such a decision.

A relatively new score being currently used on achievement test score reports is this next one.

> **d. Normal Curve Equivalent score.** The NCE scores range from 1 to 99 and coincide with percentile scores at 1, 50, and 99. NCE's have many of the characteristics of percentile ranks but have the additional advantage of being based on an equal-interval scale. This allows for mathematical manipulation of the scores, particularly desirable for special programs such as Chapter I. Like percentile scores, an NCE score that remains the same from one year to the next indicates one year's academic growth.

Two other achievement test scores, stanines and scaled scores, are seldom referred to by public educators in discussions with parents, and you are not likely to need knowledge of either of them during your annual evaluation process.

It is important to remember that the purpose of achievement test scores is primarily comparison. They are intended for comparisons among students as a measure of a common education. They are also intended to provide a basis for year-by-year tracking of an individual student's achievement. Third, they are in some instances used to evaluate particular instructional programs.

Achievement test results are sometimes used, however, in ways that go beyond their purpose. For example, they may be subtly and unofficially used within a school to reflect upon the effectiveness of the teachers who teach there. They may be used in this way to reflect upon your teaching.

Standardized achievement tests are often also accorded much value in decision-making situations relative to individual students regardless of the tests' suspected flaws and of problems related to the testing situation. Among those flaws or problems may be those mentioned earlier, such as biases and a lack of correlation with a schools' curriculum, or an insensitivity to student reactions to the test-taking environment, inflexibility regarding student health on test day, and the possible ambiguity of test items. Further, we note the areas of learning that are missing from the tests that might speak well for home-schooled children — creative writing, art, music, health, values, character development, consumer education, entrepreneurship, and others. However, while home schoolers may want to participate in such watchdog organizations as The National Center for Fair and Open Testing, they may, in the meantime, need to continue meeting achievement test requirements.

What we're hoping for you and your children, at any rate, is at least a year's academic growth — reflected in achievement test scores. You now know how to determine if such growth has taken place. Also important to note is that achievement test results are (or should be) only one factor in determining growth. Your children's daily performance, routine quiz and test scores, social behavior and development, daily exhibition of a sense of well-being, attitudes toward learning, zest and zeal, and so on, are all indicators of growth. Unfortunately, arguing this point with school officials may not be successful.

Local or State Competency Tests

A school district or state department of education may use standardized achievement test results in combination with local or state competency tests or may rely on competency tests only. Competency tests typically cover writing as well as reading and mathematics, at a basic level, and they are not ordinarily given below junior high level. They are shorter and narrower in scope than standardized achievement tests, are typically not normed and usually provide what are called "criterion-referenced" scores identifying the number of items a student answered correctly. The writing subtest, however, is likely to be holistically scored on a 1-10 point basis. Usually the formats are familiar to students and the content is based directly upon local or state curriculums. Some schools now use the competency test results as a means of screening students eligible for diplomas.

If you live in one of the states where local public schools utilize competency tests, you may be expected to arrange for your home-schooled children to take these tests. Scoring may vary among different tests, so ask for thorough explanations of the scoring procedures as well as for information related to the competency test content and formats. The results of such tests will probably become a part of your home-school annual evaluation.

Other Evaluative Documents

Also considered as part of an evaluation may be your children's student portfolios for each subject area. In some states you may be asked to submit the portfolios to officials. (See p. 140 for details on portfolios.) Other items that may be a part of your ongoing record-keeping procedure and that may become important in your annual evaluation are your curriculum outlines, lesson plans, report cards, schedules and calendars. You may be asked to have these items reviewed by a consultant, to account for them yourself in an evaluative report, or to submit them to school officials at year's end. If lesson plans are required, you may be asked to account for them or to submit them routinely throughout your home-school year.

You may also be asked to arrange for the writing and submittal of a narrative report on student progress in each subject area and/or on student social progress. You can base your student progress narrative on work and tests that have been kept in your children's portfolios and on your lesson plans for the year which show what has been taught to each child. You may need to show what is called "curriculum mastery" which involves concrete demonstration that your student has achieved the skills and knowledge that were designated as goals or objectives in the curriculum. In the narrative, then, you would need to discuss what your child's curriculum goals and objectives were at the year's beginning and which of the goals and objectives he had mastered by year's end. In a few states you may also be requested to describe your children's social, cultural, and/or character development. You may find helpful Annual Evaluation Sample One: Narrative on page 107.

You may not be expected to write the narrative yourself. Instead a consultant may be asked to investigate factors demonstrating your child's progress and to write the evaluation narrative. The consultant may, on the other hand, be asked to review and summarize evaluations that you and she had completed on a quarterly basis throughout your home-school year. She may further be asked to discuss with your child his year of home schooling.

Another possible inclusion in a yearly evaluation is a home teacher's daily diary, journal, or log which documents home-school attendance, lessons, and activities. Your personal observations of your child's academic and social progress and strengths and weaknesses may also be included. Your home teacher's log would be kept in a notebook of some sort, such as an inexpensive spiral notebook, and you would probably write in an entry each day or every other day or perhaps write a fairly detailed overview at the end of each home-school week. If turning in your log is a requirement, remember that the primary purpose of a log is to demonstrate your children's coverage of the required curriculum. So you'll want to make note of all curricular areas on an ongoing basis. A daily log might look like Annual Evaluation Sample Two: Home Teacher's Log on page 108.

Official Visits

Perhaps a visit by school officials is necessitated by statutes or procedures in your state. Such a visit may be part of an annual evaluation or separate from it. If a visit is imminent, try to identify ahead of time those elements of your home-school program about which school officials will be curious. Review the home-school requirements in your state to be sure you can demonstrate compliance with each of them. Also consider your physical setup, home library, the location and safe-keeping of your home-school records, and so on. You might create a small checklist for yourself as you prepare for the visit. Include items such as the following eight.

1. My curriculums for each child — Are they written, available, used? Do I have student work available that demonstrates that the curriculums are being taught? Am I familiar enough with the curriculums to discuss them? Do I have teaching materials on hand that I may want to show and discuss?

2. Progress assessment — Can I demonstrate how I will carry out or am carrying out ongoing assessments of each child's progress and achievement?

3. Required paper work and deadlines — Have I completed all required documents?

4. Attendance — Are my attendance records for each child available and up-to-date? Do they show that my children have been schooled the required numbers of hours and days? Are these records kept in a safe place?

5. Our home-school setup — What special aspects of our home-school arrangement will I want to point out to the visitors? Our home library? Our aquarium? Etc.?

6. Special services — Do I need for any reason to explain our use of special services by people such as a certified consultant, speech or hearing therapist, physical therapist, school psychologist? Or of facilities such as a library, gym, or science lab?

7. Socialization — Am I prepared to discuss the ways in which my children are involved in social activities that include other children, as well as adults?

8. Do I have any questions or issues I want to discuss with the visitors?

Add whatever items you wish to your checklist. Base the checklist upon those factors that involve requirements, expected procedures, exemplary teaching, and good or excellent student achievement. Then, using your checklist, prepare yourself for the official visit.

Finally, in some states you and your consultant can develop your own plan for an annual evaluation of your children's progress and of your home-school program. Whichever the case in your state, when you submit your statement of intent or a home-school proposal you may be expected to include your plans for either the required annual evaluation process or for an evaluation process planned by you. Once you have determined the choices regarding an annual evaluation that your state allows, do the needed planning for any required evaluation. At the end of your home-school year and/or at other appropriate times, you'll need to implement your evaluation plan.

An annual evaluation usually takes place when one's curriculum for the year has been completed or nearly completed. To truly reflect upon the effectiveness of your teaching and on your child's learning, the evaluation should logically correlate with goals and objectives outlined in your curriculum. If you are the designer of your evaluation, you could ensure such correlation. In most situations, however, correlation between evaluation and curriculum will be only partial. Standardized achievement tests, for instance, are based upon sets of goals and objectives unique to each test. Curriculums are established without regard for the specific content of standardized achievement tests, although curriculum framers often are generally aware of or informed of the content of the test which will be taken by the students who will use their curriculum. In your case, as a home schooler you will probably have to draft your curriculum without benefit of such awareness or information. This fact does not, however, mean that your curriculum can not be at least partially correlated with standardized tests or other evaluation devices that are used. By following the curriculum design method delineated in the next portion of this section, you will be able to plan a curriculum that does include commonly evaluated content, as well as other content that you wish to include. Let's step next, then, onto the pages of your home-school curriculum.

Annual Evaluation Sample One: Narrative

Annual Evaluation Narrative
Home Student: Billy Miller   Grade: one

Please note: General curricular categories of Billy's studies appear in capital letters below and the specific learning objectives are underlined.

With respect to CHILDREN'S LITERATURE, Billy has logged a total of 144 children's books, including 19 Caldecott Award Books and other selections of children's literature, in his self-illustrated "Books I Have Listened To" scrapbook. He has spent no less than 30 minutes each home-school day listening to complete stories and to books of children's poetry.

Having enjoyed hundreds of poems by a wide variety of poets, including young poets featured in the children's magazine Stone Soup, Billy has developed a roster of his favorite poems and poets which he names and discusses with anyone interested and he can identify poetry by both its visual configuration in magazines and books and by its aural cadences when he hears it aloud.

He is also happy to pull out stories by his favorite authors and children's book illustrators whenever friends visit after school or on weekends. Prior to his "reading" of the book to a friend, he will identify the story characters and offer an overview of the events in the story. At times, he and a friend will abandon the books in our 60-volume library and simply tell stories of their own and now and then even create skits to depict their stories and present them to any available adults.

Billy has developed a great love for books during his first years of storybook experiences. Certain books have even become his "teddy bears" for bedtime sharing and cuddling. And his favorite building in Sky, Kansas, is the Sky Public Library. At the library he has also enjoyed the monthly Storybook Puppet Shows put on by the local arts association.

[Note: This narrative is based upon the Children's Literature Curriculum outlined in "Sample Seven: Curriculum and Materials" at the end of Section Two. This portion would be only one segment of a larger evaluation narrative which would refer to all areas of the curriculum. Although actually writing the narrative will be time-consuming, if you rely on your curriculum outline and your records of daily lessons, you should quickly and easily come up with the information you need for your narrative.]

Annual Evaluation Sample Two: Home Teacher's Log

Home Teacher's Log
School Year: 1988-89
Home Student: Billy Miller   Grade: one
Home Teacher: Mazie Miller

Sept. 1: Morning, phonics — beginning consonant sounds; reading — oral paragraphs in the form of a simple recipe for no-bake cookies which Billy followed as I read; literature — an oral reading of *Frederick* by Leo Lionni followed by discussion of the central character, a mouse; math — counting and measurement — as we made the cookies; social studies — continued work on Billy's cardboard model of a metropolis he calls "Megalapatropolis. During lunch, science — watched a video documentary on African wildlife which Billy later discussed with his dad. Afternoon, literature, science, & socialization — we joined other home schoolers for a trip to the library for the monthly Storybook Puppet Show, followed by a walk through the park to find leaf samples and to play with the other kids. Later, art, literature — Billy did a painting of a giraffe on the African plains and the usual bedtime story — this time *The Grey Lady and the Strawberry Snatcher* by Molly Bang.

Sept. 2: Morning, phonics — review and on to new consonants; reading — a letter from Billy's Aunt Goldie after which Billy reiterated to me the main things about which Aunt Goldie had written; writing — Billy dictated a letter to Aunt Goldie which I typed and read back to him and then he attempted with some success his own reading of the letter; art & science — Billy made a crayon stencil of three of the leaves he'd found in the park yesterday and then dictated to me brief paragraphs describing each leaf and the tree from which each came; math — counting the leaves he'd gathered and gluing them to a sheet of paper in order of size, smallest to largest, and discussing the comparative sizes of the trees from which the leaves had come. Afternoon, literature — *On Market Street* by Arnold Lobel, followed by Billy's oral story of what he'd do during a day on Market Street; music — piano lesson; physical education — fast-walking with his sister and the planning of what they called "A Super Health Nut Backyard Picnic Supper."

Sept. 3: Morning, math — counted people lining up for our home-schoolers' field trip bus ride and compared the number of children with the number of grown-ups, the number of boys with the number of girls, and the number of bus seats with the number of people; social studies — discussed with other home schooled children and their parents the many transportation systems available in the U.S. and their advantages and disadvantages; science — visit to the Kansas City Nature Museum. Evening, literature — read *Ferdinand*, Billy's current favorite children's book.

Curriculum and Materials

A written curriculum is one of the most frequently required components of a home-school program proposal. In public school terms, a curriculum is a set of goals and objectives for student learning in each of the subject areas that will be taught. The goals and objectives usually relate to or stem from a personal (home school) or institutional philosophy of education and life. Often suggested textbooks, materials, and methods are also listed as tools with which the curriculum may be taught. You may even see the term *curriculum* used to refer to the materials themselves. However, materials in themselves are *not* a curriculum and should not be used as such. When a school uses a set of materials as the curriculum, that school has turned over its educational philosophies, its courses and course structures, and often its teaching methods to the publisher of the materials! Educational materials should only be used as *aids* to teaching the goals and objectives or philosophies of a school's curriculum. You should establish your home-school curriculum before searching for and selecting materials. During the school year, lesson planning will allow for means by which you can carry out the curriculum, and materials will aid you.

Typically, the states delineate specifically which subject areas must be included in a home-school curriculum, and the regulations or procedures often require that those subject areas must demonstrate that "the same," "comparable," or "equivalent" instruction to that given in public schools is being provided in home schools. To the required curricular areas you may add courses of your own choosing. You can check the "Basic Information Chart," your state's summary in Section Four of this book, and the information from your state department of education to determine if your state has such requirements.

If your state makes no mention of curriculum requirements for home schoolers, it is still possible that *expected* procedures have been established either statewide or locally that include the selection or writing of a curriculum. You need to identify and study such procedures. Your ability to show evidence that a suitable curriculum does exist for each of your home-schooled children may determine whether or not you'll be able to legally continue to home school should you be challenged at any time by school officials. To public school officials, no written curriculum is likely to equal no schooling.

In actuality, they may be correct. Engaging in an entire home-school year with no planned curriculum could lead to a lackadaisical effort on your part and your children's part. Little academic learning may be the result. This is not to suggest, however, that your children's interests and your own academic passions shouldn't play a role in designing curriculum and lesson plans and also in designing methods and materials with which to teach and learn. Interests, passions, philosophies, beliefs, even going off on a tangent now and then, should play a role. However, partly stemming from them and underlying all, should be a planned curriculum.

We should recognize, too, that the social, emotional, philosophical, and spiritual aspects of living that we wish to enhance and develop in our children can be and should be interwoven into the academic. The academic does not need to control a child's life. Instead, while academics are given full opportunity for development, values and philosophies can be integral to the academic content of a child's home-school curriculum to whatever extent you wish. Let's take a look, then, at curriculum.

Realize first that having a written curriculum does not dictate invariability. You may exercise some variance from any curriculum as you implement it throughout the year. It isn't, after all, your daily implementation that will be approved (if approval is necessary in your state), it is your *written* curriculum. You see, even public school teachers do not strictly adhere to curriculums. Curriculums are guides. The listed materials and methods, likewise, can be altered, deleted, and added to throughout the teaching year. But the officials who may approve, evaluate or challenge your home-school program will look for solid written curriculum outlines as the foundation of your academic program. They may also look through your student portfolios, home teacher log, or other records to determine that the curriculum areas are being addressed in some manner.

To carry out the process of designing or outlining a curriculum for each of your home-schooled children; i.e., a curriculum for each grade level you will teach, you can follow these steps.

> a. State your educational philosophies and general learning goals for your children.

> b. Decide the subject areas that will be included in each child's curriculum for one home-school year. Include those areas required and those of your own choosing.

> c. Locate sample curriculums. Select items from the samples that are age appropriate, grade-level appropriate, and in more personal ways suitable for your children's curriculums.

d. Create rosters or charts of general subject categories.

e. Insert specific goals or objectives to complete the guide for each curricular area.

f. Engage in an initial search for materials and methods that you feel will be appropriate for teaching your curriculums. Add those materials and methods you select to your curriculum guide.

Don't be discouraged; writing a curriculum can take time, but the process outlined below will make the task less complicated than you might expect. Let's take each of the above steps one-by-one. Please keep in mind that what you will end up with here is a curriculum format the public schools and state departments of education typically use. My purpose here is to show you a process and curriculum format that comes as close as possible to guaranteeing its acceptability to public school officials. The overall aim, of course, is to enable you to create curriculums that will handily win approval and/or remain unchallenged. Let's give the process a try.

a. State your educational philosophies and general learning goals for your children.

Usually a curriculum is prefaced by a statement of the educator's basic philosophy and/or goals for the overall focus of the curriculum. This preface may include beliefs about how children best learn, the lifelong aims of education, the lifestyle and learning style emphasis that is integrated into the curriculum, basic values related to reasons for learning that are held by the framers of the curriculum, and so on. The basic, broad goals for the curriculum may be given in outline form. Educational goals reflect the quality of life and uses of knowledge and skills towards which the curriculum aims. There are as many possibilities for philosophies and goals as there are parent educators. You are as capable as any other parent or teacher to establish educational philosophies and goals. Curriculum Worksheet One on pages 119-120 will help you explore and express yours. As you explore them, think deeply. What are your true and sincere philosophies and goals for your children's education? Remember that these are continuously revisable; they can be altered and added to intermittently, especially at the beginning of your next home-school year.

b. Decide the subject areas that will be included in each child's curriculum for one home-school year. Include those areas required and those of your own choosing.

Look first at the information chart and summary for your state in Section Four. When the information you've requested from your state department of education arrives, check for confirmation of any subject areas for your children's ages/grade levels that are noted in Section Four. Make a list of these required subjects. Let Curriculum Worksheet Two on page 121 help.

With the required subject areas listed, you'll have the beginnings of the legal skeleton of your curriculum. Now add subject areas that are not required, but that you wish to include. Some state's subject area requirements for home schools are very basic — math, English, reading, for example — and will allow much fleshing out. Also, of course, there may be subject areas never listed as requirements for home schoolers, but that are areas you feel important for inclusion. As long as you are careful to include the required subject areas, you can feel free to include others of your own choice. It is quite possible that you will design a curriculum that reaches far beyond the public school curriculum in offering a rich educational experience for your children.

You may, for example, be more in tune than public schools with what is being termed "the curriculum of the 21st century." In this curriculum you may wish to include critical thinking, computer literacy and practicum, environmental science, entrepreneurship or home careers. Perhaps, instead, you feel environmental science is of greatest importance and will want to consider zoology, botany, ecology, conservation, earth science, ornithology, etc., for inclusion in your curriculum. Or perhaps you are a person for whom religious instruction is of vital significance and you want to integrate such instruction into your curriculum. You may, on the other hand, be an athlete and feel that physical education subject areas must be included. You may feel that the concept of a core curriculum should have an entirely different core. Public school academics may be of least importance; values, creativity, critical thinking, etc., may be of greatest or of core importance. Whichever, enrich your required curriculum list with subject areas of your choice.

> **c. Locate sample curriculums. Select items from the samples that are age-appropriate, grade-level-appropriate, and in more personal ways suitable for your children's curriculums.**

Many curriculums can be purchased. Some private and church satellite schools sell them. See "Home-School Curriculum Suppliers" in Section Six for a list of schools that offer curriculums. Also, state departments sometimes offer curriculums to home schoolers. If your state department has no curriculums available for purchase, you might try another state's department of education. Several have designed curriculums and made them available nationwide, and they are just as usable in one state as another, generally speaking. Curriculum guides may be available, too, for loan from local public schools. Further, especially if any of your children are high schoolers and they opt to enroll in correspondence or extension courses, you could convert course syllabi into the basis for your curriculum outline. Available, too, especially in college libraries, are books which outline recommended curriculums in certain subject areas. Moffett and Wagner's *Student-Centered Language Arts and Reading K-13: A Handbook for Teachers* is an example. Also possible for the development of your curriculum is the selective integration into a curriculum framework of items covered in a grade level textbook. The outcome of your curriculum search should be a sampling of several curriculums to which your can refer as you design you own.

Remember that if you wholly adopt a textbook publisher's "curriculum" or buy a set of curriculums from some other source, you may be locking yourself into prescribed courses, prescribed item-by-item coverage, sometimes prescribed materials and methods, and possibly prescribed philosophies. So select curriculum sources carefully. If you want to buy curriculums but maintain flexibility, look for those sources that allow for flexibility. If you want those that espouse philosophies and beliefs similar to your own, search for curriculums that satisfy such needs. In addition, look closely at teaching approaches integrated into any curriculums which you examine. Are the approaches compatible with what you believe will be your style as a teacher and with your children's learning styles? Read Appendix A for descriptions of common teaching approaches that may be built into curriculum programs. If you buy curriculums, remember that they must satisfy state requirements. If they don't, you can choose others or design and add on the missing subject areas yourself.

I recommend that you obtain two to four curriculum guides from such sources as those noted above in your listed subject areas, study them, and then create your own guides. In this way you can allow for your own and your children's interests to be included and also for curricular areas that seem especially appropriate in your particular home-school environment. An estimated 50 to 75 percent of all home-schooling parents design their own curriculums. In other words, a solid majority have found the task not to be formidable. Keep in mind, too, that curriculum guides can be reused and revamped for younger children as they advance to the levels for which you have designed guides for an older child. Also, one year's guide can provide the basic outline, advanced skills inserted, for the next year's guide for one student. If your state department of education offers guides, you would be wise to include them among those you obtain. By following them to even a modest extent in the core subject areas, you will come closer to ensuring that your curriculum will be age appropriate, grade-level appropriate, and that you will be viewed as providing "equivalent instruction" at home. That means, of course, that your curriculums are more likely to be approved and/or to not be successfully challenged.

Curriculum Worksheet Two provides a column for listing any subject areas you may wish to adopt from your curriculum samples. When you've completed Worksheet Two, you'll have choices to make. Which of the possible subjects you've listed will become your final list of subjects? Do you need your children's input regarding these choices? Of course, required subjects should be included. Beyond that, think about the ages, abilities and interests of your children, the amount of time available to you each day and week for schooling, the availability of resources that you may need to teach each subject, and so on. Also, which subject areas will allow the best opportunity for your educational philosophies and your goals for your children's education to be put into action?

d. Create rosters or charts of *general* subject categories.

After rummaging through your sample curriculums, selecting, deleting, adding, and sorting items, and finalizing some selections, it's time to convert your rough list and notes into a more formal-looking curriculum. Begin with the general or broad subject areas you've selected. As you do this, remember that implicit within the phrase "equivalent instruction" is the concept of *complete* curriculums. Let your sample curriculums serve as models in your effort to create fairly comprehensive curriculums without overdoing. When you've finalized your subject area choices, create subject area rosters or charts, leaving room between each subject area heading for additional writing. Look back to Sample Seven in Section Two for an acceptable format and ahead to Curriculum Worksheet Three on pages 122-124 for guidance. Then go on to step *e* as follows:

e. Insert *specific* goals or objectives to complete the guide for each curricular area.

You may be one who is philosophically opposed to utilizing specific learning objectives. You may, in other words, oppose the step-by-step, task-by-task approach to learning and prefer more holistic learning. We need not debate the value of one versus the other approach to learning here, but only to note that public school people largely use the specific learning objectives method of designing curriculum. If you want public school officials to approve your curriculum, you will probably be wise to frame it in writing as they would frame it, as they would expect any teacher to frame it. Again, it is worth repeating here that your actual daily methods of teaching what you have written down in the curriculum is not under scrutiny during the approval process, nor could it be easily observed during an inspection of or challenge to your home-school program. Only the *written* curriculum is up for approval or denial, and likewise, the *written* curriculum is what school officials would look at were they to inspect your records. Once approved, your curriculum goes home under your arm: yours. You may then teach in whatever fashion you wish, as long as the end result is student progress which is related to the approved curriculum.

In other words, step *e* suggests that you offer the officials a curriculum format they expect to see which includes specific goals and objectives. Approval and continued acceptance of your curriculum are your aims. So let's look at step *e* in greater detail.

You'll need to think, one at a time, about each of the broad subject categories you have listed. Let your sample curriculums help you decide which specific tasks or skills a student at the designated grade level would need to learn and perform successfully in each subject category. A first grade reading curriculum, for example, might include the 21 consonants' sounds and the 5 vowels' sounds under the word attack subcategory. In math perhaps counting objects from 1 to 20 would be included. You can let your sample curriculums (and textbooks) *suggest* specific items that you might add. Add your own ideas, too, of course. Also, refer again to Sample Seven in Section Two for examples.

In your curriculum each of the tasks or skills is called a "specific learning objective." You should begin your statement of each learning objective with the words, "The student will be able to ...." A verb follows, a verb which reflects an act on the student's part. In other words, the student must in some way demonstrate the task or skill in order for the teacher to see that the student has mastered the learning objective. For example, you might write for the first grade reading student, "*The student will be able to* say all the beginning consonant sounds when presented with each consonant letter visually." For the math student, you might write, "*The student will be able to* count from 1 to 20 objects."

You'll want to avoid repeatedly writing "The student will be able to ...," so just write it once at the beginning of each list of learning objectives. It might appear in chart form as shown below or in a simple roster as shown in Sample Seven, Section Two.

Writing learning objectives may seem like a large project, and it is, but manageable. The lists of objectives under each category should be relatively short, as should be evident in your sample curriculums. Don't be surprised, however, to discover that at home you and your children are able to cover a typical curriculum at a much faster pace than public school teachers and children. First, the amount of time per day most public school classes spend on actual learning activities is three to four hours. The remainder of the time is basically wasted on routines, transitions, etc. At home you won't be involved in such etcetera. Also, you'll be functioning in a one-on-one, or two, or three, situation which is much more conducive to faster learning than the full classroom situation. With respect to your curriculum then, you may wish to add an objective or two that branches out or up into more advanced skills, to embellish your curriculum with additional subject areas that interest your children, to take frequent academic field trips, or even to conduct a shorter school day than public schools.

One final but very important note regarding step *e* — learning objectives: A curriculum must be sequential. Sequential means that the specific tasks or skills the student will master are listed in order of increasing difficulty. Also, the sequential nature of any one grade level curriculum should suggest that the sequence is sustainable from grade level to grade level, K-12, at least in the core subjects. In other words, you would not list letter identification after letter-sound association in a kindergarten reading curriculum. You would not list subtraction before counting in a first grade math curriculum. You would not list polysyllabic (many-syllable) words before two-syllable words in a third grade spelling curriculum. Obvious degrees of difficulty make it logical to list the learning objectives sequentially. Again, the sample curriculums you obtain should serve as models of the sequential nature of curriculums.

Use Curriculum Worksheet Three to formalize your rough list and to add specific goals and objectives. Ignore the "Materials/methods" line until you have read through Step *f* below. I suggest that you not write directly on these worksheet pages but that you make copies since you will need several sheets to complete an entire curriculum.

Moving now to our last step in curriculum design, we should note that some, not all, curriculums include materials and methods lists. If your state requirements for approval indicate that you will need to provide an account of materials and methods, you should complete step *f* below. If your state does not request that you submit such an account, you will sometime want to complete this step anyway, but not necessarily as part of your curriculum plan.

f. Engage in an initial search for materials and methods that you feel will be appropriate for teaching your curriculums. Add those materials and methods you select to your curriculum guide.

To start with you will need to engage in an initial search for materials and methods. It could take a lengthy, exhaustive search to find every and all materials and methods you might use in a year's time. Initially, you just want to locate major texts that you think you'd like to use, at least for core subjects (reading, math, social studies, science) or plan for other key resources to use and key methods and approaches for teaching. Some curricular areas may be taught, perhaps even best taught, without textbooks. However, if you are able to list one major text for each core subject along with any correlated workbooks that are supplied with the text, you should satisfy school officials for the sake of approval. For other subjects, list textbooks or other resources or teaching methods. Again, please realize that the materials you list initially are part of the guide, and as a guide list it is not binding. You may elect to use portions of the texts you choose and to supplement with other materials or let the texts be springboards to *real* and lively activities. You may elect to use some of the student activities presented in the texts you choose and to supplement with activities of your own design. You may supplement, too, with field trips, activity days, resource persons, educational props or equipment, and so on, to whatever extent you wish. If you plan to teach without texts, the textbooks you do list in your curriculum could serve as reference books in the way that atlases, encyclopedias and dictionaries do. You may want, too, to reread the answers to questions 7 and 9 in Section One of this book at this time. At any rate, as long as the end result is student achievement, you are free to use a wide variety of materials and methods.

You can begin your search for materials by browsing through the "Teaching Materials, Aids, and Information Suppliers" portion of Section Six in this book. Write for catalogs from which you can select.Visit bookstores. Christian bookstores in particular often carry publications of use to all home schoolers. Speak with other home schoolers about useful materials they've located. Check to see if your state department of education and your local school district have lists of recommended texts — good places to begin if you need official approval of your list. Look through your sample curriculums for any included materials lists and through home-schooling magazines and books which include materials and resources lists. (See "Readings" and "Periodicals of Interest to Home Teachers" in Section Six.) As you search, begin deciding on materials and creating a simple list of basic texts. Then, to your basic list add any other materials and resources that come to your attention that you think you'd like to use and also any methods with which you are familiar and which you plan to use. Materials can be literally anything — your kitchen as a science lab, the local forest for botanical studies, purchasable educational equipment of various sorts, local tide pools for studies of sea life, etc. Other resources can include museums, libraries, experts, home-school group activities, etc. Methods, too, can be varied and innovative. Perhaps, for example, for primary math you will emphasize the use of manipulatives and practical application as methods. Perhaps for music instruction, you will use the Suzuki method. Perhaps for creative writing instruction your methods will involve the full writing process rather than a product orientation. Perhaps for science you will use exploration and experimentation as methods. At this point in your efforts, on the other hand, you may not be aware of these kinds of methods and will need to limit your list to materials. That's fine for now. The longer you work with your children at home the more aware you will become of teaching materials and methods.

For the time being, then, just list those materials and methods of which you are aware and think you would like to use. List them on the "Materials/methods" line on the curriculum worksheets you have copied for each subject area. You don't necessarily need to be specific, but you may be. For instance, you may not wish to list specific book titles for your children's literature subject area, but rather list "a variety of children's books" as your materials. However, if one of your objectives under children's literature is "The student will be able to cite aloud examples of goodness versus evil found in children's literature," then you may wish to list specific titles in which goodness versus evil is a factor. When listing actual textbooks and workbooks, you should give the specific titles. But when listing your local forest as an environment for botanical studies, you needn't list specific items in the forest.

After initial approval has been granted, if necessary, for your curriculum and materials list, both will become ongoing aids to your teaching. By ongoing I mean that you will add to them and alter them as the year progresses. Having created them yourself, and then worked with them for a period of time, you will probably find them to be marvelously helpful guides for your teaching. They will function like cookbooks in your kitchen functioned when you first began cooking on your own or for your family. Although neither of them — curriculums nor materials lists — will dictate how you teach or what you teach, you may choose to follow their "recipes" exactly. You can refer to them frequently to determine your next step, next unit of study, next lesson, all throughout your home-school year.

Mention of lesson here, brings us to our next topic. Once you have completed your curriculum and materials/methods list, you and your children are on the brink of beginning your home-schooling year. You'll need to gather your materials, settle on your schedules and calendars, gain any needed approval, and so on. Then you're ready to teach . . . almost. Actually, lesson planning comes first; then teaching. Although you won't be submitting a year's worth of lesson plans as part of your program proposal, we should take time to discuss them as they relate to curriculum, as part of your preparation to home teach, and because in some states lesson plan samples or lesson plan books are required.

Curriculum Worksheet One: Philosophies and Goals

<u>My Educational Philosophies</u>

1. I believe children learn best by: _____
_____
_____
_____
(State how they learn best.)

2. I believe teachers teach best by: _____
_____
_____
_____
(State how they teach best.)

3. I believe the lifelong aims of my children's educations are: _____
_____
_____
_____
_____

4. I believe my children's learning should lead towards this kind of adult lifestyle: _____
_____
_____
_____
_____

5. I believe my children's lifelong learning attitude should be:
_____
_____
_____
_____
_____

6. I believe the following basic values should be integrated into my children's curriculum: _____
_____
_____
_____

7. _____
_____
_____

Curriculum Worksheet One continued

<u>Basic Learning Goals for Your Children</u>

My children's curriculum should enable them to develop the ability to:

1. _____
2. _____
3. _____
4. _____
5. _____
6. _____
7. _____
8. _____
9. _____
10. _____
11. _____
12. _____
13. _____
14. _____
15. _____

Examples: examine and use information
acquire no less than survival literacy
develop a sound sense of self-worth
develop a sense of brotherhood with other people
establish strong moral self-guides
understand and respect cultural differences
acquire a perception of *excellence*
develop personal drive
develop steadfast character traits
understand and function well in the free enterprise
     system
develop a keen sense of the value of a healthy envi-
     ronment
be curious and explorative

[Note: There are dozens of other possible long-term goals for a child's learning. The above are merely examples.]

Curriculum Worksheet Two: Subject Areas

Selecting Subject Areas to Include in Your Curriculum		
Required Subjects for Home Schoolers	Subjects I Noted in Sample Curriculums	Other Subjects I Just Want to Teach

Now you have a rough list. Ponder your possible subject areas until you can settle on those you must teach and those you additionally want to teach. Circle them. Then go on to Step *d.*

Curriculum Worksheet Three: Home-School Curriculum

<u>Home-School Curriculum</u>

Curriculum for _____ (student's name)
Academic Level/Grade _____

Broad Subject Area: _____(e.g.: SCIENCE)

Focus Area 1: _____(e.g.: zoology)

The student will be able to:

a. _____

b. _____

c. _____

d. _____

e. _____

f. _____

g. _____

h. _____

i. _____

Materials/methods: _____

_____

_____

_____

Curriculum Worksheet Three: continued

Focus Area 2: _____ (e.g.: botany)

The student will be able to:

a. _____

b. _____

c. _____

d. _____

e. _____

f. _____

g. _____

h. _____

i. _____

Materials/methods

_____

_____

_____

_____

Curriculum Worksheet Three: continued

Broad Subject Area: _____ (e.g.: LANGUAGE ARTS)

Focus Area 1: _____ (e. g.: reading)

  The student will be able to:

  a. _____

  b. _____

  c. _____

  d. _____

  e. _____

  f. _____

  g. _____

  h. _____

  i. _____

  Materials/methods:

  _____

  _____

  _____

  _____

Lesson Planning

I'm sure some resistance will crop up here: "Must I write lesson plans?!" The answer? No, not always. It is possible to teach effectively, at least at certain junctures within the progress of a unit of study, without lesson plans. Sometimes mid-lesson inspiration or intuition will steer you in the directions you and your children need or wish to go. In fact, unusually effective teaching and learning can result from taking spur-of-the-moment advantage of unplanned but excitingly teachable moments. On other occasions you may elect to let a text in some curricular area, such as intermediate math, for example, lead the way, and student progress will probably occur just as well as with lesson plans. Many times, too, your children will lead the way. Should they become enamored, for example, with a week-long project, you may want to suspend regular lesson plans and regular lessons during certain hours each day. Some projects, such as a small business, will lend themselves to unstructured studies in several curricular areas at once. On a smaller scale, should your children become fascinated with watching a snail crawl up a tree, and snails aren't in your lesson plan, please do not stop this spontaneous, momentary, child-led lesson. In fact, take advantage of the opportunity to lend a bit of the academic to the situation: "How do you suppose he crawls? Does he have legs? How does he see? Where are his eyes? Why does he lug around that shell all the time? What does he eat? Why is he crawling up this tree? How long do you think it will take him to get wherever he's going?" Open ended questions are excellent mind-stretchers, even if never answered, for such teachable moments. Curiosities may lead your youngsters to animal books or encyclopedias in search of snail information once you are all back home. Then, too, you can look for lead-ins back to your lesson plans or study unit, so the snail becomes an integral part of what you had planned all along.

Back, then, to lesson plans. Although it is true, as we saw above, that in some situations you can teach effectively without lesson plans, for the most part you should sketch out some form of lesson plan weekly for each subject and grade level you teach. In some states, in fact, lesson plans may be inspected at your home or need to be submitted or maintained for the records. In some school districts or states the format for plans may be prescribed. In others, lesson planning is an option, or the form of the plans is an option.

Lesson planning can occur in various forms, but perhaps the most commonly referred to form in our nation's public schools is the written 5-step lesson plan. Its commonness in public school rhetoric does not, of course, necessarily indicate that it is the best form to use for a home school. However, we could conclude that the 5-step plan should be most acceptable to any school officials in a position to approve or review your home-school plans. Also, you may at some point find yourself in a discussion regarding the 5-step plan and, therefore, need to know its components.

The 5-step plan is based upon a research-supported lesson format. That is, a specific format for the progress of an effective lesson has been researched and defined for use by educators. That lesson format, *per se*, is not our direct concern here, but is presented for your information in Appendix C. We are concerned with the planning process that stems from that format. The plan is presented here to inform you, to enable you to prepare, if you must, lesson plan samples that will be acceptable to school officials, and to give you some examples to work with as you develop your own lesson plan design and procedure.

The 5-step lesson plan, then, is the design basis for the samples given on pages 128 and 129. As you can see in Samples A and B, for application of the 5-step lesson we would have to include learning activities for each of five steps. The terms for the five steps are numbered and appear in bold italics in Sample A. Note that one lesson may carry over from day to day for several days before it has been completed.

Looking over the Formal 5-step Lesson Plan sample, you can see that actually not much is written down for each day. However, writing out the entire lesson plan could take 15 to 20 minutes, and in the case of this particular science lesson it would note activities for a five-schoolday period after which another lesson plan would have to be written.

It isn't likely that you will be expected to write out plans quite this complete, nor wish to, but at least now you can understand the concept of the 5-step lesson plan. After you've studied the formal plan a bit and understand its parts, you can use briefer statements to complete the plan in less time. Sometimes the briefer method omits the writing down of the objective — the objective will, after all, already appear in your curriculum for science. In fact, it is from your curriculum that you will get the objectives for your lessons. If you follow your curriculum, you may find it unnecessary to write objectives into your lesson plan, unless required. You can see how the same lesson plan would look if it were written in briefer form by reading through Lesson Plan Sample B: Brief Plan.

The brief lesson plan example would only take about 10 to 15 minutes to complete. All the components of a 5-step lesson are present; they would relate directly to an objective in the science curriculum, and should anybody ask, you could explain all of this. Your lesson plans should then be acceptable. Not only acceptable, they'll probably be effective; that is, they'll help you do a good job of teaching because they include all of the components of a good lesson.

If you feel working with the fuller plan at first would help you focus on each lesson's objective and do a better job of teaching or if you think you may need expertly written plans in order to pass inspection, by all means use the fuller form. Perhaps later on, once you've proven yourself, you'll ease into the briefer form.

Typically, public school teachers use the briefer form but may have to account for how their lessons fit into the fuller form, and they almost universally write their plans in what is called a "lesson plan book." You may be able to secure one, if you wish, from your local school administrator, or order one from a school supply catalog, or make one designed like those public school teachers use or designed in a fashion that works better for you. The public school lesson plan book is about the size of a large looseleaf binder and is much like a combination schedule and calendar with pages full of large boxes, one for each subject area lesson included each day. It is a schedule in the sense that the time of day each period occurs is noted. It is a calendar in that each pair of opened pages makes up one school week, and there are enough pages for a full year's lessons. (See Lesson Plan Sample C on page 130.)

Lesson plans and lesson plan books of this type or of your own design can be useful to home teachers for the following reasons:

a. They help the home teacher stay roughly on schedule in her attempt to complete the year's curriculum in a year's time.

b. The plan procedure helps to assure that the objectives outlined in the curriculum for each subject area will be addressed.

c. Reviewing her own plan book from time to time can help the home teacher retain focus on her stated educational philosophies and her children's long-term learning goals.

d. The plan book serves as a lesson review guide for the home teacher.

e. The plan book serves as an ongoing student assessment guide. The home teacher can review the covered information noted in the plan book in order to create tests and/or other assessments over that information.

f. The plan book can satisfy any official requirements that exist regarding lesson plans.

Lesson Plan Sample A: Formal Plan

Formal 5-Step Lesson Plan

Subject Area: <u>SCIENCE</u>   Dates _____

Focus: <u>turtles as representative of reptiles</u>

Learning Objective: <u>Students will be able to identify body parts of the turtle and their functions, explain the turtle life cycle, needs, food, dangers, reptilian characteristics, and habitat.</u>

Monday *1. anticipatory set (or introduction):* Observe turtle. Elicit and offer open-ended questions. One child records observations on a large sheet of poster paper.

2. instruction: (a) Together set up a terrarium and include two turtles for further observation. Spend some time today and each day this week observing and recording our observations.

Tuesday (b) Biologist Kelly Green will demonstrate and discuss characteristics of turtles. We will review and summarize his presentation and add items to our chart, then look through the items on the chart and try to organize them by body parts and functions, life cycle stages, needs, etc. We will also determine what information we still need.

Wednesday (c) Using our list from yesterday of those items of information we still need to find, we'll conduct further observations and also do library research using our set of wildlife encyclopedias and our book on reptiles. Then we will add our findings to the chart.

3. guided practice: Using a large drawing of a turtle on butcher paper and the items recorded on our chart, the children will work together to identify and label the body parts and also write down the functions of each body part. Then we'll begin painting a mural showing turtles' natural habitat, food, etc.

Thursday *4. closure:* One-by-one, the children and I will observe the turtles in the terrarium and I'll orally quiz each child about all aspects of turtles we've covered. Finish mural.

Friday *5. independent practice:* Each student will be given a worksheet on which will appear a drawing of a turtle. Each student will be asked to independently label the body parts of the turtle and to write down the functions of those body parts, identify the turtle's reptilian characteristics, and draw in an appropriate environment for the turtle.

Lesson Plan Sample B. Brief Plan

<u>Brief 5-Step Lesson Plan</u>

Subject Area: <u>SCIENCE</u>   Dates _____

Focus: <u>turtles as representative of reptiles</u>

Learning Objective: <u>Students will be able to identify body parts of the turtle and their functions, explain the turtle life cycle, needs, food, dangers, reptilian characteristics, and habitat</u>

Monday
Observe turtle. Open-ended questions.
Record observations on chart.
Build terrarium.

Tuesday
Biologist Kelly Green
Observe turtle.
Review, summarize, and add items to chart.
Organize chart items.
Determine what information we still need.

Wednesday
Further observations and library research.
Students identify and label turtle body parts and functions on turtle drawing on butcher paper and begin a mural showing habitat, food, etc.

Thursday
Orally quiz individual students.
Finish mural.

Friday
Individually complete turtle worksheets.
Give immediate feedback with butcher paper drawing.

[Note: In Appendix C explanation is give of each of the five lesson steps — anticipatory set, instruction, guided practice, closure, and independent practice.]

Lesson Plan Sample C: Plan Book

	Lesson Plans		
School _____ Teacher _____ Grade Level(s) _____ Week _____ 19__ — 19__			
	subject: time:	subject: time:	subject: time:
Monday			
Tuesday			
Wednesday			
Thursday			
Friday			

As you complete your lesson plans, you'll want to be conscious of the time blocks needed for the planned activities of each subject area session and the schedule of your whole day. Try to balance substantial coverage of a day's learning objectives with your need to compress the lesson segments of your day into reasonable time periods. Also consider the ages of your children and their correlated attention spans and toleration for active versus quiet activity. Aim for a mixture of types and lengths of activities. If you have more than one child, you may need to plan for some separate lessons for your children to accommodate their academic levels. However, many lessons can be taught to students of varied levels simultaneously. Children's literature, science, and language usage, for example, could be taught to more than one level, as long as the levels are not too far apart. A subject like math, on the other hand, may require separate lessons for separate levels, although practical application situations could involve more than one level. In that case, the more advanced child would perform the more difficult applications and the less advanced child the less difficult. But they could, nevertheless, work together.

When your children must be taught separately, schedule independent work for one child while you teach the second child. Then switch. Also, education research has demonstrated that students teaching students is highly effective. Consider letting an older child help you teach a younger at times. Eventually the younger child may become skilled in areas which he can in turn teach the older.

When you teach your children together, you may want to provide instruction to them jointly, but vary the difficulty levels of their independent learning activities. Your plans can allow for this.

Obviously you will need to streamline your regular daily routine to accommodate home-school lessons. However, be flexible, look for options and alternative timing possibilities. You don't, for example, need a nonstop block of lessons. You could schedule two hours in the morning and one or two in the afternoon, or vary the hours from day to day. Evening schooling hours may enable you to share the teaching of your children with your spouse. You may even discover that your children function best as learners during certain hours of the day and you will want to adjust scheduling to capture those best times. At home, you control the time choices and can allow for much variety and flexibility in the activities that fill your children's time.

You may find yourself planning activities not as a part of a particular lesson or unit of study, but simply as good learning activities. This is fine. You may find a subject area category for the activities. For example, if you plan to attend a matinee play production, you can label that time block "language arts" or "literature," since a stage play is a live performance of a written play — a work of literature. If it's an historical play, you could call it a history lesson. After a few weeks of home schooling, your children may even begin to design lessons, to an extent. Many home educators are successfully letting their youngsters lead the way with lesson planning. You'll just need to record in lesson plan format those lessons your children design.

In closure here, I'd like to urge you to carefully design your curriculums and to attempt to write lesson plans in the manner described above. Doing so will provide you with the best evidence you could possible have that your home school program is and consistently has been a good one.

Next we'll consider the various kinds of other evidence that you may want or need to keep as you home school your children.

Keeping Records

While *Why?* may be one of the first questions you answer about home schooling, in many states or school districts it may be the last question school officials ask. They may be more interested in *How? Where? When? Who?* and *What?* and in many states they will want to see the answers on paper, as evidence. They may want to see your records.

Their responsibility to both educate and protect all children within their boundaries is the primary reason many states and school districts expect home schoolers to keep, and often submit, records. While keeping home school records may not be enjoyable, many home schoolers derive satisfaction from the realization that the states attempt to protect all children in this fashion.

We might admit, too, that keeping several of the required types of records simply makes sense. Home schoolers themselves, for example, are likely to want some acceptable form of attendance, curriculum, and assessment records to demonstrate that their children have been schooled, have achieved certain academic levels, and are ready to go on to the next academic level, or to high school or college, or to a job. Home-school parents, like other parents, are preparing children to someday enter the adult world for which they need to be realistically equipped. Entrance to training programs, colleges, and/or jobs usually involves "admittance tickets" in the form of school records. Children don't necessarily need diplomas and degrees to enter that world, as discussed in question 11 in Section One, but usually do need evidence of having been schooled.

Also, if you think you may enroll your children in public school or in a Christian or other private school at some future time, you will need records to verify to those schools that your children have been attending home school, have studied certain subjects, have achieved certain levels, demonstrate special skill in certain areas, need particular assistance in other areas, and so on.

Another reason for keeping good records is as a contingency for potential home-school litigation. In 1984 John Holt estimated that well over 90 percent of this country's home schoolers function with no hassles from authorities, but that estimate leaves room for a hassled 10 percent. While the latter percent has probably decreased slightly since 1984, keeping careful records, and keeping them all the years you home teach and longer, may be the key to ensuring that you remain within the unhassled group. In my state, for example, when one longtime home-school mother, upon request, emptied two boxfuls of well-prepared and well-kept home-school records on a local school superintendent's desk and proceeded to provide a two-hour description of her program, she was politely thanked and dismissed. No further questions were asked. Evidence easily won. While what is outlined below is certainly not meant to be a legal brief, nor am I qualified to offer one, should you become one of the hassled at some point in time, the presentation of complete records as outlined here would surely be welcomed by a lawyer.

There are several kinds of records you either may be required to maintain and/or submit, or may simply want to maintain:

a) Home-school legal and procedural information.

b) Statement of intent (potentially eleven segments).

c) Annual evaluation documents.

d) Lesson plans, logs, and curriculum outlines.

e) Ongoing progress assessment results and report card

f) Schedules and calendars.

g) Communications with officials.

h) Consultant's activities.

i) Home-school attendance register.

j) Portfolios of student work.

k) Student socialization activities.

l) Special student services information.

m) Year-by-year, cumulative, permanent records.

Sounds like quite a drawerful? To some extent it is, especially if you elect to maintain all of these possible records. While all of them could be important in your case, you'll need to determine for yourself which you must keep or wish to keep. Realize too that to begin you will need to complete some records, such as schedules and a calendar, but for other records only set up a design or system for later maintenance. The greatest amount of work occurs in setting up your record-keeping system; later, routine should take over. Also, as your home-school year progresses, you'll find yourself fine tuning your record-keeping routines to save yourself time and trouble.

Several of the records you might keep have already been noted in Section Two and earlier in this section, Section Three, but we will touch upon these again here to clarify fully which initial and continuing records may be kept. Let's take a closer look now at the possible contents of your records drawer.

First, if you've been working on gathering legal information and on the segments of your statement of intent since your reading of Section Two, you have already begun two record files:

> **a) Home-school legal and procedural information.** As you recall, in your legal file you'll include statutes, codes, regulations, requirements, guidelines, procedures, etc., related to home schoolers in your state.

> **b) Statement of intent.** In your statement of intent file you'll insert those of the eleven segments of the statement that you've selected to complete, as outlined in Section Two.

Several of the items in your statement of intent file initiate the need for further record keeping, as you'll see below. Also, other records aside from those that stem from your statement may need to be kept.

> c) **Annual evaluation documents.** As indicated in Sections Two and Three, at the end of each home-school year or intermittently during the year you may need to conduct or arrange for some form of formal evaluation of your children's progress and of your overall program. If such an evaluation is a requirement, you will want to document the evaluation activities and results.

The evaluation records may take one of the many forms noted on page 93 in this section. Each item included should be dated to show that the elements of the evaluation were carried out when appropriate. You should complete the evaluation records and file them in your file drawer as soon as possible after each element of the evaluation is carried out, keep the records or copies of them in a permanent file at your home, and submit original copies, if required, to the local school district.

> **d) Lesson plans, logs and curriculum outlines.** Keep your ongoing lesson plans and/or log in a notebook, plan book, or logbook throughout each of your home-schooling years and thereafter until your youngsters finish school. Also, once you have created your curriculum outlines or charts, plan to keep them indefinitely.

As explained earlier, you may be asked to submit lesson plan samples as a portion of your initial home-school proposal, or to submit lesson plans throughout the year, or to maintain lesson plans in a lesson plan book open to inspection throughout the year. In some states a log or diary/journal may do. Likewise, you may be asked to submit or maintain your written curriculum. On the other hand, you may not be asked to write or keep any of the three. In any case, as noted, it is wise to keep at least sketchy lesson plans, even if completed in log or journal form after the lessons are taught, and to create some form of written curriculum that documents your effort to teach required subjects in your state. (Refer to Section Two and earlier portions of this section for detailed information about and samples of lesson plans, logs, and curriculums.)

> **e) Ongoing progress assessment results and report cards** (if needed). As noted in Section Two, in most cases ongoing progress assessments must be periodically carried out and results recorded. Assessments may include quizzes, tests, observed progress, paperwork that demonstrates progress, oral responses to assessment situations, projects, and so on. See Section Two for other possibilities. Some form of recording the results of those assessments is often required, and in a few states, report cards must be completed and submitted.

The assessments themselves may be kept — most likely in a student portfolio for the appropriate subject area. Assessment papers would provide hard evidence that your children have progressed and that they are studying the approved curriculum.

If you are required to complete a report card, you might choose to record assessment results in a grade book of some sort. If so, you could secure one from the local school administrator, buy one from a school supplier, use a simple ledger book or sheets of graph paper, make one, or make copies similar to Record-Keeping Sample One: Grade Book shown on page 146. You would for the grade book write in your children's names in the farthest left column, write dates and identify the assignments or assessments atop the vertical columns whenever you were going to enter a grade, and consistently enter either percentage scores or letter grades. You may record significant daily assignments and assessment results, or just assessment results (with some of the assignments stored in portfolios). In a few states progress reports or progress narratives are required in lieu of report cards. Such reports would likely include various areas of growth — academic, social, cultural, ethical — and be written in a fashion similar to Annual Evaluation Sample One: Narrative on page 107.

As explained in Section Two, even casual observations can be recorded as assessments. Your daily observations of student progress — academic, social, behavioral, self-developmental, emotional, etc. — are valid measures as long as they are recorded somewhat consistently, objectively and in sufficient detail. You could keep such observation records quite easily in a log or journal. Doing so could prove to be fun, and at year's end you and your children will have a wonderful account of their growth. If your children attend public school before home school, you may be able to use the observation journal to document affective as well as academic improvements that result from removing your children from the public school environment. In fact, such a journal may be your only means of verifying affective improvements.

Sometimes you will find commercial progress charts that could be useful for recording assessments. They may be found in teacher's manuals that are companions to textbooks your children use. They may be separately published checklists, such as the "Barbe Reading Skills Check List" published by Prentice-Hall. They may accompany a mastery learning or diagnostic/prescriptive program if you are using one. You can create your own checklists or progress charts by utilizing your curriculum objectives. Such charts or checklists are not mandatory, of course, but could provide an easy means for recording student progress.

You may have occasion to record the results of an oral assessment during which you informally quizzed your children. Then you could jot down the contents of your quiz and the degree of success your children demonstrated by their answers. A score or grade could even be given if you wish.

As you can see, a variety of assessment records are possible. Remember, it is imperative that such assessment records show that you have been assessing those curricular areas required by your state for home-school education programs. It will be obvious to school officials that if you have been assessing achievement in the required curricular areas, you have indeed been teaching the required subjects to your children.

f) Schedules and calendars. As indicated in Section Two, schedules of daily and weekly home-school hours and semester or yearlong calendars must be established by home schoolers in some states and maintained with other home-school records. Please see Section Two for a complete explanation of this form of record keeping.

Let's move on now to records not previously discussed in Section Two or earlier portions of this section, but which you would likely be wise to keep and some of which you may be required to keep.

g) Communications with officials. As a parent teacher you will probably engage in several sorts of interactive situations with school officials, particularly while you are setting up your program and trying to secure official approval for it, if needed. You should record the focus and results of each of those situations in log or journal format and keep copies of all written communications, yours and theirs.

This could be one of the more important of your sets of records. As you progress through the home-school approval process, if approval is mandatory in your state, you will interact with school officials by phone, by letter, or face-to-face. It is important that you record each and every one of those communications so that you will not skip over something you have agreed to do, so that you can keep tabs on what the officials have agreed to do, so you can prevent deviations from or inconsistencies in the officials' dealings with you by reminding them of their communicated statements and yours. Using communication records to keep the process moving along according to agreed upon dates or dates acknowledged as required deadlines can also be important.

Many states, in fact, provide a chronology for the approval process. You must follow certain timelines, and likewise must the officials. Only if you have dated copies of communications exchanges can you justifiably prompt procrastinating officials. Remember, too, that should your own communications to the officials reveal laxness on your part, the officials may have reason to delay or deny approval. Furthermore, most states have well-defined appeal processes for parents whose home-school proposals are denied. But in order for an appeal to succeed, you very likely would need to demonstrate that you had followed carefully all timelines and met all deadlines. It could also obviously be beneficial to provide written evidence that the officials did not follow the timelines, if, of course, such is the case. Only by keeping regular, dated records of all communications with officials, beginning with your very first contact with them, would you be prepared to provide such evidence.

If program approval by school officials is not required of potential home schoolers in your state, you will probably be wise to keep communications records just in case questions or challenges arise further down the road weeks, months, or even years later.

h) Consultant's activities. If you will use the help of a certificated consultant, create a file into which you can slip a calendar or simply a lined sheet of paper that can be dated and filled in periodically as your consultant completes the items of your mutual agreement. You can begin this calendar/log by listing and dating items the two of you established as to-be-completed by her. Then as she becomes a participant in your program, record all of her activities, with dates, on the calendar or log and continue to record them throughout your home-school year. Be especially sure to clearly show that the consultant has assisted you in any activities for which you are required to have assistance.

If your state is one that requires you to work with a consultant, this log will serve as proof of your consultant's active involvement in your home-school program. If your state doesn't require a consultant but you've independently secured one anyway, you still will want to keep track of your consultant's activities, your interactions with her, dates you need to remember with respect to her activities, and so on. Always remember, too, that if your right to home school is ever challenged or your program ever questioned, you can demonstrate with your consultant's activity file that in your attempt to be a legitimate and effective teacher to your children, you've gone so far as to secure the assistance of a certified teacher — someone whose legitimacy the state already recognizes. Then, too, with the specifics of her activities recorded and dated consistently by you, you will be able to demonstrate exactly how she has participated in your planning or teaching, in assessing your enrollees' ongoing progress, or in the overall evaluation of your program.

> **i) Home-school attendance register.** The attendance register is typically a record booklet, somewhat like a ledger, with columns and squares and lines at the left for entry names. In it are kept students' names and a record of their days of absence and attendance in school.

You can design a register yourself by making or purchasing a few sheets of graph paper, by actually using a few ledger sheets, by securing a register booklet from you local school if possible, or by making a few copies of a page from a local school register booklet. If you use separate sheets, bind them together somehow, write your children's names in on lines in the column furthest to the left, and write in the dates that will be included in your home-school year (a week or month at a time will do) at the top of each vertical column of little squares. It would look like Record-Keeping Sample Two: Attendance Register on page 146.

Once you have the graph or register itself set up you'll need to devise a marking system. For example, an "A" could be inserted in a square whenever one of your children is "absent" from home school. A "P" could represent "present." An "H" could represent "present half the day, absent the other half." Or you could use a system of plus and minus and zero symbols. You might even check with a local school teacher to find out how local teachers mark their registers and then use that system for your register. Write a note at the top of the first page or on a cover sheet explaining your marking system. You could later teach the system to your children and let them record the marks.

You will also need to reserve a section of your register for noting the reasons for absences when they occur. If you wish instead, you could attach an extra sheet of paper for this purpose, dating each entry as you record it.

A grade level line at the top of the register page would appear if the register were a published one. The teacher would write in the grade level of the students in the particular class listed on each page. If you are teaching more than one of your children at home, you probably are teaching more than one grade or academic level. In that case, you may wish to record grade levels,

Then all you need to do is regularly record your marks for each child's days of absence and attendance. Remember, *absence* means *no school* for that child on the date recorded. If you take your children on a science field trip or to an art workshop or a piano lesson, and those activities are a part of your day's lesson plan and reflect your curriculum, then your children are indeed in attendance.

At the end of each quarter, semester, and year, tally the total numbers of days of absence and attendance for each child. You will want to be sure that by year's end your attendance register shows that your children attended home school the number of required hours and/or days noted in the "Basic Information Chart" in Section Four of this book or in the material you've received from your state department of education. If you are expected to turn in your register, compliance with these time-in-school requirements will be what the officials will look for.

Another routine form of record keeping, but one frequently asked for by officials and oftentimes fun to keep, is the student portfolio. Let's look at what might constitute student portfolios for your home-schooled children.

> **j) Portfolios of student work.** Home-school student portfolios contain samples of work that a student has completed. Typically a portfolio would be kept for each subject of the student's curriculum, and the samples would include a wide array of student work — drawings, reports, worksheets, project reviews, creative writings, lists of books read, cassette tapes of musical performances, photographs depicting learning activities, pressed and identified plants — virtually any student work small enough to fit into the file.

In most portfolios you would not insert *every* item of student work that your children complete. Select such items as those that are exemplary, that demonstrate the central focus of a unit of study, or that culminated a unit of study. In some portfolios you may wish to include every item completed in an area of study — an art portfolio, for example. Remember, you'll be maintaining portfolios in order to document that your children have been truly studying those curricular areas that are required and those that you indicated in your home-school proposal you would cover.

You and your children will probably discover that keeping portfolios is actually quite rewarding because you'll be able to concretely see an accumulation of work that represents learning. Also, if you date the items you include and keep them in chronological order in your children's portfolios, you and they can use them to measure progress. Your children may find themselves amazed at their own productivity as they return to their portfolios throughout the home-school year. In fact some portfolios, such as an art or creative writing portfolio, can become treasures, kept and enjoyed for years to come.

Looks like your record file drawer is going to fill up fast. The next category of home-school records, however, won't become quite so portly. Let's consider the records that we hope will show that you can answer with a confident smile one of the questions asked most frequently of home schoolers, "How will your children learn to socialize?" The answers can be found in this file:

> **k) Student socialization activities.** These records can appear in the form of logs or journals, written by you or perhaps written at least in part by your children. In these logs or journals, one for each child, date and enter brief descriptions of any activities that involve persons in your children's learning community other than you, their teacher.

The socialization logs may become a fun writing activity for your children. As you or your children complete them, recognize that school officials, who often worry about the socialization of home-schooled children, will want particularly to know that your children have contacts with other children. So be sure to note even out-of-school-time interactions that your children have with their peers. Of course, also note interactions with children cther than their peers and with other adults. You can include family activities, too, noting sibling and parent-child relationships in action. Write your descriptions with an emphasis on common socialization factors — teamwork, cooperation, self-confidence, adaptability, independence, conversational skills, friendliness, etc.

> **l) Special student services information.** In this record file you would keep notations of any special needs of your children that led to the services of such people as a physical therapist, speech therapist, school psychologist, special education teacher, a teacher of the gifted or talented, or a Chapter I remedial reading or math teacher. Then you would date and record those services that were

delivered by such people. If one of your children meets on a regular basis with a special services person, you may want to slip a service calendar into this file.

As I noted above, this set of records may be nonexistent in your case if none of your children have the special needs that would necessitate the services of the persons listed above. If, however, you are aware or become aware that one of your children has a physical or speech problem, emotional problem, or a reading problem, or is gifted or talented, or is learning disabled or mentally retarded, check your state statutes and procedures regarding such home-schooled children, and seek help. Child neglect could quickly become the charge against you if you are aware of such special needs and try to handle them entirely on your own. However, there are two potential exceptions.

First, it is possible that school officials won't have identified giftedness or unusual talent or a learning disability in your children, especially if your children are in the primary grades. If you have never been contacted by a school to discuss a special need of one of your children, then probably the school has not officially identified such a need. (Federal law dictates that schools contact parents in cases of identified handicaps or identified giftedness to discuss special services.) In this case, then, you would not need to seek special services yourself, unless you wanted to. I would suggest, in fact, as noted in answers to question 11 in Section One, that you may be able to do a better job of facilitating the learning of a gifted or talented child and of a learning disabled child than can the public schools. However, you may want to explore, rather quietly, the available services.

Second, if your child is severely mentally retarded, school officials may be delighted to let you school your child without interference from them. It may be necessary to go through the legal channels to home school a retarded child, but you may be able to function quite independently after that.

One final note about special services. You may at some time be offered an opportunity for your child to participate in a special instruction program, such as Chapter 1 remedial reading or math. Be skeptical, however, of remedial programs, especially if the services will be carried out by an aide. Aides are indispensable persons on public school staffs, but they are not typically trained in methods of teaching reading or other subjects, remedial or otherwise. Usually they simply follow a teacher's instructions and present brief skills lessons. Perhaps you would want to schedule an observation session before deciding to utilize the services of a remedial program.

At any rate, if you do perceive a need for special services for any of your children, investigate the possibility of securing those services. Record your observations that led to realizing your child's special need, the steps you take to secure appropriate services, the responses you get, and the services that actually are delivered. You want to be able to demonstrate that you did not neglect any of what school officials would consider your children's special needs.

> **m) Year-by-year, cumulative, permanent records.** At the completion of each year's schooling a simple record is prepared of the student's courses for the year with grades or pass/fail status or other symbol of achievement for each course. The student's total days present and absent are also recorded. These are written in a file or on a sheet of paper which has room for twelve, or with kindergarten thirteen, such yearly records. Typically achievement test results are also recorded or glued onto these records.

When a public school student finishes his schooling, he normally would have a completely filled in cumulative, permanent record which could be copied and sent as a transcript to college admissions departments and to potential employers. The permanent record is also used as a transcript at any grade level during which a student transfers from one school to another. It serves as a record of all the courses he has completed thus far and his achievement record in those courses, as well as a year-by-year attendance record. Having such a cumulative record for your home-schooled children could prove useful, particularly if you give your home school a schoolish sounding name and create a "perm record" that looks somewhat professional. The perm record or transcript should be mailed from the old school (yours in this case) to the new, or to the employer, or to the college, rather than delivered by hand by you or your child.

Legally you have a right to see and copy any public school permanent record that might already exist for your child if she has previously been a public school student — if you can do so without removing the record from the school. If the school has a copying machine, just ask to use it to copy your child's permanent record. Then you will have not only a sample of a legitimate perm file, but a record you can continue for your child. If you can't copy your child's school file, perhaps a friendly school secretary, teacher or administrator would let you have one blank permanent file folder in which the cumulative record format is printed. (Public schools buy them already printed.) Also, some of the home-school support organizations or a satellite school might supply you with a cumulative record folder.

If your child has not previously been a public school student, or if you are unable to secure a permanent file folder, you can create your own. Type it out or print it on a computer printer. It should include segments that look like those in Record-Keeping Sample Three: Cumulative Permanent Record on page 147.

We've come to the end of our roster of records to keep. You can refer to the Record-Keeping Checklist on page 145 for a quick review.

Then select those records you will need to maintain, and finally plan for and set up your record-keeping system.

I'd like to conclude this segment with a final acknowledgment. I know there are many potential home schoolers and practicing home schoolers who immediately cringe at restrictions placed upon any aspect of their lives, including home schooling, by *the authorities*. It follows, too, that these home schoolers will not take lightly the right states claim to require that certain records be kept. I understand and concur in many instances, but can only advise you here to try to determine the most efficient route to gaining the right to educate your children at home, and to follow that route. Doing so will no doubt mean that you will select from above the types of records **you** feel you should and must keep in the interest of establishing for your children schooling at home. My purpose in presenting the full range of records that can be kept is to show you how to set up a reliable body of documents which demonstrates that you have planned your program exceedingly well, that your plan correlates closely *on paper* with public school expectations, and eventually that you teach your children very successfully. Then if you did choose the route your state has laid for home schools, chances are you'll make it, legally and efficiently, all the way *home.*

With this we close the home-school planning process — in this book, but not in your life. Still in the offing are working through each of the components you elect to complete, preparing those you must for presentation to school officials, and using the completed components to seek approval and/or to begin your home-school year. and maintaining and revising them throughout your home-school year. Thus you will have taken that first major step towards your home-school door. When you arrive, you will discover an extraordinary world of educational possibilities for you and your children. And the steps continue — pathways to choose, trees to climb, rivers to swim — educational byways winding into and around and over and through your home and your family. A wonderful journey — enjoy.

Record-Keeping Checklist

Required	Desired	Type of Record	Record Ready and Active
		Home-school legal and procedural information.	
		Statement of intent. (See checklist at end of Section Two for those segments you elected to include.)	
		Annual evaluation documents.	
		Lesson plans.	
		Log. Purpose: _____	
		Curriculum outlines.	
		Ongoing progress assessment results and/or report card.	
		Schedules and year's calendar.	
		Records of communications with school officials.	
		Consultant's activities record.	
		Home-school attendance register.	
		Portfolios of student work. Subject areas: _____ _____ _____	
		Record of student socialization activities.	
		Special student services information.	
		Year-by-year, cumulative permanent records.	

Record-Keeping Sample One: Grade Book

School _____			Teacher _____								
School year _____			Semester ____ Quarter ____								
Course/Subject _____											
dates											
	M	T	W	T	F	M	T	W	T	F	M	T
students												
1. Mary Miller												
2. Susie Miller												
3. Tom Miller												

Record-Keeping Sample Two: Attendance Register

School term _____			School _____								
Teacher _____			Academic Level(s) _____								
			Month _____								
dates											
students	M	T	W	T	F	M	T	W	T	F	M	T
Mary Miller												
Susie Miller												
Tom Miller												

Record-Keeping Sample Three: Cumulative Permanent Record

Cumulative Record

School _____

Student's full name _____ Birthdate _____

Father's name _____

Mother's name _____

Parents' address_____

_____

Elementary

spelling	reading	math	science	soc st	music	art	health				absent	present	gr level	teacher

[Subjects may vary; use blank columns to add others.
Final grades are recorded on the grid for each subject area.]

Junior High High School

[Grids similar to the one on the right are used to record each year's academic work for grades 7-12]

		Grade ___			
	course	sem 1	sem II	final grade	teacher
1.					
2.					
3.					
4.					
5.					
6.					

State Regulations and Procedures

From the States

The information presented below has been gleaned from documents sent to me by the fifty state departments of education and the District of Columbia's Public Schools Office. Note that the information presented here does not necessarily apply to private or correspondence schools within your state. Although many of the same regulations and requirements may apply to such schools, most states have alternate or additional regulations that address those schools. The "Basic Information Chart" below provides quick reference to four home-school regulatory items: 1) compulsory school ages, 2) teacher certification requirements, 3) courses to be taught and 4) in-school time. Following the Basic Chart is a "Summary of State Regulations and Procedures" which includes recommendations for home schoolers in each state.

Keep in mind, incidentally, that home-school regulations change from time to time in the individual states; you are responsible for securing updates. You would be wise to confer with established home schoolers in your state regarding procedural changes and adaptations. Fellow home schoolers may be aware not only of changes in statutes and procedures, but of legitimate loopholes and alleyways through which you can most easily take your first step to home schooling. You may even discover from practicing home schoolers that the school board in your school district ignores known home schoolers and home-school statutes.

While Idaho law, for example, indicates that a home school teacher must be certified unless the certification requirement is waived by the local school board, in parts of Idaho, where I live, the issue is often not addressed. Many home schoolers in these areas do not approach their local school boards regarding certification or any other matter, and are not sought out by school officials. Only by contacting an experienced home schooler in these locales would a newcomer find out about this mutual silence. However, while similarly rare, prosecutions are not unheard of. In one area town recently a home educator was taken to court because she had no written curriculum to present when asked for one. On the other hand, the educator mentioned on page 134 in Section 3 overcame a superintendent's challenge (out of court) when she presented complete home-school records. Home schoolers do need to know their state's requirements and procedures and keep good records which demonstrate compliance with those requirements and procedures.

You'll quickly discover that the most common state requirement is that the home-school curriculum "equally well serve," be "the same as," or be "equivalent to" that of the public schools. In the summaries below, the specified course requirements for such equivalency are given for each state. Be aware, however, that *equivalency* is a vague term in the education laws; in other words, it is a term still open to interpretation in many states. Also recognize that the equivalent curriculum requirement represents minimums not maximums. You may freely add other courses as you wish. Also, as noted in Section Three, to remain able to demonstrate equivalency you should keep your curriculum in written form and store it in a file at home, as well as submit it, of course, if required.

Usually, scheduling also allows some freedom. The required number of home-school days is most often stated; the number of hours, less often. But seldom are how-to-use recommendations given for scheduling those hours and days. In other words, having to home school four or five hours daily does not mean you must spend those hours at desks as if you and your children were literally in school. Many possible uses of those hours can be justified as learning time or home-school time. Sometimes the hours requirement will be stated in terms of *contact time.* This means that you must be present with your children in educational pursuits during the specified number of hours. *Contact time* does not mean contact with a desk and chair!

Another frequent requirement you'll discover is standardized achievement testing. As you study your state's summary, be sure you understand if achievement testing is legally required, and if so, exactly which test must be administered, when and where the test is to be given, and by whom. This understanding will aid you in deterring any public school attempts to test your children beyond the degree required. Psychological, IQ, readiness, textbook, and interest tests, for example, are not commonly the kinds of tests to which your children must submit. Standardized achievement tests are common. You may be opposed to all testing, but if ignoring a testing requirement will result in the denial or closure of your home school or lure school officials into the courtroom in a case against you, please think carefully about your decision to test or not. As you consider this issue, you may wish to return to Section One's question 2, *e* regarding typical home-school test results and to the discussions of annual evaluations in Sections Two and Three.

If you walk through the planning procedure and compose as complete a plan as you deem advisable, and yet find your proposal denied or challenged by school officials, calmly ask them to tell you exactly how it is deficient. What must you add or alter in order for your plan to become acceptable? Then revise as you see fit, relative to your rights and theirs. Foremost, remember your goal.

Recognize, too, that some school officials may take the law into their own hands in zealous attempts to live up to their self-perceived responsibilities by molding home-school regulations to their own perspectives. To prevent yourself from being taken in by such overstepping of school officials' rights and responsibilities, you need to be well-informed of the extent and the limits of your state's home-school laws. Then, should inquiries be made by school officials, you can review the limits of their authority as defined by the laws in your state and respond to the officials with written assurances that you are meeting the specific legal requirements of your state, notations of those requirements, and explanations and/or documentation of your means of meeting those requirements.

Let's set out then to map the legal footpath to your home school, to draw in the route that will take you and your children home. Note that wording in the "Basic Information Chart" is as found in the actual state statutes. Thus, for example, "between 7 and 16" and "7 through 15" both appear in the chart in order for the wording to remain consistent with each state's laws. However, please remember that what follows here is a layman's summary and does **not** constitute legal consultation.

Basic Information Chart

state	compulsory attendance	certification required	state-required subjects/courses	hours per day days per year
AL	between 7 and 16	yes, if a "private tutor;" no, if a local church "ministry"	yes	3 hrs daily between 8 a.m. and 4 p.m. 140 days
AK	between 7 and 16	no, if approved by your local school board	if non-religious, either state or school district correspondence courses that "equally well-serve" the student	time as needed to complete correspondence courses, grade levels, or time to "equally well serve" the student. 180 days
AZ	between 8 and 16	no, but must pass the state reading, math and grammar proficiency exam	yes	175 days or equivalent
AR	7 through 16	no	yes	150 days
CA	between 6 and 16	no, if you enroll in the Independent Study option with local school, or claim your home to be a private school	yes	3 hrs daily 175 days
CO	7 and under 16	no	yes	average 4 hrs daily; 172 days
CT	over 7 and under 16	no, but your qualifications are subject to local board review	instruction equivalent to public schools	equivalent to public schools
DE	between 5 and 16	no	same as public schools.	180 days
DC	between 7 and 16	no	equivalent to public schools	substantially equivalent

state	compulsory attendance	certification required	state-required subjects/courses	hours per day days per year
FL	6 and under 16	no	sequentially progressive instruction	same as public schools
GA	between 7 and 16	no	yes	4.5 hours 180 days
HI	6 through 17	no, but must have at least a bachelor"s degree	basically yes	no minimums
ID	7 to 16	yes, unless waived by local school board	yes	2.5-3 grade K 4.5 grade 1- 3 5 grade 4- 8 5.5 grade 7-12 180 days
IL	between 7 and 16	no	equal to or superior to public schools	equal to or superior to public schools 176 days
IN	7 to 16	no	equivalent to public schools	same number of days as public schools where you reside
IA	7 to 16	yes	equivalent instruction	at least 120 days
KS	7 and under 16	no	yes	substantially equivalent hrs. 180 days
KY	between 6 and 16	no	yes	185 days
LA	7 through 15	no	a sustained curriculum at least equal to that of the public schools	180 days

state	compulsory attendance	certification required	state-required subjects/courses	hours per day days per year
ME	7 and under 17	no	equivalent instruction	adequate hrs to accomplish the proposed education plan 175 days
MD	6 and under 16	no	studies as usually taught in the public schools	regular instruction during school year of suffic- ient duration to implement the instruc- tional plan
MA	between 6 and 16	no	yes	180 days
MI	6 to 16	yes	yes, comparable to those taught in the public schools	continuous and consecu- tive with local school year; daily hours determined by state supt. 180 days
MN	between 7 and 16	no	yes	170 days
MS	6 and under 14	no	no	5-8 hours daily;155 days or a term sufficient for promotion from grade to grade
MO	between 7 and 16	no	yes	1000 hours (See further note in sum- mary below.)
MT	7 through 15	no	yes	180 days or equivalent

state	compulsory attendance	certification required	state-required subjects/courses	hours per day days per year
NE	between 7 and 16	no	yes	elem. 1,032 hours yearly second. 1,080 hours yearly 175 days
NV	between 7 and 17	no	equivalent instruction	days of appropriate length 180 days
NH	between 6 and 16	no	equivalent instruction	instructional hours appropriate to child's age, ability and needs 180 days
NJ	between 6 and 16	no	equivalent to public schools	equivalent to public schools
NM	5 to 18, or high school completion	no, but must have a baccalaureate degree unless waived by state superintendent	a basic academic educational program	2.5 grade K 5.5 grade 1-6 6.5 grade 7-12 180 days
NY	6 to 16	no	substantially equivalent	5 hours daily 180 days
NC	between 7 and 16	no, but must have at least a high school diploma	such minimum curriculum standards as are required of public schools	must run concurrently with local public schools 180 days
ND	7 to 16	yes	yes; same as local schools	5.5 elementary 6 jr/sr high K 30 days min 1-12 180 days
OH	between 6 and 18	no, but a baccalaureate degree recommended	no	same as public schools 182 days

state	compulsory attendance	certification required	state-required subjects/courses	hours per day days per year
OK	7 and under 18	no	equivalent to public schools	180 days
OR	between 7 and 18	no	courses usually taught in public schools	equivalent to that required by public schools
PA	8 to 17	no	yes	daily hours: 2.5 grade K 5.0 grade 1-6 annual hours: 450 grade K 900 elementary 990 secondary 180 days
RI	between 7 and 16	no	yes, substantially so	substantially equal to that required in public schools
SC	5 to 16	no, but must have at least a high school diploma or the equivalent	yes	4.5 hours daily 180 days
SD	6 and under 16	no	competent alternative instruction in basic skills	equivalent to public schools
TN	7 through 16	no for K-8; baccalaureate degree for 9-12 unless waived	no	4 hours daily 180 days
TX	7 through school year including child's 16th birthday	no	yes	170 days
UT	between 6 and 18	no	yes	same as the public schools

state	compulsory attendance	certification required	state-required subjects/courses	hours per day days per year
VT	between 7 and 16	no	yes	same as local public schools or affiliate private school; 175 days typical
VA	5 through 16	no	yes	same as the public schools
WA	8 and under 18	no (See Summary below.)	yes	180 days; (See Summary below for yearly hours
WV	7 to 16	no	yes, the basics	equal to local public schools
WI	between 6 and 18	no	yes	875 hours yearly
WY	7 and under 16	no	must provide a sequentially progressive curriculum of instruction	175 days

Summary of State Regulations and Procedures

In all states you could choose to follow the procedures outlined in Sections Two and Three of this book. The home-school regulations and procedures of your state, summarized below, are in most instances already incorporated into the contents of Sections Two and Three. However, remember that you may need to *adapt the form* of required documents — however indicated in your state's procedures.

The terms *core curriculum* and *basic curriculum* are used below to refer to the typical, basic five courses of reading, language arts, math, science and social studies. If a *three-course core curriculum* is noted, just reading, language arts, and math are designated in the state regulations and procedures as mandatory.

Language arts typically includes spelling, grammar, creative writing, and related areas. Although reading is often listed as a separate subject area, it is actually one of the language arts subcategories and, when understood as such, is not listed separately. Math courses are sequentially based, progressing in plateaus of prerequisite skills and include the usual roster of math skill areas — number recognition, counting, measurement, geometry, problem solving, fractions and so on up to the higher math skill areas and courses. Computer education is sometimes included in the math sequence. Science and social studies may include any or all of the commonly taught, age-appropriate knowledge and skill areas. For typical course lists, check state or local curriculum guides, private or satellite school curriculums, or commercial home-school curriculums, as recommended in the curriculum portion of Section Three. Also, take advantage of your at-home freedom to embellish any required basic curriculum. You do need a written account of your curriculum that reflects compliance with regulations, but in everyday practice, please remember that most important home-school word: flexibility.

The summaries provided below are meant to be read in combination with the information in the chart above for your state. Both, of course, are to be considered along with information received from your state's department of education and information obtained from experienced home schoolers in your state. Again, too, all home schoolers should remain alert to any changes in laws affecting them.

One of the best ways to do this and to gather information about the legal atmosphere in your local area and state is to communicate with active home-school organizations. Also, please remember that the following is a layman's summary and does not constitute legal consultation. Note that the word *form* appears in italics below if a prepared form is provided for your use by your state or local school officials. This is to signal you that you will need to secure the designated form.

ALABAMA: A statement of intent including your children's names, the subjects you will teach and the amount of time you will devote to each subject must be delivered prior to instruction to either your county superintendent or city superintendent of schools. (See Section Two and write to your state department of education for "Alabama Private School License Law" & "Certain Laws and State Board Resolutions That Pertain to Private Schools in Alabama.") Following approval you will be issued a certificate by the state superintendent allowing you to hold school. Then you will need to register your home school (annually) by October 10th with the state department of education and provide statistics on student and instructor numbers, enrollment and attendance, courses, instructional term, tuition costs, funds, property values and conditions, as applicable to you, on uniform *forms provided* by the state superintendent of schools. After the fifth day of the local public school year, you must report the names and addresses of your children enrolled in your home school — on *forms provided* by your local superintendent (who should secure them from the state). During the instructional year, you will need to keep a register of course work completed, hours and attendance, and submit any reports that the state board, state superintendent, county superintendent, or local board may require. The language of instruction must be English. If you're not a certified teacher and not able to qualify as a "ministry," see question 3 in Section One. To qualify as a ministry, you may form a nonprofit church-affiliated school. In this case, you would notify the local school district that your children are satellite students of a local church school or that your home school is sponsored by a local church. Ask your state department of education for a copy of Alabama codes related to church schools. Courses of study are available from your state department and curriculum guides from your local school district. Plan to include no less than a basic curriculum, plus physical education and health. (See Section Three on curriculum.)

ALASKA: You have the option of establishing your home school through your state's Centralized Correspondence Study program, or as a religious school or private school (not difficult, but must be under the aegis of a religious organization), set up tutoring for your children by a certified teacher, or establish a home school that "equally well-serves" its enrollees. In the latter case, your home-school proposal and your qualifications to home teach will be reviewed for approval by the local school board. (See outlined procedure in Sections Two and Three and secure a curriculum guide handbook from your state department of education.) You may wish to request from your state department its "Correspondence Study Handbook" to see which courses are available. Plan to include no less than a three-course core curriculum.

ARIZONA: You will need to file with the county school superintendent an affidavit stating that your children are being taught at home. To qualify for home teaching you must pass the state's reading, grammar and math proficiency exam before or within six months after beginning your home school. Your children must take a standardized achievement test annually, and you should file a copy of the test results with the county superintendent. You may request a copy of an achievement test from your state department of education, and the test must be administered by a public or private school. Plan to include in your curriculum no less that the core subjects. You would probably be wise to follow the procedures outlined in Section Two and Section Three, particularly the curriculum and record-keeping segments.

ARKANSAS: A notice (aka *statement*) of intent must be delivered to your local public school superintendent by August 15th of each year (or December 15th for second semester) and Notice of Achievement Test Selection by November 15th. (See "Statement of Intent" and "Annual Evaluation," in Sections Two and Three.) The Arkansas state department of education *provides* a notice of intent *form* and test registration *form.* If new to the state, you have twenty school days to file these documents. Request "Regulations and Procedures for Home-schools" from your state department for yearly standardized test requirements, approved test list, test administration process, & satisfactory test results information. Plan to include no less than a core curriculum.

CALIFORNIA: You have three options: private tutoring as a certified teacher, independent study through your public school under the supervision of a certified person, or filing an affidavit claiming your home to be a private school. Write to your state department of

CO – CT

education for specifications of each of these three options and for all available information regarding the procedures involved in carrying out these options. Whichever option you select, you'll be expected to provide your child instruction in the areas required for public education (English & all language arts, math, social sciences, fine arts, health, science, physical education), to keep necessary records (See "Keeping Records" in Section Three.), and to demonstrate your competency; but each of the three options comes with its own set of requirements. To purchase curriculum guides or frameworks, ask your state department for its "Selected Publications" catalog. California, you'll soon discover, has a large number of home-school support groups to whom you can appeal for help. (See Section Five.)

COLORADO: Fourteen days prior to the beginning of your home-school program each year you must provide written notification to the local school district of the establishment of your home school, including basic personal information, i.e., names, ages, address, attendance hours, for each child. You should plan for a record-keeping system including attendance data, test and evaluation results, immunization records. If the superintendent of your local school district has probable cause to believe that your home-school program is in noncompliance with your state's home-school guidelines, he may request that you submit your records to the district within fourteen days of his written notice. (See "Keeping Records" in Section Three.) Plan for a sequential program of instruction including communication skills (reading, writing, speaking), math, history, civics, literature, science, and the U.S. Constitution. (See "Curriculum and Materials" and "Schedules and Calendars" in Sections Two and Three.) Arrange for achievement tests at grade levels 3, 5, 7, 9, 11, using the same standardized test as used by the local public schools. Results must be submitted to your local district or an independent or parochial school in Colorado whose name is then submitted to your local district. If composite test results for your home-schooled children are not above the 13th percentile, you will need to select another educational alternative for your children — although you may retest with another approved test first. Ask your state department for a current copy of "Rules for the Administration of an Established System of Home Study" and a copy of Senate Bill 56 passed in 1988.

CONNECTICUT: Suggested procedures which are likely to be *expected* by your local public school officials: File your request to home school with your local school officials "within a reasonable period of time" prior to your school year, allowing for no less than a ten-day board approval time. (See "Statement of Intent" in Section Two.) Your local superintendent or a designee should then invite you to meet with him so that he may explain procedures you should follow in presenting your request to the local board. Following that meeting, you will need to notify the superintendent of your desire to present your home-school proposal to the local board. Along with that notification, you should send a written program of home instruction to the superintendent who will approach the board at its next scheduled meeting with your proposal and plan. (See Sections Two and Three.) You, too, may discuss your proposal with the board at that time. The board will then have ten days in which to determine if you will be providing "equivalent instruction" and to approve or disapprove your plan. Subject matter should include the areas of reading, language arts, math, U.S. history and government, local and state government, geography, citizenship. Although standardized achievement testing isn't required, you should include some means of evaluation in your plan. (See "Annual Evaluation" in Section Three.)

DELAWARE: Delaware rules and regulations do not speak directly to home schooling, but rather to school attendance. However, proceed as you deem advisable with Sections Two and Three for your own benefit. The state asks that you submit an enrollment statement to your local superintendent both before July 31st and by the last school day in September. Include a statement and evidence to the effect that your child is receiving a regular and thorough education at home. Some means of measuring progress should be shown; i.e., testing. Note that although you aren't officially required to complete the entire procedure outlined in Sections Two and Three, by privately following most of those procedures you are likely to be well equipped to respond to challenges that arise.

DISTRICT OF COLUMBIA: Your home school must be approved as a private school. You must present for local school board approval a completed "Application for Approval of Private Instruction" *form*, a yearly home-school calendar, evidence of teacher qualifications, and a curriculum substantially equivalent to the public schools. (See Sections Two and Three.) Although teacher certification is not required, evidence that your teacher qualifications are substantially equivalent to public school teacher qualifications must be submitted. You must supply the local school district with personal information on each of your children — name, address, race, sex, date and place of birth. Plan to maintain attendance records open for inspection. You may also be asked to verify the suitability of your home-school building and the availability of any needed school counseling services. Monitor your legislature and state department of education for upcoming home-school legislation and procedural specifications.

FL – HI

FLORIDA: You must *either* hold a Florida teaching certificate for the grade levels you intend to home teach *or* comply with the following requirements: 1) File with your local superintendent a notice of intent to home teach. Include names, addresses, and birthdates of all children you will home teach. 2) Maintain a portfolio, including a daily teacher's log which shows titles of textbooks used, sample writings and other work, worksheets, workbooks, creative materials used or developed by the student. The portfolio is to be kept for two years and be available for inspection. Better yet, keep the portfolio at least as long as your children are home schooled. Upon any future discontinuation of your home school, you will be expected to submit requested records to your local district. 3) Arrange for annual student evaluation by one of the following methods: a) review of portfolio and discussion with student by a certified teacher; b) standardized achievement test administered by a certified teacher; c) state student assessment test; d) "any other valid measurement tool" agreed upon by you and your district superintendent. (See Section Three.) The results of the evaluation will be reviewed by your superintendent, and if he determines that student progress has been unsatisfactory, you will be placed on a one-year probationary period. This allows you one more year of home teaching to help your student improve his progress record. Plan to include no less than a core curriculum. Finally, your state maintains a data base of educational institutions for which you are required to file a data base survey *form.*

GEORGIA: You must submit a declaration of intent to your local school superintendent on a *form provided* by him by September 1st or within thirty days after your home-school program has begun. Names and ages of your enrollees, address of your home school, and your school year calendar should be included. If you parent teach, you must have a high school or GED diploma. If a tutor teaches, the tutor must hold a baccalaureate degree. Plan to include no less than a core curriculum. You will need to submit monthly attendance reports — *forms available* from your local superintendent. Arrange to administer standardized achievement tests in consultation with a person trained in the administration and interpretation of such tests, every third year beginning at the end of third grade. You will be expected to write annual progress assessment reports in each subject area for each of your home-schooled children. (See "Annual Evaluation" in Section Three.)

HAWAII: You will need to secure a copy of Form OIS 4140, "Annual Request to Withdraw School-age Child" from your state department. You will then need to complete it and submit it to the local school district, along with verification (transcripts) of your qualifications as a parent educator (bachelor's degree required) and an account of your planned curriculum, schedules, testing procedures, and materials. Quarterly, you must submit a narrative report, test copies, and a report card for your child to your local school principal and submit any other reports that your principal requests. (See Section Three.) Your narrative will need to demonstrate subject area progress and growth in social awareness, self-understanding, societal and cultural understanding, and in character/ moral/ ethical values. Elementary courses must include the areas of language arts, math, social studies, science, art, music, health, and physical education. Secondary courses must include the areas of social studies, English, math, science, health, physical education, guidance. Your child may be issued a diploma by your community school for adults if she scores satisfactorily on your state's General Educational Development Test. If you don't hold a bachelor's degree, see question 3 in Section One.

IDAHO: You may offer a statement of intent and curriculum outline to the local school board for approval as "comparable." Special curricular areas to be taught in addition to a core curriculum: U.S. Constitution, American flag use, national colors, Pledge of Allegiance, the national anthem, the anthem "America;" health, physical fitness, drug awareness; and Arbor Day from a preservation perspective. You may need to demonstrate that you have access to library/research facilities; speech, hearing, and psychological assessment and counseling; social services; music, art, and physical education programs, and the availability of a certificated "supervisor" for you as a parent-educator. (See Section Two.) You may need to account for your child's "normal social growth and development" through planned group interaction activities. (See question 4 in Section One.) Do remember that if you approach your local school board and the members find you qualified to offer "comparable education" to that of the public schools, the board may waive a certification requirement. If a certification requirement is imposed, see question 3 in Section One and "Evidence of Home-teacher Qualifications" in Section Two. Your "school" may need to meet local, county, and state fire and building codes and ordinances. Check with your state department regarding the availability of course syllabi and curriculum guides. Maintain thorough records so you are prepared for any official challenge to your status as a home schooler. (See Section 3.)

ILLINOIS: In your state a home school is a private school. You may complete and submit to your local superintendent a "Statement of Assurance" *form provided* by your state department. You would probably be wise to submit the form. However, if you choose not to, be prepared to do so should you at some time be challenged. In

IN – IA

other words, plan well — in writing — and keep good records from which you can later derive information for completing the form and/or meeting any challenge to your home-school program. The burden of proof will be on you. Plan to include no less than a core curriculum. The language of instruction must be English.

INDIANA: Home schools in Indiana are treated as private schools, subject only to requirements including a core curriculum and the "same number of days" as public schools. However, recent case law in Indiana indicates that you must furnish information regarding your home school to school officials. That information should include the basic specifics (names, ages, teacher, etc.), student learning objectives (particularly in reading, writing, & math), methods you will utilize in order for your students to achieve the learning objectives, a one-year time schedule/calendar, and evaluation methods (See Sections Two and Three.) Contact other home schoolers in your area or a state home-school organization to determine your school district's expectations regarding these submissions. Plan to keep attendance records. The language of instruction must be English. Curriculum guides are available from your state department of education.

IOWA: In your state the school year must begin no sooner than September 1st and must be in session no less that 120 days — to which compulsory attendance applies. Home schools, therefore, need not run concurrently with the local school term and should not be challenged by school officials until the final 120 days of the September to May school year (followed by a typical summer vacation). (Refer to State v. Trucke, a 1987 Iowa Supreme Court case.) However, check with local school officials to determine common practices in your district. The compulsory education law provides that within ten days of receiving notice from your local school secretary, you must furnish a certificate stating names and ages of your home-schooled children, the period of time during which those children have been and are being home schooled, details of their instruction, and the name of their teacher. (See Sections Two and Three.) Also maintain immunization records. If you are not certified to teach, see the note below regarding the current one-year moratorium and also see question 3 in Section One. The language of instruction in your home school must be English. Plan to include art, English, handwriting, literature, reading, spelling, health, physical education, math, music, science, social studies, traffic safety, and career education in your grades 1-6 curriculum. Plan to include art, reading, spelling, grammar, writing, health, physical education, math, music, science, social studies, and career education in your grades 7-8 curriculum.

Prepare an outline of your curriculum and a materials list. Request from your state department its "Equivalent Instruction Standards" for further specifications. If your reasons for home schooling are religious, you may file proof of the conflicts you hold with the public schools regarding your religious tenets and principles and the names, ages, and addresses of your home-school enrollees to the director of your department of education. If such proof is approved by your state board, you and your enrollees will be exempted from compliance with the compulsory education and educational standards laws. NOTE: Recently in Iowa a committee was established to study the Iowa education laws, and a one-year moratorium forestalls enforcement of the present compulsory education laws. During this period, through July 1, 1989, it is likely you can teach at home without certification but under the supervision of a certified teacher. However, you must submit names and ages of your children and weekly lesson plans and other items delineated above. (See Section Three for lesson planning information.) Monitor the activities and recommendations of the education law committee.

KANSAS: To establish your home school you must register it with your state department as a private school. Although you may not be challenged, do be prepared to show evidence that you are "competent" as an instructor. See "Evidence of Home-Teacher Qualifications" in Section Two and follow as you feel advisable the other procedures outlined in Sections Two and Three, particularly with respect to curriculum and record keeping. Maintain copies of your curriculum design, records, daily plans, etc.; do not discard them. Plan to include no less than a core curriculum.

KENTUCKY: Within the first two weeks of the local school district's school year, you must submit to the local school district the names, ages, and address of your home-schooled children. The superintendent of schools may request further information necessary to carrying out the compulsory attendance and employment of children laws in your state. Keep an attendance register, which will remain open for intermittent inspection. (See "Keeping Records" in Section Three.) School officials may inspect your home school as deemed necessary. Plan to include no less than a three-course core curriculum. The language of instruction must be English.

LOUISIANA: Within thirty days after you begin home schooling submit an application to the state department of education for review and recommendation to the state board of education. The initial application should include attached copies of your home-schooled children's birth certificates. (Yearly renewals are due Oct. 1 or within

ME

12 months of initial approval, whichever is later.) You will need to demonstrate that you are providing a "sustained curriculum;" i.e., a curriculum that is sequential — provides for learning by steps or degrees of difficulty in a consistent fashion. You can offer evidence of a sustained curriculum in one of four ways:1)documentation: complete outlines of each subject taught, a list of books and materials used, a portfolio of students' work and tests, statements by third party observers of your children's progress, or other evidence; or 2) verification of your children's performances on the State Basic Skills Test — at or above the state performance standard established for their grade levels; or 3) verification of your children's performances on the state board-approved standardized achievement test — at or above their grade levels or progress at a rate equal to one grade level per year; or 4) a statement from a certified teacher indicating that his or her examination of your program reveals that your children are being taught a "sustained curriculum" of *at least equal* quality to that of the public schools. If you follow the procedures outlined in Section Two and Section Three, you should be able to accomplish *1* herein as evidence — if you wish to proceed according to *1*. Plan to include no less than a core curriculum.

MAINE: Thirty days prior to the beginning of the school year you must submit a thorough request to "provide equivalent instruction;" i.e., to home school, to your local superintendent (who upon local approval of your request will send it for further approval to your state's commissioner of education). Also note that your state department has made an application *form available* to local schools; check with your local superintendent regarding its use in your school district. Plan for your curriculum to be sequential (in order of steps or degrees of difficulty) and to include no less than a core curriculum plus physical education. You will need to submit a syllabus and description of your curricular program. *Forms* for such are available. Arrange for testing quarterly and either for a yearly standardized achievement test or a locally developed test based upon your curricular plan or for an annual review and approval by a certified Maine teacher. Keep thorough attendance and other records. (See Section Three.) If you are not certified or eligible for certification, arrange for a certified teacher or a successful, experienced home-school teacher or a public or private school to assist and advise you at least four times during the school year. Or you may design your own support system to the satisfaction of the Maine Commissioner of Educational and Cultural Services. (See "Certificated Home-School Consultant" in Section Two.) With local school officials' approval, your home-schooled child may use public school facilities and may participate in public school student activities. Secure a copy of "Guidelines for

Equivalent Instruction Through Homeschooling" from a practicing home schooler or from the Maine Homeschool Association — address in Section Five. If you wish to avoid the above approval process, look into enrolling at least one unrelated child in your school and calling your school a "nonapproved private school."

MARYLAND: You will be asked to complete and sign an "Assurance of Consent *Form*," regarding your compliance with Maryland education laws at least fifteen days before you begin home teaching. Plan to include no less than a core curriculum plus art, music, health, and physical education and to maintain thorough home-school records, particularly a portfolio of your initial and ongoing plans, materials, samples of your child's work, and tests. (See Sections Two and Three.) Your portfolio will be reviewed by a local school official at the end of each semester to verify that you are providing "regular and thorough instruction." However, you may opt instead to step under the supervisory umbrella of a state-approved nonpublic school. You may volunteer to participate in the yearly standardized test administration carried out by the local public school. Ask your state department for a copy of the home-education bylaw, which delineates the procedure for setting up a home school and which sets limits on public school officials' involvement in your program.

MASSACHUSETTS: While the approval process is currently being debated in Massachusetts and may soon be altered, traditional expectations are presented here. Prior to withdrawing your children from public school, you will need to gain approval to home school from your local school committee. You must demonstrate that you are complying with schooling requirements in the state by submitting curriculums to be taught, a list of materials and aids to be used, lesson plans, schedule and calendar, your qualifications as a home-teacher, plans for ongoing student progress assessment, plans for annual evaluation. (See Sections Two and Three) You have the right to present your proposal and to present witnesses on your behalf, if necessary, during a school committee meeting. Should approval of your proposal be denied, its inadequacies should be delineated for you so that you may revise your proposal. The school committee *may* require standardized achievement testing and *may* arrange for visits or observations of your home-school environment by school officials. Plan to include no less than a core curriculum plus art, music, physical education, and principles of "good behavior."

MICHIGAN: You must declare your intent to home school to the local intermediate school district at the beginning of your home-school year on a *provided form*. Also, you must keep attendance records and

MN – MO

instructional records. Plan to include no less than a core curriculum plus U.S. & Michigan constitutions and histories, and the political subdivisions and municipalities of Michigan. (See Section Three.) By November 1st, you must file "Home School Membership Report" *forms* with the intermediate district. If you home school six or more students, your home-school building must meet fire and health standards. Ask your state department for compulsory education acts and all publications regarding home-school compliance procedures. If you're not a certified teacher, see question 3 in Section One. Check with your state department regarding the availability of curriculum guides.

MINNESOTA: By October 1st you must submit a notice of intent to your local school superintendent. You should include the names, ages, and addresses of your enrollees; the name of each home-school teacher along with evidence that each either holds an appropriate teaching certificate, or is supervised by a certified person, or has completed a teacher competency exam, or holds a baccalaureate degree, or is the parent of a child who is assessed yearly using a standardized achievement test, arranged in cooperation with the local school superintendent. If you, as home-school teacher, are the latter ("the parent of..."), then you will need to complete a quarterly report card which indicates your child's progress in each required subject area. Plan to include the areas of reading, writing, literature, fine arts, math, science, history, geography, government, health, and physical education in your curriculum. You should keep and make available an annual instructional calendar and documentation that reflects your compliance with subject area requirements, such as class schedules, materials used, and testing or other assessment methods. (See Section Two and Section Three.) The language of instruction must be English. Your local superintendent or designee may visit your home school annually.

MISSISSIPPI: By September 15th each school year you must complete a certificate of enrollment, the *form* of which will be prepared by the state board of education and which will include names, addresses, ages of your home-schooled children and a description of your educational plan and scope. (See "Curriculum" in Section Three.) Plan to keep an attendance register along with a log of valid reasons for your child's absence from home-school lessons. (See "Keeping Records" in Section Three.) Ask your state department for a copy of its "Curriculum Structure" manual.

MISSOURI: According to state law, within thirty days after you begin home schooling you *may* file a signed, written declaration of enrollment and notice of intent to home school with your county recorder or local school superintendent. However, such registration is not required. (Consult with practicing home schoolers.) Names and ages of your enrollees; address and phone number of your home school; teachers' names; and names, addresses, and signatures of each person making the declaration of enrollment would be included, if you elect to register. While you need to provide at least 1000 hours of home instruction, at least 600 of those hours should be in the core curriculum areas; and at least 400 of the 600 should occur at home. Maintain a plan book or other written record of subjects taught and activities carried out, a portfolio of your child's academic work, and a record of tests and other measures of your child's academic progress. (See Sections Two and Three.)

MONTANA: Notification of your intent to home school should be submitted to the county superintendent of schools. Plan to maintain attendance and immunization records, which should be available to the county superintendent, and to provide "an organized course of study," including those subjects basic to the instructional programs of the public schools. (See Section Three.) Your home-school building must meet local health and safety regulations. Ask your state department for a copy of its "Rural Education Curriculum Guide."

NEBRASKA: To obtain exemption from compulsory attendance requirements for your children, you will need to sign and have notarized a "Statement of Objection and Assurances" *form*, indicating that the requirements for school approval and accreditation required by law and the rules and regulations of your state board of education violate your "sincerely held religious beliefs." Then, thirty days prior to the beginning of your home-school session, you must file an "Affirmation of Appointment as Authorized Parent Representative" *form*, indicating your understanding of your duties as a "parent representative" of the parents of the children who attend your home school. Also, prior to your school session, you must submit to the commissioner of education an information summary, including a 175-day calendar; a list of names, addresses, ages, educational levels, and experience of any instructional monitors who will work in your home school; a scope and sequence instructional chart or summary including no less than a core curriculum plus health, a list of all classes or courses and grade levels, and the names of the monitors responsible for those classes or courses. You must show evidence of your basic literacy; i.e., your qualifications to teach; or take a minimum competency test. (See Section Two regarding home-teacher qualifications.) Your state or local superintendent may elect to visit your home school at mutually agreed upon times.

NV – NH

NEVADA: You must prepare and submit to your local superintendent a request to have your children excused from compulsory attendance. In that request you must include a statement about the home teacher (you) and the location of the home school; an educational plan; a 180-day calendar; and evidence of <u>one</u> of the following:1) you are certified; 2) you qualify for certification; 3) you have available to you a certified teacher consultant (at least twenty-five hours of planning, development, review, and learning problem consultation); 4) your children's enrollment in an approved correspondence program. If you choose option 3, the requirement may be waived after one year if your home-schooled children demonstrate reasonable educational progress. Plan to arrange with your local superintendent for annual achievement testing of your elementary home-school enrollees with the same test used locally, unless you have chosen option 4. In that case, correspondence course transcripts may be used as evidence with local district acceptance. For high school enrollees, you and your local school board may jointly determine an acceptable means of demonstrating educational progress. Plan to keep records and follow other procedures similar to those outlined in Sections Two and Three. Also, plan to include a typical core curriculum, plus the U.S. and Nevada constitutions, in your curriculum.

NEW HAMPSHIRE: Ninety days prior to beginning your home-school year, you must make initial application to your local school board by following the procedures outlined in the booklet "Regulations and Procedures for Home Education Programs in New Hampshire," which you can obtain from your state department. If your initial request is based upon religious reasons, and if approved, your home school may be granted exemption from regulations. If not exempt for religious reasons, sixty days prior to the school year a written application statement must be submitted and must meet the requirements laid out for "manifest educational hardship" and include the child's educational program, parent qualifications, and a plan for evaluation of the child's educational progress. It is imperative that you obtain, read carefully, and follow the procedures outlined in the above noted "Regulations and Procedures..." booklet. Also consult Sections Two and Three of this book. You must provide courses and learning experiences reasonably the equivalent of those commonly taught in the public schools: reading, writing, spelling, grammar, English, math, history, government, U.S. & state constitution, geography, physiology, music. Again, refer to "Regulations and Procedures...," particularly to Appendix A, "Recommended Standards for the Development of the Required Instruction in Home Education Programs." You, as parent, must be able to demonstrate your competency as the potential teacher of your child, and your application statement must include a plan for the evaluation of your child's progress. (See the "Regulations and Procedures..." booklet and "Annual Evaluation" in Section Three.) State department personnel may be available to assist you with all of these procedures, and I encourage you to secure the help of established home schoolers and of public school certificated personnel as well. Following your first home-school year, a "Request for Continuation of Approved Status" must annually be delivered to your local school superintendent at least ninety days prior to the beginning of your school year.

NEW JERSEY: One of your tasks in setting up and carrying out a home school is to maintain continuous records/documentation that show that you are providing your home-schooled children with "instruction equivalent to that provided in the public schools for children of similar grades and attainments...." You would be wise to complete major components of the statement of intent outlined in Section Two in order to effectively establish that you are providing equivalent instruction. If challenged, you must present evidence that you are and have been in compliance with the equivalent instruction requirement. Plan to include no less than a typical core curriculum.

NEW MEXICO: You must complete a "Notification of Establishment of a Home-school" *form issued* by your local school district, attach immunization records for your home-schooled children, and submit the documents to your local district within thirty days prior to the beginning of your home-school year (and by April 1st for each subsequent year). Plan to include no less than a core curriculum. Plan to continue maintaining immunization records and to maintain attendance records. (See Section Three.) Between November 1st and 6th, you should complete a "Home-school Enrollment Report," a *form issued* by and returned to the local school district. Arrange with the local district for yearly standardized achievement testing. If you do not hold a baccalaureate degree, you may file an "Application for Waiver of Baccalaureate Degree Requirement"*form* or consider suggestions given under question 3 in Section One. Ask you state department for a copy of "Procedures for Home-schooling in New Mexico."

NEW YORK: Although there is no statutory requirement in New York that a parent must obtain school district approval to remove a child from public school, you are expected to file a notice of intent by July 1st, or 14 days prior to beginning your home school if you begin midyear. You are also expected to meet with your local superintendent to present your home-school proposal — names, ages, and grade levels of your enrollees; course outlines and materials lists;

NC – ND

instructional plans for each child; a year's home-school calendar; description of your qualifications to home teach; and plans for evaluations of progress. (See Sections Two and Three.) Check with local experienced home schoolers regarding specific expectations of the local school district. Annual evaluation plans should include either standardized tests or a narrative review of each child's progress, but in grades 4, 6 and 8 standardized achievement tests must be given. Testing is also required after 8th grade. Evaluation must include reading and math at grade 3, writing at grade 5, reading and math at grade 6. An Application for Home Instruction *form is available.* A diploma may be granted provided competency is shown through your state's Preliminary and Regents Competency Tests during grades 8-12. Plan to keep attendance and other records. (See "Keeping Records" in Section Three.) Plan to include no less than a core curriculum plus physical education. Curriculum guides and other publications are available from your state department.

NORTH CAROLINA: You must notify the director of nonpublic education in your governor's office of your intent to home school. Home schools in your state fall under the jurisdiction of the governor's office, so that you are not legally accountable to your state board of education or to your local school district officials. However, your state considers your local school superintendent to be the watchdog of compulsory attendance requirements in your school district and that his overseer's role includes your child's home-school attendance. To be fully in compliance with your state's expectations, to prepare yourself to home teach, and to prepare yourself to meet the requirements of any upcoming North Carolina home-school legislation, you would be wise to complete major segments of the procedures outlined in Sections Two and Three. Your curriculum should include reading, spelling, grammar, English, music, Americanism, free enterprise, physical education, health. You will need to arrange for the purchase, administration, and scoring of standardized achievement tests at the appropriate level for each of your children beyond second grade. When writing to your state department for a copy of the Compulsory Attendance Act and the nonpublic schools acts, ask for a current copy of the "School Management Advisor" for the answers to some of your initial questions.

NORTH DAKOTA: You should contact the local superintendent of schools to begin the process of home-school approval. A private schools *form* will be needed, available from the state department of instruction. Your home school must meet the same statutory requirements as public or private schools, including teacher certification, subjects taught, length of session, and compliance with municipal and state health, fire, and safety laws. You should make your contact early enough to be ready to sign the annual "Certificate of Compliance" by October 1st. The local and state superintendents will jointly decide approval or disapproval of your home-school program. Ask the state department for a copy of "North Dakota Statutory Requirements for the Funding of Public Schools and the Approval of Private and Parochial Schools." Also, watch for home school vs. North Dakota litigation, particularly regarding the certification requirement. If you're not certified, see question 3 in Section One. Plan to include no less than a core curriculum plus agricultural science. Check with the state department of education regarding the availability of curriculum guides and other materials. Watch for upcoming changes in home-school regulations.

OHIO: You must file a request for your children to be excused from public school attendance and apply to the local school superintendent for approval to home school. You will be expected to present your qualifications to home teach and to propose a home-school curriculum and materials list, a variety of which have been approved, but you would be wise to plan for the inclusion of no less than a core curriculum plus physical education. The superintendent will make a judgement as to your qualifications — so describe them fully. Your having or not having a college degree may become the pivotal point in the superintendent's decision. (See Sections Two and Three). The local superintendent may impose a testing requirement. Monitor your legislature for pending home-school legislation.

OKLAHOMA: To date, the state of Oklahoma recognizes your right to "in good faith" home educate your children and places few regulations, requirements, or restrictions upon your family's procedures as home schoolers, beyond what is "reasonable." Do plan to include the array of subjects typically taught in Oklahoma's public schools, as your curriculum must be "equivalent" to that provided in public schools. This, of course, means that you should include no less than a core curriculum. Also, do plan careful record-keeping. (See Section Three.) Lastly, keep an eye on your legislature — home-school legislation may be imminent.

OREGON: At least ten days prior to home schooling, you should notify your education service district superintendent or county school district superintendent, who according to legal procedure should then notify your local district superintendent. When writing your state department for the Oregon laws, ask for the state board's approved comprehensive examination list (with publishers and addresses) from which you may select the test you wish to have administered to your child (yearly) by a qualified neutral person. Plan to include a core curriculum.

PA – SC

PENNSYLVANIA: Your home-school proposal and your qualifications to home teach are subject to the approval of your local school superintendent. "Written assurance" from you that you are complying with official expectations and are providing quality home education is required before consideration for approval. To provide written assurance and evidence of compliance, I recommend that you selectively follow the procedures outlined in Sections Two and Three. For elementary instruction plan to include the areas of reading, writing, spelling, English, math, geography, United States and Pennsylvania history, science, civics, loyalty to the state and national governments, safety, humane treatment of wildlife, health, physical education, physiology, music, art. For secondary instruction include the areas of English, math, art, health, music, physical education, science, social studies, United States and Pennsylvania history.

RHODE ISLAND: You will need to contact the local school committee for approval of your home school. I recommend, however, that before you contact local school officials, you consult with members of Parent Educators of Rhode Island (address in Section Five). Until you are able to discuss the home-schooling climate in your county with other home schoolers, you may wish to maintain a low profile. When you do proceed, follow carefully the procedures outlined in Sections Two and Three of this book so that you will have a sound home-school proposal to present for approval and well-kept evidence of the quality of your children's home schooling. Plan to include no less than a core curriculum. The language of instruction must be English. Your attendance register should be a duplicate of that used in your local public schools. You may be able to secure a register book from your local school, or make copies of pages from one of their books, or order one from the company who prints theirs.

SOUTH CAROLINA: While a high school diploma or the equivalent is sufficient for home teaching in South Carolina, according to current law, you will need to pass a basic skills test before you will be granted the right to home teach unless you hold a baccalaureate degree. You will need to present your qualifications, curriculum, record-keeping system, access to library facilities, and plans for participation in the statewide standardized achievement and basic skills assessment programs. (See Sections Two and Three.) While approval of these items by the local school board is required, if all items are completed and presented, approval is virtually assured. Plan for no less than a core curriculum, plus composition and literature in grades 7 through 12. Record keeping should include a plan book, diary or other written record of subjects and learning activities, a portfolio of student academic work, and a record of ongoing assessments of student progress. Semi-annual progress reports are required. The statewide tests must be administered by a certificated employee of the local school district either with public school students, or (at the parent's cost) in the student's home. Home-schooled first graders must take a readiness test within the first fifteen instructional days — using the same readiness test given at the public school. You will be advised of the results, including a determination of your child's status as a first grader or kindergartner.

SOUTH DAKOTA: You must file an "Application for Excuse from Attendance," a standard *form provided* by your state superintendent. If approved, your local school board president will issue you a certificate of excuse — a right to home school. Your state superintendent may determine your "competency" for home teaching. English language mastery must be one of your child's goals, and your curriculum should include no less than a core curriculum plus free enterprise, U.S. and South Dakota constitutions, patriotism, and moral instruction. Your child must take the same achievement test as is administered in your local school (and will be provided by your local school) and its administration may be monitored by a local school designee. Plan to keep records of attendance and reasons for absences for your child. (See Section Three.) When writing to your state department, ask for its "Instructional Services Order Blank for K-12 Curriculum Guides and Materials."

TENNESSEE: By August 1st you must submit a notice of intent to your local superintendent, including basic enrollee information, home school location, curriculums, instructional hours, your qualifications. Plan to include no less than a core curriculum. Vaccination/immunization records must also be submitted. Arrange for standardized achievement testing when your home-schooled children have achieved grade levels 2, 5, 7, and 9 (same test as approved by state board for public schools) to be administered by your state commissioner of education or a designee on public school premises or by a professional testing service (if you wish to hire one) which is approved by your local school district. Public school facilities may be used by home schoolers upon the approval of the local superintendent, particularly for special needs courses (lab sciences, special education, etc.). Maintain attendance records, which are subject to periodic inspection and must be turned over to your local superintendent at year's end. (See Section Three.) If you are not certified but wish to home teach secondary students, you may apply for an exemption to the certification requirement.

TX – VT

TEXAS: Your children are legally excused from compulsory attendance in the public schools if they are attending a private or parochial school that teaches no less than reading, spelling, math, grammar, and good citizenship. A home school is considered a private school. However, do be prepared — plan well, as outlined in Section Two and Section Three, so you have documentation, so you build a valid record of your child's achievement. Your records should demonstrate that you are using books, workbooks, and other written materials. In particular, you must write out and maintain a well-planned curriculum. (See "Curriculum and Materials" in Section Three.) School officials may verify the attendance of your school-age children in home school and request assurances from you that you are complying with the law. Keep watch over your state legislature. Laws related to home schooling in Texas are currently undergoing a period of transition.

UTAH: You are expected annually to seek a public school attendance "release" for your children from the local school board. You should establish and maintain evidence sufficient to satisfy the local school board that your curriculum and the length of your school days/years are the same as prescribed by law for the public schools, that you are a competent teacher, that your home-school materials are adequate, that records such as attendance are kept, and that your children make at least minimal academic progress. (See Section Three herein.) Many districts in Utah provide a home-school approval/registration form and will offer help with books, curriculum and testing. Your home-schooled children may opt to attend selected courses and/or extracurricular activities at the local public school with school official approval. Plan to include no less than a core curriculum. Ask the Utah Office of Education for a copy of "CORE Standards for Utah Public Schools" to determine acceptable curricula for your home school.

VERMONT: Any time after March 1st of the year prior to the beginning of your home-school year, you must complete and send to your state's department of education an "Enrollment Notice for Home Study Program" *form provided* by the state department. Basic information is included on the form, and you will be expected to attach a detailed outline of each of your courses of study. Plan to include no less than a core curriculum plus physical education and health. (See "Curriculum and Materials" in Section Three.) Within fourteen days of receipt of your Enrollment Notice, you should receive word that either your Notice is complete enough or that further information is needed, information which you then have fourteen more days to provide. Your state commissioner of education *may* then order that a hearing be held within forty-five days, if he deems it necessary. (You can see that you will need to allow sufficient time for your Notice to be processed.) Arrange for yearly assessment of your child's progress in each subject area by one or more of the following: a Vermont certified teacher, an approved private school teacher, a publisher's teacher advisory service report along with a portfolio of your child's work, a report prepared by you along with a portfolio, or standardized achievement test results (administered by a qualified person or by an approved Vermont school).

VIRGINIA: In August each year you must notify your local superintendent of your intent to home school (an optional form is available), including your children's names, a description of your planned curriculum, and verification that *one* of the following four conditions exists: 1. you hold a baccalaureate degree; 2. you meet the qualifications for a teacher prescribed by your state board of education; 3. you enroll your children in an approved correspondence course; 4. you provide in writing a program of study (curriculum) which, in your local superintendent's judgment, includes your state's "Standards of Learning Objectives" for language arts and math and provides evidence that you are able to provide an adequate education for your children. Plan to include no less than a core curriculum. Ask the state department of education for a copy of its "Standards of Learning Objectives" and see "Curriculum and Materials" in Section Three. If you decide to enroll your children in a correspondence school, ask your state department for a copy of its approved "Correspondence Courses for Home Instruction." Plan to arrange for achievement testing (SRA test supplied) with your local superintendent or to provide for an alternative evaluation or assessment to be approved by your superintendent. (See "Annual Evaluation" in Section Three.) If one of your children scores below the 40th percentile on an achievement test, further assessment may be conducted by the local superintendent to determine if home schooling may (legally) continue for that child. If your intent to home school is based upon conscientious religious opposition to public school attendance, secure a copy of law 22.1-257 from the state department of education.

WASHINGTON: When you write to your state department, ask for "Washington State's Laws Regulating Home-Based Instruction" in which you will find responses to questions regarding compulsory attendance, home-based instruction as an extension of a private school, and home-schooled students' part-time attendance in public schools; tables showing your responsibilities as a home educator; your state's Declaration of Intent form; and a list of approved tests. You will need to submit your Declaration of Intent to your local

WV – WI

superintendent by Sept. 15th or within two weeks of the beginning of the upcoming quarter during which you intend to home school. You will need a certificated supervisor unless you have earned forty-five college quarter credits or completed a course in home-based instruction, or have been deemed qualified by your local superintendent. (Your local superintendent *may* declare you unqualified if you do not possess a teaching certificate, but this is not likely to happen.) Immunization records, instructional/learning activities records, and test records must be kept. Required hours of instruction: 2700 during the three-year period of grades 1,2,3; 2970 hours during the three-year period of grades 4,5,6; 1980 hours during the two-year period of grades 7,8; 4320 hours during the four-year period of grades 9,10,11,12 and units the equivalent of graduation requirements. Your curriculum should include no less than a core curriculum plus music, health, occupational education, United States and Washington constitutions. (See Section Three.) Your home courses may be approved for credit provided you submit to the local school district an acceptable proposal for such prior to course implementation.

WEST VIRGINIA: Two weeks prior to withdrawing your child from public school or prior to the beginning of the local school year, you must submit a notice of intent and a plan of instruction for the upcoming year to your county superintendent or school board. (See Sections Two and Three.) Plan to include no less than a core curriculum. You must also include evidence that you hold a high school diploma or equivalent *and* that your formal education extends four years beyond the most academically advanced of your home-schooled children *or* you may take the National Teacher Examination and earn a score sufficient for certification in West Virginia. You need to arrange for the administration of a standardized achievement test by a certified educator at your local public school, or by a licensed psychologist, or by a person authorized by the test publisher, or by a person authorized by your county superintendent or board. If composite scores fall below the 40th percentile, a remedial program must be initiated. If such score occurs a second year, home schooling must be (legally) discontinued. Your county superintendent or a designee "shall offer" textbooks, other teacher materials, and other resources that might help you in your efforts to home school, and your child may enroll in any class offered by the county board. Your superintendent or board may request information from you periodically regarding your child's attendance, instruction, and progress.

WISCONSIN: By October 15 you must submit to your state department a statement of your home-school enrollment tallied on the third Friday of September - *form provided* by your state department. You must include a statement that your home-school program provides private or religious-based education, that it is privately controlled, that you provide at least 875 hours of instruction yearly, that you are not attempting to circumvent the compulsory attendance requirements of your state, that you will allow no less than two months for summer vacation, and that your instructional program provides a sequentially progressive curriculum - including no less than a core curriculum plus health. Maintain a written curriculum which verifies the scope of your instructional program. (See Sections Two and Three.) Ask your state department for its curriculum and course materials "DPI Publications Listing."

WYOMING: Each home-school year you must submit a curriculum to your local school board showing that your home-education program provides a "basic academic educational program;" i.e., a sequential curriculum including fundamental instruction in reading, writing, math, civics, history, literature and science. A sequential curriculum, simply put, is one that builds upon itself — involves sequential steps or degrees of difficulty. (See Section Three.) Maintain records which demonstrate that your teaching is based upon that curriculum and that your children are home schooled the required number of days.

State Departments of Education

Use the following addresses to request further information, such as the actual education statutes and procedural information for home schoolers.

Alabama Department of Education, Room 483, State Office Bldg., Montgomery AL 36130. (205) 261-5156

Alaska Department of Education, Pouch F, Juneau AK 99811. (907) 465-2800

Arizona Department of Education, 1535 W Jefferson, Phoenix AZ 85007. (602) 255-5057

Arkansas Department of Education, Education Bldg., 4 State Capitol Mall, Little Rock AR 72201-1021. (501) 371-1461

California Department of Education, 721 Capitol Mall, Room 524, Sacramento CA 95814. (916) 445-4338

Colorado Department of Education, 201 East Colfax Ave., Denver CO 80203. (303) 866-6806 (Also: Department of Field Services, 866-6806)

Connecticut Department of Education, 165 Capitol Ave., Hartford CT 06106. (203) 566-5061

Delaware Department of Public Instruction, Townsend Bldg., Dover DE 19901. (302) 736-4602

District of Columbia, D.C. Public Schools, 415 12th St. NW, Washington DC 20004. (202) 724-4222

Florida Department of Education, The Capitol, Tallahassee FL 32301. (904) 487-1785

Georgia Department of Education, 205 Butler St. SE, Atlanta GA 30334. (404) 656-2800

Hawaii Department of Education, 941 Hind Luka Drive, Honolulu HI 96821. (808) 548-6583 (Department: Office of Instructional Services, Student Personnel Services Section.)

Idaho Department of Education, Len B. Jordan Bldg., 650 W State St., Boise ID 83720. (208) 334-3300

Illinois State Board of Education, 100 N First St., Springfield IL 62777. (217) 782-2221

Indiana Department of Public Instruction, 227 State House, Indianapolis IN 46204. (317) 232-6667

Iowa Department of Public Instruction, Grimes State Office Bldg., Des Moines IA 50319. (515) 281-5294

Kansas Department of Education, 120 E 10th St., Topeka KS 66612. (913) 296-3201

Kentucky Department of Education, Capital Plaza Tower, Frankfort KY 40601. (502) 564-4770

Louisiana Department of Education, P.O. Box 94064, Baton Rouge LA 70804-9064. (504) 342-3602

Maine Department of Educational & Cultural Services, State House Station #23, Augusta ME 04333. (207) 289-5802

Maryland Department of Education, 200 W Baltimore St., Baltimore MD 21201. (301) 659-2100

Massachusetts Department of Education, 1385 Hancock St., Quincy MA 02169. (617) 770-7300

Michigan Department of Education, 520 Michigan National. Tower, P.O. Box 30008, Lansing MI 48909. (517) 373-3354

Minnesota Department of Education, 550 Cedar St., 8th Floor, St. Paul MN 55101. (612) 296-2358

Mississippi Department of Education, 501 Sillers Bldg., Jackson MS 39201. (601) 359-3513

Missouri Department of Elementary & Secondary Education, 515 E High St., Box 480, Jefferson City MO 65102. (314) 751-4446

Montana Office of Public Instruction, State Capitol, Helena MT 59620. (406) 444-3654

Nebraska Department of Education, 301 Centennial Mall S, P.O. Box 94987, Lincoln NE 68509-4987. (402) 471-2465

Nevada Department of Education, 400 W King St., Carson City NV 89710. (702) 885-3100

New Hampshire Department of Education, State Office Park S, Concord NH 03301. (603) 271-3144

New Jersey Department of Education, 225 W State St., Trenton NJ 08625. (609) 292-4450

New Mexico Department of Education, Education Bldg., Santa Fe NM 87501-2786. (505) 827-6635

New York Department of Education, Education Bldg., Albany NY 12234. (518) 474-5844

North Carolina Department of Public Education, 116 W Edenton St., Raleigh NC 27603-1712. (919) 733-3813 (Department: Governor's Office for Non-Public Education.)

North Dakota Department of Public Instruction, 11th Floor, State Capitol, Bismarck ND 58505. (701) 224-2261

Ohio Department of Education, 65 S Front St., Room 808, Columbus OH 43215. (614) 466-3304

Oklahoma Department of Education, 2500 N Lincoln Blvd., Oklahoma City OK 73105. (405) 521-3301

Oregon Department of Education, 700 Pringle Pkwy. SE, Salem OR 97310. (503) 378-3573

Pennsylvania Department of Education, 10th Floor, Harristown Bldg. #2, Harrisburg, PA 17108. (717) 787-5820

Rhode Island Department of Education, 22 Hayes St, Providence RI 02908. (401) 277-2031

South Carolina Department of Education, Rutledge Bldg., 1429 Senate St., Columbia SC 29201. (803) 734-8465

South Dakota Department of Education & Cultural Affairs, Kneip Bldg., Pierre SD 57501. (605) 773-3243

Tennessee Department of Education, 100 Cordell Hull Bldg., Nashville TN 37219. (615) 741-2731

Texas Education Agency, 201 E 11th St., Austin TX 78701. (512) 834-4000

Utah Office of Education, 250 East Fifth Street South, Salt Lake City UT 84111. (801) 538-7743

Vermont Department of Education, 120 State St., Montpelier VT 05602. (802) 828-3135

Virginia Department of Education, P.O. Box 6-Q, Richmond VA 23216. (804) 225-2023

Washington Public Instruction, Old Capitol Bldg. FG-11, Olympia WA 98504-3211. (206) 753-6717 (Department: Office of Private Education)

West Virginia Department of Education, 1800 Washington St. E., Bldg. 6, Charleston WV 25305. (304) 348-2681

Wisconsin Department of Public Instruction, 125 S Webster St., P.O. Box 7841, Madison WI 53707. (608) 266-1771

Wyoming Department of Education, Hathaway Bldg., Cheyenne WY 82002. (307) 777-7675

❋❋

section **5**

Support for Home Schoolers

Mutual-Support Groups

Wisely, most home schoolers communicate with other home schoolers. As pointed out at the beginning of Section Four, legal information and atmospheres can be clarified for you by practicing home schoolers in your area. Also, as noted in the introduction, when your faith in yourself lags or you begin to experience burnout, support from home-schooling friends may rejuvenate you. Likewise important are the idea exchanges, home-school news, issue updates, shared activities including children, meetings, and so on, that can be brought to you through interaction with other home schoolers. One way to reach other home schoolers is through involvement in a home-school support group. Hundreds of such groups exist throughout the United States.

Within the list below you will find informal local support groups, larger regional or state networks, and national networks. Those listed here are respondents to my nationwide survey of hundreds of such organizations, but no doubt there are many others whose addresses were unavailable to me, but which you may locate as you begin making contacts with the home-schooling community. Remember, too, that most organizations listed here are primarily *mutual support* organizations, although several offer services and resources beyond support. At the end of this section you'll find a list of organizations more commercial or formal in nature which offer services to home schoolers. In Section Six further educational resource suppliers are listed.

As you begin to contact support groups, you will learn that many have evolved around the shared educational philosophies of the members. Some, for example, may include mostly members who feel the Bible should be the core of all curriculums, or who share a maverick attitude towards governmental controls, or who believe in integrating life with learning. Some simply feel that parents are the best teachers for their children. A few may be composed of parents dealing with special educational situations, such as teaching a handicapped child. You may need to shop for a group whose philosophies and purposes are most compatible with your own. Many groups, on the other hand, are eclectic in composition so that varied philosophies are accepted and encouraged, and support remains the focus of the group.

191

Useful to note, too, is that although you will want to contact support organizations within your state, you may also benefit by looking beyond your state to those organizations in other states whose offerings appeal to you and whose scope ranges across state boundaries. At the same time, don't avoid organizations that appear to be small. A tremendous home-schoolers' network exists in the United States, and even the small organizations are likely able to help you consider options, locate information and make needed connections. You will discover, in fact, that many of the larger organizations listed here will connect you with one of the yet hundreds of local groups not listed here. Also, incidentally, support group contact persons, addresses, and phone numbers change from time to time, but frequently if a phone call or letter to a support group draws no response, it doesn't mean the group no longer exists. It just means the contact person has changed and you may have to do some tracking to locate him or her.

One final note — Since the organizations listed below are non-profit, you are more likely to get a response if you enclose a stamped, self-addressed envelope with any mailed request for information.

Alabama

Alabama Home Educators (819 Joryne Dr., Montgomery AL 36109): A nonprofit, nonsectarian organization which supports parents wishing to educate their children at home. Offers information dissemination, materials, networking, ten branch groups throughout Alabama, quarterly newsletter, public awareness activities, support, idea exchanges, meetings, field trips and activity days, publications, curriculum/materials fairs, certificated consultants and consultation services, legislative monitoring. (205) 277-1614

Alaska

State Correspondence Study (CCS, P.O. Box GA, Juneau AK 99811): A complete roster of elementary and secondary correspondence courses using returnable free materials, with no tuition fee, including close contact with advisory teachers. Includes an optional student activities program involving cost-free travel to locations around the state, a 15,000 item lending library, a secondary academic counselor, and testing and record-keeping services. (907) 465-2835

Valley Homeschoolers Network (HC30 Box 5370-A, Wasilla AK 99687): Offers support and encouragement, information dissemination, networking, idea exchanges, meetings, field trips, activity days, a 10-issue/yearly newsletter. (907) 373-0740

Arizona

Arizona Families for Home Education (639 E. Kino Dr., Mesa AZ 85203): An umbrella support organization. Offers information, newcomers assistance, and support, networking, annual state convention, newsletter. (602) 964-7435

Arizona Families for Home Education (P.O. Box 31674, Phoenix AZ 85046-1674): Offers information dissemination, resource guidance, networking and phone tree, newsletter, public awareness activities, legislative monitoring and action, conferences. (602) 971-3090

Blue Sky Learning Center (P.O. Box 460, Arivaca AZ 85601): A private, nonprofit, educational program for children age six and above with a staff that includes a program director, parents, and volunteers. Purpose — to encourage children to take responsibility for and derive pleasure from learning and doing; to develop the ability to learn. Offers parental involvement in a child's learning, family goals development, and Skills Exchange Program. Also, home-school consultations,

AR – CA

curriculum assistance, record keeping, testing, networking, and student sessions three afternoons per week at the center.

Making Contact (3543 E. Bellevue, Tucson AZ 85716) Purpose — cooperation among home schoolers and the sharing of resources. Offers support and encouragement, information dissemination, family-to-family networking.

Tucson Home Education Network (2080 N. Via Condesa, Tucson AZ 85718): Offers support and encouragement, information dissemination, monthly newsletter, meetings, field trips and monthly picnics, consultation services, curriculum assistance, materials and aids for home teaching, publications of interest to parent teachers. (602) 299-8130

Arkansas

Arkansas Christian Home Education Association (P.O. Box 501, Little Rock AR 72203): Purpose — to provide help and information to home schoolers, to organize efforts to obtain and keep favorable home-schooling laws, to help organize local support groups. Offers monthly newsletter, information packet, encouragement, annual home-school teen day. (501) 337-0221

California

California Coalition of People for Alternative Learning Situations (P.O. Box 92, Escondido CA 92025): Purpose — to support learning situations alternative in intention, form, and content. Offers support and encouragement, sharing, information dissemination, newsletter, meetings, statewide communications network, field trips and activity days, publications of interest to home teachers, legislative monitoring and lobbying efforts, public awareness activities, statewide conference, consultation services. (619) 749-1522

Christian Home Educators Association (P.O. Box 28644, Santa Ana CA 92799-8644): Offers information and support, training, newsletter, magazine subscription, materials (at discount), speakers bureau, workshops and seminars, group networking, legislative representation, regional conventions. (714) 537-512

Christian Home Educators of California (P.O. Box 28644, Santa Ana CA 92799-8644): Offers information, support, training, regional convention, materials, speakers bureau, networking, representation to the community and the media, bimonthly newsletter. (714) 537-5121 — A 15-minute informational message will describe services, literature and statewide events.

Homeschoolers for Peace (P.O. Box 74, Midpines CA 95345): Offers support and encouragement, information dissemination, networking, monthly newsletter, idea exchanges. (209) 742-6802

Monterey County Home Learners (P.O. Box 4667, Salinas CA 93912): Offers information networking, idea exchange, newsletter, field trips, park days, camp outs, workshops, a newspaper published for kids by kids, special classes for students, other special events.

North Santa Clara Valley Homeschoolers (795 Sheraton Dr., Sunnyvale CA 94087): Offers support, field trips, special children's classes, science fair participation, informal meetings. (408) 735-7525

Northern California Homeschooler Association (2214 Grant St., Berkeley CA 94703): Purpose — to ensure that members are informed of and are represented in major legislative decisions of statewide impact. Offers statewide survey results, representative to attend county chapters of NCHA, assistance to NCHA county chapters, newsletter, communications networking, political education and action. (415) 674-1294. Alternate address: 3345 Santa Paula, Concord CA 94518; (415) 674-1294

San Gabriel Valley Homeschoolers (486 W. Leroy Ave., Arcadia CA 91006): Offers support and encouragement; information dissemination; newsletter; public awareness activities; idea exchanges; meetings; workshops, seminars or courses; field trips; activity days, such as choir sessions, folk dancing, art classes, sports days; and science, art, pet, and book fairs. (808) 447-8067

School of Home Learning (P.O. Box 92, Escondido CA 92025): An accredited private school. Purpose — to encourage and support "invited teaching" in the home and community. Offers group networking, individual consultations, skills exchange service, materials catalogs, special events and field trips, joint educational projects. (619) 749-1522

South Valley Homeschoolers (Box 961, San Martin CA 95046): Offers support, assistance for new home schoolers, newsletter, meetings, field trips. (408) 683-4802

CO – CT

Colorado

Colorado Home Educators' Association (1616 17th St., Box 372, Denver CO 80202): Purpose — to provide a statewide voice for Colorado home educators without partiality to any one perspective or approach. Offers statewide networking, newsletter, promotion and encouragement of local support groups, a home-school state fair, public awareness and education programs, CHEA state fair, promotion of favorable legislation and legal action, promotion of sound home-education programs, bibliography of home-school research studies, legal and resource information handbook.

Colorado Home Schooling Network (7490 W Apache, Sedalia CO 80135): Purpose — to provide support for Holt/unstructured home-schoolers. Offers bimonthly meetings for idea exchange and support, bimonthly newsletter, 30-page legal packet. (303) 789-4309 or 688-4136

Homes Offering Meaningful Education (P.O. Box 543, Loretto Station, Denver CO 80236): Offers Bible-based group support, encouragement and help; monthly meetings, field trips, activity days, resource library, conferences, curriculum fairs, volunteer consultants. (303) 567-4800

Northern Colorado Home School Association (4721 Harbor View Lane, Fort Collins CO 80526): Offers support and encouragement, news, meetings, field trips, legislative monitoring.

W. A. T. C. H. (1518 Brighton Dr., Brighton CO 80601): Offers support and encouragement, meetings, field trips. (303) 659-9282

West Metro Denver Home Educators (2680 Gray St., Edgewater CO 80214): Offers support and encouragement, news, get-togethers, field trips and other group activities. (303) 238-8706

Connecticut

Connecticut Homeschoolers' Association (98 Bahr Rd., Deep River CT 06417): Offers support and encouragement, information dissemination, networking, bimonthly newsletter, idea exchanges, meetings, field trips and activity days (talent show, Christmas party, summer picnic), legislative monitoring and action, consultation services, curriculum packages, conferences, curriculum and materials fairs. (203) 526-9762

Delaware

Delaware Home Education Association (P.O. Box 55, Dover DE 19903): Offers encouragement and stimulation, monthly meetings, newsletter. (302) 492-3453

Florida

Florida Association for Schooling at Home (1000 Devils Dip, Tallahassee FL 32301): Offers help to families getting started in home schooling, statewide networking.

Florida Parent Educators Association (Star Rt. 1, Box 3871, Tallahassee FL 32300): Purpose — to promote sound home-education programs, to educate public officials and the general public of the virtues of home education, to assist in legal proceedings involving home-school families. Offers support and encouragement, assistance, information, advice and counsel, legislative lobbying, liaison with Florida Department of Education and county superintendents of public schools, networking, idea exchanges, annual statewide meetings, curriculum/materials fairs, statewide conferences, workshops for parent educators, bimonthly newsletter. (904)576-8729. Alternate address: 4381 73rd Ave. N., Pinellas Park FL 34665. (813) 546-3938

Georgia

Christians Concerned for Education (Rt. 3 Box 1180, LaFayette GA 30728): Offers support and encouragement, information, newsletter, legislative monitoring and action, curriculum assistance and consultations. (404) 397-2941

Georgians for Freedom in Education (4818 Joy Lane, Lilburn GA 30247): Offers support and encouragement, information, legislative input and monitoring, promotion of public awareness, meetings, newsletter, field trip planning assistance, seminars, workshops, consultation service. (404) 923-9932

Gwinnette Christian Home Educators (328 Omega Dr., Lawrenceville GA 30245): Offers support and encouragement, information dissemination, newsletter, idea exchanges, meetings, consultations, curriculum assistance, curriculum/materials fairs, programs, networking, public awareness activities, field trips and other activities (international dinners, field days, parties), special classes, parent workshops. (404) 921-4646

HI – ID

Mountain Homeschoolers (Rt.1 Box 1426, Clayton GA 30525): Offers support and encouragement, information dissemination, networking, newsletter, meetings, field trips, activity days (fairs, cultural days, workshops). (404)782-3920

Hawaii

Hawaii Home Based Educators (Alejado's 91-824 Oana St., Ewa Beach HI 96824): Offers support and encouragement, information dissemination, networking, monthly newsletter, public awareness activities, idea exchanges, meetings, field trips and activity days, testing service, legislative action and lobbying, informal consultations and curriculum assistance, publications of interest to parent teachers, conferences, workshops, curriculum and materials fairs. (808) 689-6398 or 235-0220

Idaho

Idaho Home Educators/Southern Idaho (Box 4022, Boise ID 83704-4022): Purpose — to train and instruct as commanded by the Holy Scriptures. Offers support, information, idea exchange, resource and reading lists, testing and evaluation by fee, monthly skating parties, monthly mom's breakfasts, meetings, buddy system, home-teacher inservice training, school board liaison. (208) 362-0449 or 286-7727

LDS Support Group (1217 W. First, Meridian ID 83642): Offers support and encouragement. (208) 888-4259

Magic Valley Home Educators (Box 304, Hazelton ID 83335): Offers support and encouragement, meetings, special activities and field trips, spring track meet, curriculum fair. (208) 829-5574

North Idaho Home Education Association (W. 805 Wyoming, Hayden Lake ID 83835): Offers support and encouragement, first-timer's assistance, information dissemination, newsletter, monthly field trips, activity days (such as art fairs, field days and picnics, skiing), testing service, publications of interest to home educators, and periodically offers workshops, seminars, courses, and curriculum/materials fairs. (208) 772-2241

Payette C.H.A.M.P. (10592 Virginia Dr., Payette ID 83661): Offers support and encouragement, special group classes and other group activities, parties, parent gatherings, a "Meet Your Legislator" night. (208) 642-9227

Port Cities Home Educators (1880 Old Spiral Highway, Lewiston ID 83501): Offers support and encouragement, meetings, field trips and special classes.

Southeast Idaho Home Education Association (5321 Hawthorne Rd., Pocatello ID 83202): Offers support and encouragement, field trips, parties, annual science fair, newsletter, parent workshops. (208) 237-2312

Illinois

Illinois Christian Home Educators (P.O. Box 261, Zion IL 60099): A ministry to home educators in Illinois. Purpose — to aid in the formation of local support groups and statewide networking. Offers publications of interest to home educators, seminars, magazine, encouragement.

Home Oriented Unique Schooling Experience (P.O. Box 578291, Chicago IL 60657): Offers support and encouragement, information dissemination, networking, public awareness activities, idea exchanges, group meetings, field trips and activity days, legislative monitoring and action, consultations, recommendations regarding materials and aids, conferences, workshops, curriculum/materials fairs. (312) 328-2248

Reba Place Fellowship Home Schoolers (P.O. Box 6017, Evanston IL 60204): Offers support, oversight, and structure for area Mennonite home schoolers.

Indiana

Central Indiana Home Educators (7262 Lakeside Dr., Indianapolis IN 46278): Offers educational and emotional support, monthly meetings, monthly field trips. (317)293-0371 Alternate address: RR 1 Box 215A, Pittsboro IN 46167. (317) 852-2730

Fort Wayne Area Home Schoolers (4321 Mirada Dr., Ft. Wayne IN 46816): Purpose — to encourage home-schooling excellence. Offers bimonthly newsletter, book fair, orientation meetings, get-togethers and field trips, some materials, moms' meetings, achievement testing. (219) 447-0425

Greater Lafayette Home Educators (926 N. 19th St., Lafayette IN 47904): Offers support and encouragement to Christian home educators (nondenominational), information dissemination, public

IA

awareness activities, consultations, curriculum assistance, publications of interest to home educators, field trips, group activity days, picnics, curriculum sharing and idea exchanges, physical fitness activities, art classes. (317) 448-4988

Huntington County Home Educators (1138 Byron St., Huntington IN 46750): Offers support and encouragement primarily to Christian home educators, calendar of events. (219) 356-8471

Indiana Association of Home Educators (P.O. Box 50524, Indianapolis IN 46250): Offers support and encouragement to Christian home educators, legislative monitoring and lobbying, newsletter, publications of interest to home educators, conventions, seminars, networking, a roster of home-school support groups in thirty-seven Indiana counties. (317) 849-3780

Madison County Home Educators (Rt. 11 Box 41, Anderson IN 46011-8503): Offers mutual support and encouragement, fellowship, information and help, meetings, idea exchange, field trips and other group activities. (317)779-4029

Midnorth Indiana Homeschoolers (926 N 19th St., Lafayette IN 47904): Offers field trips and special activities.

Wabash Valley Homeschoolers Association (RR 53 Box 260, Terre Haute IN 47805): Offers — support, field trips and other group activities, meetings for sharing and encouraging, information exchange. (812) 466-9467

Iowa

Iowa Home Educators Association (P.O. Box 213, Des Moines IA 50301): Offers support and encouragement, information dissemination, support group coordination, monthly newsletter, legislative monitoring and action, parent workshops, curriculum and materials fairs, a few publications of interest to home educators.

Southwest Iowa Home-Education (RR 3 Box 143, Missouri Valley IA 51555): Offers support and encouragement, information dissemination, public awareness activities, idea exchanges, meetings, field trips and activity days, legislative monitoring and action, consultations, curriculum assistance, publications of interest to parent teachers, workshops, curriculum and materials fairs. (712) 644-2322 or 566-2802. Alternate address: SW Iowa Home-Education, Rural Route, Underwood IA 51576

Kansas

Kansans for Alternative Education (19985 Renner Rd., Spring Hill KS 66083): Offers statewide networking, information and resource ideas, newsletter, legislative monitoring, annual state meetings with workshops and seminars. (913) 686-2310

Kentucky

Kentucky Christian Home School Association (1301 Bridget Drive, Fairdale KY 40118): A Christian group primarily for parents in the Jefferson County area. Offers support and encouragement, information dissemination, networking, bimonthly newsletter, public awareness activities, idea exchanges, meetings, field trips and activity days, testing service, legislative monitoring and action, consultations, curriculum packages, certificated consultants, materials and aids, publications of interest to parent teachers, workshops, curriculum and materials fairs, science and craft fair. (502) 363-3104

Kentucky Home School Association (817 Perennial Dr., Louisville KY 40217): Offers support and encouragement, information dissemination, networking, semi-annual newsletter, idea exchanges, legislative monitoring and action, home-schoolers state picnic in June. (502)634-1846. Alternate address: 3310 Illinois Ave., Louisville KY 40217. (502) 636-3804

Kentucky Home Schoolers (3310 Illinois Ave., Louisville KY 40213): Offers support and encouragement, information dissemination, semi-annual newsletter, idea exchanges, yearly picnic, legislative monitoring and action, consultation services. (502) 636-3804

Lexington Homeschoolers (c/o Morley, 3522 Greentree Rd., Lexington KY 40502): Offers support and encouragement, information dissemination, networking, bimonthly newsletter, idea exchanges, bimonthly meetings, field trips and activity days, informal consultations, assistance with materials and publications of interest to parent teachers, and an annual fair for the display of student projects. (606) 273-7816

Louisiana

Louisiana Citizens for Home Education (3404 Van Buren, Baker LA 70714): Offers support and encouragement, information dissemination, networking, public awareness activities, idea exchanges, meetings, field trips and activity days, testing service, legislative monitoring and action, conferences, workshops, curriculum and materials fairs, bimonthly news, information packet. (504) 775-5472

ME – MA

Maine

Maine Homeschool Association, Inc. (P.O. Box 3283, Auburn ME 04240): Offers support and encouragement, information dissemination, basic information brochure, group networking, newsletter, idea exchanges, meetings, field trips, consultation services, conferences, curriculum and materials fairs, confidentiality.

Maryland

Maryland Home Education Association (9085 Flamepool Way, Columbia MD 21045): Purpose — to provide long-term service and support for home educators regardless of political or religious orientation and to function as a legislative watchdog and initiate action in favor of home schooling. Offers legal information, statewide networking, statewide conferences and other similar functions, books at discount, research information, and a starter kit. (301) 730-0073

Montgomery County Support Group (26824 Howard Chapel Dr., Damascus MD 20872): Offers support, information, get-togethers and play groups, youth club, assistance to newcomers to home schooling, newsletter. (301) 253-5467 or (301) 428-0217

Massachusetts

Apple Country Homeschooling Association (Box 246, Harvard MA 01451) Offers support and encouragement as a local support group.

Massachusetts Home Learning Association (P.O. Box 248, Harvard MA 01451): Offers support and encouragement, information dissemination, networking, newsletter, idea exchanges, meetings, activity days, legislative monitoring, informal consultations. (617) 485-3765

Massachusetts Home Learning Association (16 Anderson Rd., Marlboro MA 01752): Offers support and encouragement, information dissemination, networking, quarterly newsletter, idea exchanges, meetings, consultation services. (508) 485-3765

South Shore Home Schoolers (163 Hingham St., Rockland MA 02370): Offers support and information.

Southeastern Massachusetts Home Educators Support Group (P.O. Box 4329, Fall River MA 02723-0403, Dept. B-32): Offers support, information, a home-education packet, networking.

Worcester Area Homeschooling Organization (246 May St., Apt. #2, Worcester MA 01602): Offers support and encouragement and occasional meetings. (508) 755-9553

Michigan

Copper Country Education Cooperative (P.O. Box 713, Houghton MI 49931): Offers support group meetings and activities. (906) 334-2788

Minnesota

Minnesota Association of Christian Home Educators (Box 188, Anoka MN 55303): Offers curriculum fairs, quarterly newsletter, seminars, picnics and other activities, support group networking.

Mississippi

Mississippi Home Schoolers' Support Group (#1 Tally Ho Drive, Starkville MS 39759): Offers support and encouragement, newsletter, meetings, conferences, workshops, curriculum and materials fairs, publications of interest to parent teachers. (601) 324-2666

Missouri

Christian Home Educators Fellowship (601 Madison Drive, Arnold MO 63010): Purpose — to support and train Christian home educators; to educate the Christian community about home education; to work with statewide home-education organizations to protect parents' rights. (314) 296-1020

Families for Home Education (21709 E. Old Atherton, Independence MO 64058): Offers statewide local and regional support group networking, information dissemination, lobbying and other political activities, monthly newsletter, seminars, educational materials dispersion, library and resource center, testing service, home teacher's conferences and workshops, science fairs and other curricular fairs, group sports activities, special group academic events including field trips. (816) 796-0978

Ozark Homeschoolers (Rt. 6 Box 70D, Rolla MO 65401): Offers informal support group, aid and information, get-togethers, field trips, newsletter. (314) 341-3216

MT – NV

Springfield Area Homeschoolers (Rt.1 Box 193, Fair Grove MO 65648): Offers support and encouragement, information dissemination, networking, bimonthly publication "The Learning Letter," meetings, field trips, activity days including cooperative games, track and field, roller skating. (417) 759-7544

Montana

Homeschoolers of Montana (Box 40, Billings MT 59101): Purpose — promotion of the intellectual, spiritual, emotional, and physical development of children. Offers support, information related to school readiness and alternative education, sharing of resources, encouragement, group activities, input regarding parenting skills, legal information, legislative updates and activities. (406) 248-6762

Nebraska

Lincoln Educated at Residence Network (7741 E Avon Lane, Lincoln NE 68505): Offers informal support and discussion of home-school issues, field trips, meetings as needed. (402) 464-8551

Mothers' Home School Support Group (2441 Bretigne Dr., Lincoln NE 68512): Offers meetings, newsletter, family activity days, annual arts and sciences fair, local art exhibits, sports days and picnics, used book fair, statewide curriculum exhibit, special classes for kids.

Nebraska Home Educators Association (5000 Grandview Lane, Lincoln NE 68521): Offers support and encouragement, facilitation of support group formation, information dissemination ("NHEA Alert"), networking, bimonthly newsletter, public awareness activities, meetings, legislative monitoring and lobbying, consultations, publications of interest to home educators, annual convention including workshops, curriculum/materials fair and prominent speakers. (402) 476-9925

Nevada

Home Schools United - Vegas Valley (P.O. Box 26811, Las Vegas NV 89126): Offers support and encouragement, information dissemination, networking, monthly newsletter, public awareness activities, meetings, legislative monitoring and action, consultations, curriculum packages, certificated consultants, publications of interest to home educators, curriculum/materials fairs, field trips, activity days (picnic, demonstration/exhibit fair, grade promotion and graduation ceremony). (702) 870-9566

New Hampshire

New Hampshire Home Educators Association (9 Mizoras Dr., Nashua NH 03062): Offers communication facilitation, information dissemination, assistance to new home educators, support meetings, organized activities, newsletter, information packet.

New Jersey

New Jersey Unschoolers Network (2 Smith St., Farmingdale NJ 07727): Offers information dissemination, phone consultations, telephone question-answer service, support group networking, a monthly bulletin, a large newsletter three times yearly, workshops and seminars. (201) 938-2473

New Mexico

National Home Schoolers (Box 167, Rodeo NM 88056): A national support organization in the planning stage at the time of this printing. Purpose — recognition of the rights of home school parents to legally educate their children at home. Potential programs include apprenticeship exchanges, travel information, legal aid, high school-age student exchange program.

New Mexico Christian Home Educators, Inc. (7417 Santa Fe Trail NW, Albuquerque NM 87120): Offers support and encouragement, assistance, information dissemination, networking, bimonthly newsletter, public awareness activities, promotion of home schooling, information dissemination, legislative monitoring and action, monitoring of and assistance to the State Department of Education in the development of home-schooling guidelines, mediation between home schoolers and education officials/institutions, an annual information and materials fair/convention (including workshops). (505) 897-4739

New Mexico Family Educators (678 Lisbon Ave. SE, Rio Rancho NM 87124): Offers support and encouragement, information dissemination, newsletter, idea exchanges, meetings, field trips and activity days, testing service, curriculum assistance, materials and aids of interest to home schoolers, parent workshops, curriculum/materials fairs. Serves the Albuquerque region. (505) 892-5783

New York

Central New York Homeschoolers (Side Hill Springs, Becker RD, Skaneateles NY 13152): Offers mutual support, encouragement,

NC – ND

sharing of information, periodic meetings, social functions, and field trips. (315) 636-8481

Home Schoolers' Exchange (RR 1 Box 172 E, East Chatham NY 12060-9725): Offers information and support, lending library of educational materials & books, field trips, legislative monitoring and information dissemination. (518) 392-4277

Long Island Family Educators (P.O. Box 283, Sayville NY 11782-0283): Purpose — to give support to Christian home teachers; to serve as a resource center, to provide legal information, to offer interaction opportunities for our children. Offers monthly support meetings, curriculum and teaching aids catalogs, a library, legal start-up handout, educational and recreational activities for kids.

Loving Education at Home (P.O. Box 332, Syracuse NY 13205): Offers monthly meetings and other activities, legal information, curriculum information and resource assistance, telephone hotline, networking, bimonthly 40-page magazine, legal packet, inservice programs, publications of interest to home teachers. LEAH Hotline: (315) 469-0564

New York State Home Schoolers (Rt. 1 Box 8, Ghent NY 12075): Purpose — to make the voice of home schoolers heard; to put home school families in touch with each other, to provide a statewide resource information network. Offers quarterly newsletter including articles and resource lists; a directory of members, resources, and support groups; legislative information.

North Carolina

North Carolinians for Home Education (P.O. Box 30443, Raleigh, NC 27622): Offers information, networking, newsletter, public awareness activities.

North Dakota

North Dakota Home School Association (P.O. Box 539, Turtle Lake ND 58575): Offers support and encouragement, information dissemination, networking, newsletter, testing service, legislative monitoring and action, consultations, curriculum packages, publications of interest to home educators, conferences, curriculum/materials fairs. (701) 448-9193

Ohio

Christian Home Educators of Ohio (P.O. Box 1224, Kent OH 44240): Offers support and encouragement, information dissemination, phone consultations, conventions, educational materials, information phone tree, newsletter, speakers bureau, legislative and state board liaison and monitoring.

Ohio Coalition of Educational Alternatives Now (P.O. Box 94, Thompson OH 44086): Offers support and encouragement, information dissemination, networking, idea exchanges, consultation services with certificated consultants.

Oklahoma

Family Learning Connection (P.O. Box 1938, Durant OK 74702) Offers support, encouragement, and information through round robin letter groups. (405) 924-1436

OK Central Home School Support Group (508 Tumbleweed Drive, Yukon OK 73099): Purpose — to serve home school families and to espouse Christian principles in home education. Offers support groups, legal and legislative initiatives, newsletter, information packets. (405) 324-2310

Oklahoma Christian Home Educators Association (Box 102, Jenks OK 74037): Purpose — to keep the Oklahoma home-school law intact. Offers support group referrals, information, bimonthly magazine. (918) 299-7647

Oregon

Douglas County Home Schoolers Connection (4053 Hanna St., Roseburg OR 97470): Offers assistance and connections for new home schoolers, legal information, curriculum resource list, reading list. (503) 679-4571

Parents Education Association (P.O. Box 1482, Beaverton OR 97075): A political action group. Purpose — to promote quality Godly education outside the state school system; to ensure like-minded supporters an adequate voice in the political arena. Offers lobbying, legislative watchdog, seminars, information exchanges. (503) 241-4585

Portland Area Tri-County Homeschoolers (28901 SE Davis Rd., Estacada OR 97023): Offers support, advice, and information, field

PA – SC

trips at least monthly, informal family get-togethers, legal and resource information to new home schoolers, materials file, individual and group networking. (503) 630-4935

Pennsylvania

Home Educators of Pennsylvania (Rd. 2 Box 334-A, Munson PA 16860): Offers support and encouragement. (814) 345-6273

Parent Educators of Pennsylvania (3334 Disston St., Philadelphia PA 19149) Offers legislative lobbying and other legal/political endeavors.

Pennsylvania Homeschoolers (RD 2 Box 117, Kittanning PA 16201) Offers support and encouragement, networking, information dissemination, newsletter, public awareness activities, idea exchanges, legislative monitoring, consultation services, certificated consultants, conferences, announcements of field trips and activity days, meetings, list of cooperative school districts. (412) 783-6512

Pittsburgh Area Homeschoolers (3562 Foxwood Dr., Murrysville PA 15668): Offers monthly meetings, monthly bulletin, idea exchange. (412) 687-0385

South Hills of Pittsburgh Support Group (3485 South Park Rd., Bethel Park PA 15102): Offers support and encouragement, information, annual seminars. (412) 854-4188

Rhode Island

Parent Educators of Rhode Island (P.O. Box 546, Coventry RI 02816): Offers statewide networking, statewide newsletter, field trip arrangements, legislative monitoring, curriculum library, information dissemination, legal case profiles. (401) 828-8724

South Carolina

Piedmont Home Educators' Association (111 Robinwood Lane, Pelzer SC 29669): Offers support and encouragement, information dissemination, networking, 10 to 12-issue newsletter, idea exchanges, meetings, field trips and activity days, legislative monitoring and action, consultations, workshops, curriculum and materials fairs, annual spelling bee, science fair, art show and field day. (803) 947-1926

South Dakota

South Dakota Home Schools Association (1616 S. 4th, Sioux Falls SD 57102): Offers support, legislative representation. (605) 334-2213

Western Dakota Christian Home Schools (8016 Katrina Court, Rapid City SD 57702): Offers support and encouragement, information dissemination, networking, monthly newsletter, public awareness activities, idea exchanges, meetings, legislative monitoring/action/lobbying, informal consultations and curriculum assistance, conferences, workshops and seminars for parent teachers, curriculum and materials fairs, field trips and activity days (science fairs, art fairs, drama and speech fairs, music festivals, field days). A support group directory and speakers bureau are being established. (605) 343-6523

Tennessee

Tennessee Home Education Association (3677 Richbriar Court, Nashville TN 37211): Offers support and encouragement, information dissemination, networking, bimonthly newsletter, public awareness activities, idea exchanges, meetings, legislative monitoring and action, consultations, publications of interest to home educators, conferences, workshops and courses, curriculum and materials fairs, field trips. (615) 834-3529

Texas

Christian Home Educators of San Antonio (Phone only.): Offers support and encouragement, consultation services, workshops for parent educators, monthly roller-skating nights. (512) 649-1792

El Paso Home Schoolers Association (Star Rt. Box 87, Anthony TX 79821): Offers support and referral information. (915) 877-2417

Southeast Texas Home School Association (P.O. Box 436, Tomball TX 77375): Offers support and encouragement, information dissemination, monthly newsletter, public awareness activities, idea exchanges, meetings, field trips and activity days, legislative monitoring and action, informal consultations, publications of interest to parent teachers, workshops, curriculum/materials fair, annual conference, networking among 26+ support groups, testing service.

Texas Home School Coalition (P.O. Box 835105, Richardson TX 75083): Purpose — to preserve through political action parents' right to educate their children at home. Offers information dissemination,

UT – WA

legislative monitoring and news bulletins, a booklet titled "Home Education: Is It Working?" Affiliated with Hearth & Home Ministries. (214) 231-9838

Utah

Utah Home Education Association (657 W. 960 N., Orem UT 84057): Offers support and encouragement, information dissemination, networking, monthly newsletter, public awareness activities, idea exchanges, meetings, field trips and activity days, testing service, legislative monitoring and action, consultation services, curriculum assistance, publications of interest to parent teachers, conferences, workshops and seminars for parents, curriculum and materials fairs. (801) 488-3676 or 224-8583

Vermont

Vermont Home Schoolers Association (RFD 1 Box 150, Jeffersonville VT 05464): Offers support and encouragement, information dissemination, group networking, legislative monitoring, informal consultations.

Virginia

Home Educators Association of Virginia (P.O. Box 1810, Front Royal VA 22630-1810): Offers statewide local and regional support group networking, materials of interest to home school parents, student testing service, newsletter, support group leader conferences, help for parents dealing with courts and boards of education, information dissemination, home educators conferences, a Virginia home-schoolers manual. (703) 635-9322

Northern Virginia Homeschoolers (2519 Buckelew Drive, Falls Church VA 22046): Offers support and encouragement, information dissemination, networking, newsletter, idea exchanges, meetings, field trips and activity days, consultations. (703) 573-6976

Washington

Family Learning Organization of Washington State (P.O. Box 7256, Spokane WA 99207-0256): Offers family learning advocacy, legislative representation, school district liaison, networking, information, testing and evaluation, courses and workshops for home schoolers. Also sponsors the Family Learning Fair, a curriculum fair which attracts

WV

hundreds of home schoolers and would be home schoolers from throughout the Pacific Northwest and southwestern Canada. (509) 467-2552

Homeschoolers' Support Association (23335 264th Ave. SE, Maple Valley WA 98038): Purpose — to assist potential and novice home schoolers, to foster community awareness of home schooling, to support and inform home schools of all philosophical persuasions. Offers support meetings, information, monthly newsletter, home-school family activities, school membership with the Pacific Science Center and Channel 9. (206) 432-3935 or 537-7192

Issaquah Homeschoolers' Support Association (1926 W. Beaver Lake Dr. SE, Issaquah WA 98027): Affiliated with Homeschoolers' Support Association of Maple Valley, WA. *See above.* (206) 392-8514

Teaching Parents Association (16109 NE 169 Pl, Woodinville WA 98072): Offers support and encouragement, information, networking, monthly newsletter, public awareness activities, idea exchanges, meetings, field trips and activity days, legislative monitoring and action, lending library of publications of interest to parent teachers, seminar/meetings with speakers. (206) 483-6642

Washington Homeschool Organization (23335 264th Ave. SE, Maple Valley WA 98038): Offers networking, annual Washington State Homeschool Convention, information dissemination, newsletter, public awareness activities, idea exchanges, meetings, field trips and activity days, testing and record keeping services, legislative monitoring and action, consultations, curriculum assistance, certificated consultants, publications of interest to home educators, curriculum and materials fairs, and workshops, seminars, or courses. (206) 432-3935

West Virginia

West Virginia Home Educators Association (P.O. Box 266, Glenville WV 26351): Purpose — to promote high quality home education which will satisfy the intellectual, spiritual, physical, and social growth needs of children. Offers aid through local support groups throughout West Virginia, information regarding home schooling, parent information and training opportunities, study and analysis of governmental and moral issues affecting home education, resource information for potential home-teaching parents, newsletter, booklist of titles available through WVHEA. (304) 462-8296

WI – WY

Wisconsin

Wisconsin H.O.M.E. (Home Offered Meaningful Education) (1428 Woodland Ave., Eau Claire WI 54701): Offers support and encouragement, information dissemination, networking, legislative monitoring, and a newsletter supportive of child-directed learning and containing statewide home-school news. (715) 835-2869

Wisconsin Parents Association (P.O. Box 2502, Madison WI 53701): Purpose — to watch, promote, and defend the rights of parents, families, and children. Offers quarterly newsletter, bulletins, regional phone tree, regional meetings, statewide conferences, handbook on home education in Wisconsin.

Wyoming

Wyoming Home Educators Network (1084 Sybille Creek Rd., Wheatland WY 82201-9801): A "file box of very independent statewide home schoolers." Offers networking, legislative input, support and encouragement especially to new home schoolers. (307) 322-4976

Wyoming Home Schoolers (Box 1386, Lyman WY 82937): Offers small group support, information, resource assistance. (307) 787-6728

Support Services

California

Baldwin Park Christian School (13940 E Merced, Baldwin Park CA 91706): Offers assistance with materials choices, curriculum planning and quarterly evaluations, teaching advice, start-up counseling. (818) 337-8828

California Home Education Clearinghouse (P.O. Box 1014, Placerville CA 95667-1014): Offers assistance in locating teaching materials, designing reading courses in various subject categories, and consultations.

Cascade Canyon School (P.O. Box 879, Fairfax CA 94930): Offers homeschoolers' enrollment in sign language, arts, physical education and foreign language (Spanish, French, Russian) classes; field trips and overnight programs. (415) 459-3464 or 488-4502

Center for Educational Guidance (P.O. Box 445, N. San Juan CA 95960): Purpose — to empower family, child and community as an interrelated whole, to serve as a model for Integrated Holistic Education. Offers programs designed to allow family and community to reclaim responsibility for the education of the young, community courses for home-school children and parents in academics, the trades, crafts, art, movement, computer literacy, etc.; an apprentice program; a learning tools library; assistance to support groups; family counseling and conflict resolution; cooperative game days for kids, families, and others; workshops in California and Oregon about such topics as how children learn, communicating with children, conflict resolution, holistic curriculums, evaluating educational options; a Special Events Program through which professionals are brought to the community to share their expertise. (916) 292-3623

Discovery Christian School (5547 Alabama Dr., Concord CA 94521): A network of independent and home schools. Offers training and curriculum seminars, materials lists, curriculum information, record and report forms, record-keeping services, annual achievement testing and scoring, annual state report of private school filing service, consultations, newsletters and bulletins regarding current educational and legal developments. (415) 672-5670

Educational Spectrums (P.O. Box 1014, Placerville CA 95667): Purpose — to provide people with information on home and/or alternative education. Offers information for home schoolers, assistance with custom designed reading courses for home-schooled children, mail-order book store, consultations.

Keystone Academy (P.O. Box 1888, Norwalk CA 90651-1888): Keystone Academy is a private Christian School. Offers curriculum development assistance, optional quarterly in-home visits, phone counseling, record keeping, special study projects, support group activities with kids, achievement testing, newsletter, local support group referrals.

Montessori World Education Institute (P.O. Box 3808, San Luis Obispo CA 93403): Offers training in Montessori teaching methods for use in home schools.

Pilgrim School (P.O. Box 1776, Porterville CA 93258): Purpose — to provide legal cover and accountability and to challenge families to live increasingly Godly lifestyles. Offers local support group, field trips, records, newsletter, tapes, and an Independent Study Program based on individually prescribed and negotiated learning contracts. (209) 782-0402

Rudolf Steiner College (9200 Fair Oaks Blvd., Fair Oaks CA 95628): Offers parenting and teaching courses, complete bookstore including books and materials related to Waldorf Education. (916)961-8727

Colorado

Pinewood School (Rt. 2 Box 409, Pine CO 80479): Purpose — to individualize the learning process according to the interests and needs of the students and parents involved. Offers initial curriculum consultation, development of an individualized curriculum, a coordinating Pinewood teacher, monthly curriculum update consultations, record keeping, national network. (303) 838-4418

Connecticut

Emanuel Homesteaders (P.O. Box 355, Woodstock Valley CT 06282): A Christian home-education resource center. Offers publications of interest to home educators, curriculum materials, consultations, assistance with designing curriculums and schedules, workshops and seminars, high school transcripts. (203) 974-2416

District of Columbia

Family Research Council (515 Second St. NE, Capitol Hill, Washington DC 20002): Purpose — to ensure the interests of the family in the formulation of public policy. Offers publications related to family issues.

Florida

Circle Christian School (3300 Edgewater Dr., Orlando FL 32804): Offers curriculum packages, newsletter, field trips and activity days, workshops and curriculum fairs, publications of interest to home schoolers.

Georgia

Perimeter Christian School (5701 Spalding Dr., Norcross GA 30092): Offers a home satellite program with monthly consultations, standardized testing, field trips, vision and hearing screenings, curriculum assistance, record keeping. (404)662-8134

Hawaii

Learning at Home (P.O. Box 270, Honaunau HI 96726): Offers a catalog of numerous materials, curriculum guides, and resource units "which offer support and structure but which emphasize the questions and interests of the learner." (808)328-9669

Idaho

Textbooks for Parents (Box 209, Kendrick ID 83537): Purpose – to provide quality texts and to make individualized accelerated or remedial curriculum possible. Offers textbooks and teacher's guides from a good variety of publishers for K-12 home teaching; curriculum advice and assistance (by mail or phone). (208) 883-0991. Alternate address: 405 N. Jefferson, Moscow ID 83843.

Illinois

Constitutional Rights Foundation (1 Quincy Court, Suite 730, Chicago IL 60604): Offers a quarterly newsletter, curriculum packages, and publications of interest to home educators.

Ad Hoc Committee for Illinois Home Education Legal and Legislative Matters (P.O. Box 6609, Evanston IL 60204): Purpose — to educate and unify home schoolers regarding legislative and legal issues; to protect home schools from regulations that infringe upon educational liberties; to advance the principle of academic freedom for all.

Indiana

WE CAN Inc. (601 Brandywine Dr., Goshen IN 46526): Purpose — to provide information, support and advocacy in these areas: education, health care, nutrition, life patterns, parenting, and childbirth; to encourage self-determination — the belief in our ability to choose our own best course in life; to promote self-worth. Offers information about alternative educational methods, about health care options and natural foods; about birthing issues; about parenting (discipline, communication, safety), about life patterns (assertiveness, mental health, marriage and families, lifestyles). (219) 831-2072

Iowa

Nonprofit Group (Rt. 2 Box 11, Fontanelle IA 50846): Offers "Homeschool Marketplace News," a flyer of advertisements for home school materials and information and other publications.

Kansas

Bureau of Educational Measurement (Emporia State University, Emporia KS 66801): Offers the California Achievement Test, Iowa Tests of Achievement and Proficiency, the Stanford Achievement Test Battery, and other kinds of tests.

Maryland

Alliance for Organic Learning (9085 Flamepool Way, Columbia MD 21045): Networking in the interest of exploring and supporting the theory and practice or organic learning and living; a clearinghouse for information, resources, and legal issues; encouragement for the personal growth and empowerment of individuals; newsletter.

Association for Childhood Education International (111141 Georgia Ave., Suite 200, Wheaton MD 20902): Offers a newsletter, conferences, and informative publications of interest to home educators.

The Centering Institute (6109 Broad St., Bethesda MD 20818): Offers support and encouragement, information dissemination, networking, public awareness activities, idea exchanges, meetings, testing service, consultations, publications of interest to home educators, conferences, workshops, etc. (301) 229-8890

National Committee for Citizens in Education (10840 Little Patuxent Parkway, Suite 301, Columbia MD 21044): Offers many publications related to parental involvement in the education of children and parents' rights, primarily with regards to public schools.

Massachusetts

Holt Associates Inc. (2269 Massachusetts Avenue, Cambridge MA 02140): Offers information dissemination, networking throughout the nation, many publications of interest to home educators (John Holt's Book and Music Store catalog), and Quadro construction toys. Publishes *Growing Without Schooling*, a well-known national, home-schoolers' newsletter. (617)437-1583

National Center for Fair and Open Testing (P.O. Box 1272, Harvard Square Station, Cambridge MA 02238): Offers activities and a newsletter to promote fairness in standardized testing and to inform people about testing practices and problems.

Michigan

Clonlara School (1289 Jewett, Ann Arbor MI 48104): Clonlara is both a campus school and a home-based education program. Offers a newsletter, curriculum programs, family tuition, state math and communication skills guidebooks, home school start-up assistance (including liaison between you and your public school), monthly record sheets, networking, pen pals, legal consultation, instructional video tapes and audio cassettes, linkages to certificated teachers, standardized testing, class time schedules, student interest surveys, report cards, transcripts, diplomas, networking, teacher education workshops, seminars, conferences. (313) 769-4515

Home School Supply House (3254 E. Mitchell, Petoskey MI 49770): Offers textbooks, science kits, art supplies, kids literature.

Minnesota

Basic Learning Network (9669 E 123rd, Hastings MN 55033): Purpose — to restore the teaching of intensive phonics, to enhance basic education, to acknowledge and learn from successful educators, to fight drug use by children, to assist parents who decide to take responsibility for their children's education. Offers a quarterly newsletter, The Basic Learning Center for children in Hastings (4-hours daily/basic subjects and rehabilitation of the desire and ability to learn), conferences, tutor training, networking, workshops, resource list.

GWS Travel Directory (Rt. 2, Winona MN 55987): Offers a list of home school families with whom you could exchange visits as they or you travel.

National Association for Gifted Children (4175 Lovell Rd., Suite 140, Circle Pines MN 55014): Purpose — to disseminate information to parents, public officials, and schools; to serve as a public advocate of the gifted; to promote research and development related to gifted education; to assist the development of gifted education support organizations. Offers an information network, encouragement and assistance to gifted education support groups, research and development journal, newsletter including parent ideas and legislative monitoring, materials, annual convention and institute, a "Private Schools for the Gifted Directory," a catalog of materials of interest to parents of gifted children. (612) 784-3475

T.E.A.C.H.(4350 Lakeland Ave. North, Robbinsdale MN 55422): Purpose — quality Christian home education. Offers an independent home-school program for preschool through grade 12, consultations and supervision by certified teachers, curriculum assistance, materials and aids for instruction, publications of interest to home teachers, workshops, conferences, curriculum/materials fair, record-keeping service, local support group training and assistance, meetings and idea exchanges, newsletter, student socializing opportunities, field trips, networking, achievement testing, legislative monitoring and action. Serves as an accrediting association able to give home educators a certificate of accreditation upon meeting certain criteria. (612) 535-5514

Missouri

Educational Freedom Foundation (20 Parkland Place, Glendale MO 63122): Purpose — preservation of freedom of choice in education and the survival of alternative schooling. Offers information, publications, participation in the legal defense of freedom in education. Affiliated with Citizens for Educational Freedom, a political action association of parents and other citizens.

National Assessment of Educational Progress (P.O. Box 2923, Princeton NJ 08541): Offers research information related to the performance of our nation's children and young adults in the basic skills of reading, math, and communication.

New Mexico

Peloncillo Primary (Box 91, Rodeo NM 88056): Offers a private school for "home learning" and an opportunity to join in the creation of a high school for home-schooled teens.

Santa Fe Community School (P.O. Box 2241, Santa Fe NM 87501): A state-recognized, alternative nonpublic school which also provides assistance to home schoolers. Offers home-school planning, development, and supervisory assistance, record keeping, a children's exchange newsletter.

New York

The Christian Homesteading Movement (RD 2, Oxford NY 13830): Offers a workshop to help parent teachers develop skills needed to deal with home-education requirements, to integrate learning into daily life and through celebration of family customs.

National Coalition of Alternative Community Schools (417 Roslyn Rd., Roslyn Heights, New York NY 11577): NCACS is an informational organization involving parent educators as well as people in various other alternative educational programs. Offers information, a directory which includes resources for home schoolers, field trips, national newsletter, regional meetings and conferences, national conferences, contact with schools that cooperate with home schoolers. A branch group is currently being formed — National Home Schoolers. (516) 621-2195

Oregon

Christian Home Schools (8731 NE Everett St., Portland OR 97220): Offers a Christian home school magazine, information, assistance.

Christian Life Workshops (180 SE Kane Ave., Gresham OR 97030): Purpose — devoted to restoring the Christian family household to its biblical place of significance. Offers The Home Schooling Workshop and other family-oriented workshops; publications about education, home schooling, and families. (206) 834-2372

Home School Researcher (B. Ray, Science Education Dept., Oregon State University, Corvalis OR 97331): Offers home-school information and extensive bibliographies of readings and research related to home schooling.

National Home Education Guild (515 NE 8th St., Grants Pass OR 97526): The N.H.E.G. "is a vehicle through which its members can exercise their constitutional right to redress the Government for grievances as they pertain to laws that govern education." Offers home-education legal strength, individual K-12 learner curriculums, materials, newsletter. (503) 474-1501

Parents Education Association (P.O. Box 1482, Beaverton OR 97075): Purpose — to help parents preserve their right to instruct children in accordance with their conscience and the Word of God. Offers political action with respect to home schooling and related issues; newsletter. (503) 241-4585

The Teaching Home (P.O. Box 20219, Portland OR 97220-0219): Offers publications of interest to home schoolers, including a "Basic Resource Guide of Christian Education Materials," and a national convention. Publishes *The Teaching Home*, a well-known, national Christian home-school magazine.

Whole Earth Farm School (3661 Seminole Rd. NE, Silverton OR 97381): Offers support and encouragement, information dissemination, assistance with curriculum design, an umbrella school for home schoolers who wish to avoid the standardized testing requirement. (503) 873-3371

Pennsylvania

Association for Children and Adults with Learning Disabilities (4156 Library Rd., Pittsburgh PA 15234): Offers publications related to the education and lives of children with learning disabilities.

Open Connections (312 Bryn Mawr Ave., Bryn Mawr PA 19010): Open Connections is a nonprofit educational organization whose purpose is to promote self-directed learning and flexible thinking in children and their families. Offers a Family Resource Center with an assortment of programs and workshops for parents and for children, publications regarding self-directed learning & flexible thinking, speeches and slide presentations, family consultations, booklist, book fair. (215) 527-1504

Rhode Island

Rhode Islanders for Constitutional Education (46 E. George St., Providence RI 02906): Purpose — to create a workable understanding of the concept of freedom. Offers classes, workshops, consultation regarding the retention of your rights. (401)274-8897

Texas

American Mensa Special Interest Group (P.O. Box 832, Bellville TX 77418): Offers the "Gifted Child Home-Schooling" newsletter and a home-school data base.

Cornerstone Christian Academy (P.O. Box 380111, San Antonio TX 78280): Offers record keeping, testing, field trips, support group meetings, newsletter. (512) 649-1740

Virginia

Council for Exceptional Children (Reston VA 22091): Offers publications and bibliographies related to the education of exceptional children, both handicapped and gifted, including the professional journals *Exceptional Children* and *Teaching Exceptional Children.*

Home School Legal Defense Association (P.O. Box 950, Great Falls VA 22066): An information and legal service center whose purpose is to research, coordinate, and support legal actions involving nonpublic education; also to help others locate, evaluate, and/or create alternatives to traditional schooling. Offers legal insurance, newsletter, support and help as noted above, networking, publications. (703)759-7577, or in Washington DC (202) 546-2335

Rutherford Institute (P.O. Box 510, Manassas VA 22110): A legal (not religious) organization that protects the freedom of religious expression, founded and directed by John Whitehead, a well-known voice for religious freedom in the United States. Free legal service, home-school consultations, monthly action newsletter, and quarterly journal. Also offers other publications of interest to home educators, including the *Home Education Reporter* — a state-by-state analysis of compulsory education laws and relevant court rulings. (703) 369-0100

Washington

Hewitt-Moore Child Development Center: (P.O. Box 9, Washougal WA 98671): Offers nondoctrinal and nonsectarian, Christ-centered learning programs and materials for preschool through grade twelve. Placement assessments, teacher's yearly manual, bimonthly journal, record keeping, information, procurement of your child's public school records, progress evaluations, parent-teacher counseling, transcripts, home-school research information, achievement test supplies, and programs for children with special needs. Publishes *Parent Educator and Family Report*, a well-known, national home-schoolers' newsletter. (206)835-8708 or 835-8541

Home Education Press (P.O. Box 1083, Tonasket WA 98855): Offers a variety of publications of interest to home educators and parents in general, including *Home Education Magazine*, a national magazine for home school parents and which includes children' s pages.

"Homeschool Connection" A radio program in Seattle (KGNW, 820 AM) that presents ideas and support for home educators. Produced by the Washington Homeschool Organization which has a list of program tapes available. See *WHO* under *Washington* in the above Mutual-Support Group list.

Moby Dick Academy (P.O. Box 236, Ocean Park WA 98640): Offers support and encouragement, information, networking, newsletter, idea exchanges and meetings, field trips, testing service, consultation service, teaching materials, publications of interest to parent teachers, conferences, workshops, curriculum/materials fairs, curriculum assistance. Several of these offerings are in cooperation with the Washington Homeschool Organization.

Washington Homeschool Report (10029 48th Ave. West, Everett WA 98204): Offers a bimonthly newsletter, information dissemination, legislative monitoring, publications of interest to home educators. (206) 348-0574

✳✳

Readings
and
Resources

Readings

The following list of readings includes those mentioned earlier in this book and also others useful to home educators. Some are philosophical or theoretical in nature — concentrating on home education as a schooling concept — while several are more practical — presenting activities, lesson formats, children's book titles, experiments, checklists, and so on. A few include commentaries on public education. Like the other lists in this section, this one is not intended to be definitive, and although the titles noted are recommended, they are not necessarily recommended above all other possible titles. You will find here, however, many of the books considered by home schoolers to be key readings.

[Note: Publishers' addresses are given only the first time each appears in this list of readings.]

"A, B, C, or F; Test Your Child's School." *Parents Magazine*, November 1987, p. 138-142. (On informing yourself about a public school.)

Arbuthnot, May Hill, et. al. *The Arbuthnot Anthology of Children's Literature, 1976.* Scott, Foresman & Co., 1900 E. Lake Ave., Glenview IL 60025. (Children's tales and poetry.)

"Barbe Reading Skills Check List." Prentice-Hall, Prentice-Hall Bldg., Sylvan Ave., Englewood Cliffs NJ 07632. (K-6 reading skills listed by grade level. Useful for developing a reading curriculum and for designing ongoing assessments of student progress.)

Barrata-Lorton, Mary. *Math Their Way,* 1976. Addison-Wesley, 2725 Sand Hill Rd.,Menlo Park CA. (A manipulative, activity-centered math program for early childhood and primary education.)

Buscaglia, Leo. *Living, Loving & Learning,* 1982. Ballantine, 400 Hahn Road, Westminster MD 21157. (Segments emphasizing the importance of warmth and love in teaching.)

Coles, Gerald. *The Learning Mystique: A Critical Look at Learning Disabilities,* 1987. Pantheon, 201 E. 50th St., New York NY 10022. (A careful dismantling of the "learning disabled" category so heavily used by our public schools.)

Colfax, David and Micki Colfax. *Homeschooling for Excellence, 1987.* Mountain House Press, Box 246, Booneville CA 95415. (Home-schooling philosophies and experiences of the Colfax family whose sons were offered admittance to Harvard, Princeton, and Yale after years of home schooling.)

Collins, Marva and Civia Tamarkin. *Marva Collins' Way*, 1982. J.P. Tarcher Inc., 9110 Sunset Blvd., Los Angeles CA 90069. (Descriptions of the teaching techniques of the highly successful educator Marva Collins. Includes much on the teaching of phonics.)

Copperman, Paul. *Taking Books to Heart; How to Develop a Love of Reading in Your Child*, 1986. Addison-Wesley. (For parents of children 2 to 9. Clear explanations of basal readers, beginning reading instruction, comprehension instruction, and thorough descriptions of at-home reading sessions. Includes activities and book lists.)

Cox, J., N. Daniel & B.D. Boston. *Educating Able Learners*, 1985. University of Texas Press, Austin, TX. (On educating the gifted/talented.)

Cummings, Rhoda and Cleborne Maddux. *Parenting the Learning Disabled: A Realistic Approach.*. Charles C. Thomas Publishing, 2600 So. First St., Springfield IL 62717. (Parenting skills for parents of learning-disabled children.)

Dobson, James C. *Parenting Isn't for Cowards*. 1988, Word Books, 4800 W. Waco Drive, Waco TX 76703. (Parenting skills.)

The Doubleday Illustrated Children's Bible, Retold by Sandol Stoddard, 1983. Doubleday & Co., 501 Franklin Avenue, Garden City NY 11530. (Useful for Christian education and sessions in the Bible as literature.)

Duffy, Cathy. *Home Educator's Curriculum Manual*, 1986. Home Run Enterprises, 12531 Aristocrat Ave., Garden Grove CA 92641. (A guide to establishing a Christian home curriculum.)

Dyer, Wayne. *What Do You Really Want for Your Children?*, 1985. Doubleday. (Educational choices and decisions parents must make.)

Elbow, Peter. *Writing Without Teachers*, 1973. Oxford University Press, Inc., 200 Madison Ave., New York NY 10016. (A guide to teaching and facilitating the writing process. You will want to be your children's writing classmate as you set up a teacher-less writing class.)

Elbow, Peter. *Writing With Power; Techniques for Mastering the Writing Process*, 1981. Oxford University Press. (Written for the secondary or college writing student, but useable by the parent educator as he teaches writing to his children. Most methods are useful for any level, and the book will offer parents a good introduction to the writing process.)

Elkind, David. *The Hurried Child: Growing Up Too Fast Too Soon*, 1981. Addison-Wesley. (About the stresses caused by hurrying the growth and education of children.)

Elkind, David. *Miseducation: Preschoolers at Risk*, 1987. Knopf, 400 Hahn Road, Westminster MD 21157. (About the negative effects of enrolling children in preschools and attempting to create super-learners/superkids.)

"The Evidence Continues to Grow, Parent Involvement Improves Student Achievement." National Committee for Citizens in Education, 10840 Little Patuxent Parkway, Suite 301, Columbia MD 21044. (An annotated bibliography of available studies that document the effects of parent involvement in children's educations.)

Fluegelman, Andrew, editor. *The New Games Book*. Doubleday. (Cooperative games.)

Freeman, Judy. *Books Kids Will Sit Still For: A Guide to Using Children's Literature for Librarians, Teachers, and Parents*, 1984. The Alleyside Press, Box 889, Hagerstown, MD 21741. (An annotated list of 1200 read-aloud children's books and chapters on the use of children's literature for improved reading comprehension.)

Gorder, Cheryl. *Home Schools: An Alternative*, 1985. Blue Bird Publications, 1713 E. Broadway No. 306, Tempe AZ 85282. (Getting started at home schooling.)

Gordon, Edward. "Home Tutoring Programs Gain Respectability." *Phi Delta Kappan*, February 1983, p. 398-399. (A report on the status of home schooling in the U.S.)

Graubard, Allen. *Free the Children*, 1972. Random House, 201 E. 50th St., New York NY 10022. (An analysis of the free schools movement and school reform literature.)

Harris, Gregg. *The Christian Home School*, 1988. Christian Life Workshops, 182 SE Kane Road, Gresham OR 97080. (The Christian home-school perspective, answers to common home-school questions, and how to start a Christian home school.)

Henderson, Anne. "Parents Are a School's Best Friends," *Phi Delta Kappan*, October 1988. (On parent-participatory education.)

Hoffman, Jane. *The Backyard Scientist*. P.O. Box 16966, Irvine CA 92713. (Experiential science activities.)

Holt, John. *How Children Fail*, 1982. Delta Books, 1 Dag Hammerskjold Plaza, New York NY 10017. (An analytical diary of observations of children in school and how they do and don't learn there.)

Holt, John. *How Children Learn*, 1971. Dell Publishing. (About how children learn and how teachers and parents should nurture children.)

Holt, John. *Teach Your Own*, 1981. Delacorte Press, 245 E. 47th St., New York NY 10017. (Home-school reasons, explanations and experiences, with comments from many experienced home schoolers.)

Holt, John. *What Do I Do Monday?*, 1970. Dutton, 2 Park Ave., New York NY 10016. (Philosophies for teaching and specifics on teaching math and writing.)

Holt, John. "So You Want to Home-School." *Mother Earth News*, Jan./Feb. 1984, p. 139-141. (Start-up suggestions.)

"Home Education; Is It Working?" 1986. Texas Home School Coalition, P.O. Box 835105, Richardson TX 75083. (A booklet citing positive home-school research.)

Hubbs, Don. *Home Education Resource Guide*. Blue Bird Publishing. (A directory of home-education resource materials.)

Hughes, Thomas. "Home Education: A Bibliography." University of Colorado. Boulder CO 80302 (Bibliography.)

Hunt, Tamara and Nancy Renfro. *Puppetry in Early Childhood Education*. Nancy Renfro Studios, Austin TX (A complete guide to making, enjoying, and teaching with puppets.)

The Illustrated Children's Bible, 1982. Retold by David Christie-Murry. Grosset & Dunlap, 51 Madison Ave., New York NY 10010. (Useful for Christian education and sessions in the Bible as literature.)

"I'm Not Stupid," 1987. Association for Children and Adults with Learning Disabilities, 4156 Library Rd., Pittsburgh PA 15200. (A video about the learning disabled.)

Judy, Stephen N. and Susan J. Judy. *An Introduction to the Teaching of Writing*, 1981. John Wiley & Sons, 605 3rd Ave., New York NY 10158. (A sound introduction.)

Kaufman, Felice. *Your Gifted Child and You*, 1983. Council for Exceptional Children, Dept. CS88M, 1920 Association Drive, Reston VA 22091-1589. (On fostering creativity and helping gifted children develop their interests at home.)

Koch, Kenneth. *Rose, where did you get that red? Teaching Great Poetry to Children*, 1973. Random House. (A useful guide for teaching poetry to children.)

Koch, Kenneth. *Wishes, Lies, and Dreams: Teaching Children to Write Poetry*. Harper & Row, 10 E. 53rd St, New York NY 10022. (An easily used guide to teaching children how to write poetry.)

Kohn, Alfie. "Home Schooling." *Atlantic Monthly*, April 1988, p.20 - 25. (An overview of home schooling in the U.S.)

Larrick, Nancy. *A Parent's Guide to Children's Reading*, 1983. Double-day. (On reading instruction.)

Laughy, Linwood. *The Interactive Parent; How to Help Your Child Survive and Succeed in the Public Schools*, 1988. Mountain Meadow Press, P.O. Box 447, Kooskia ID 83539. (A most useful guide to the why's and how's of remaining in control of your child's education should your child now be enrolled in public school or should you wish to reenroll your child in public school. Also highly helpful for home schoolers who must deal with public school officials in any way.)

Leonard, George B. *Education and Ecstasy*, 1987. North Atlantic Books, 2320 Lake Street, Berkeley CA 94704. (Describes both what public education unfortunately is and what education could be and poses the question: Do we really need or want public schools?)

Lines, Patricia M. "An Overview of Home Instruction." *Phi Delta Kappan*, March 1987, p. 510-517. (About the home school movement today.)

Lopez, Diane. *Teaching Children*, 1988. Goodnews Publishers, 982 W. Roosevelt Rd., Westchester IL 60153. (K-6 curriculum guide.)

Love, Robert. *How to Start Your Own School*, 1973. Macmillan, 866 3rd Ave., New York NY 10022. (A description of how Robert Love and others began and maintained a nonpublic school, with advice for parents who wish to do the same.)

McLean, Mollie and Anne Wiseman. *Adventures of the Greek Heroes*. Houghton-Mifflin, 2 Park St., Boston MA 02108. (Includes Greek myths retold for children.)

Medveseek, Chris. "Everybody Wins." *Parents Magazine*, April 1988, p. 121-124. (An article which discusses and gives examples of cooperative games.)

Merrow, John. *Learning Disabilities: The Hidden Handicapped.* National Committee for Citizens in Education. (A video discussing learning disabilities for parents who have children who appear to be learning disabled.)

Miles, Bernard. *Favorite Tales from Shakespeare*, 1977. Rand McNally, 8255 Central Park Ave., Skokie IL 60076. (An illustrated anthology for children.)

Mintz, Jerry. "National Directory of Alternative Schools." The National Coalition of Alternative Community Schools, 417 Roslyn Heights, New York NY 11577. (A directory.)

Moffett, James and Betty Jane Wagner. *Student-Centered Language Arts and Reading, K-13: A Handbook for Teachers,* 1983. Houghton

Mifflin. (A comprehensive description of a K-13 language and reading curriculum, including activities.)

Moore, Raymond. *Better Late Than Early*, 1976. Reader's Digest Press, 200 Park Avenue, New York NY 10000 (On school readiness and reasons to delay school entry.)

Moore, Raymond and Dorothy Moore. *Home Grown Kids; A Practical Handbook for Teaching Your Children at Home*, 1984. Word Books. (Home-school rationale and how-to; lists of resources.)

Moore, Raymond and Dorothy Moore. *Home-Spun Schools*, 1982. Word Books. (On the benefits of being schooled at home.)

Moore, Raymond. *Home-Style Teaching*, 1984. Word Books. (On home instruction)

Moore, Raymond. *School Can Wait* 1979 Brigham Young University Press, Provo, UT (On the importance of the home in nurturing children and on school readiness.)

Moore, Raymond. "What Educators Should Know About Home Schools," Family Research Council of America, Inc., 515 Second Street, Northeast Capitol Hill, Washington D.C. 20002. (Also available from Hewitt Research Foundation, 36211 S.E. Sunset View, Washougal, WA 98671.) (A 12-page discussion of home schooling, educational authority, and recommendations to public educators regarding home schools.)

Naturescope. National Wildlife Federation, 1412 16th St. NW, Washington DC 10036. (A series of teaching guides for nature/science education — very useful for home teaching. Ask for a catalog of all available issues.)

Orlick, Terry. *The Cooperative Sports and Games Book* and *The Second Cooperative Sports and Games Book*. Pantheon. (Cooperative games.)

*Our Nation at Risk: Imperative for Educational Reform,*1983. National Commission on Excellence in Education. (A report on the state of public education in the U.S.)

Pagnoni, Mario. *The Complete Home Educator*, 1984. Larson Publications, 4936 Rt. 414, Burdett NY 14818. (Home-school ideas with a large section on computer education.)

"Parents Can Understand Testing." 1980. National Committee for Citizens in Education. (A booklet on test interpretation.)

Pride, Mary. *The Big Book of Home Learning*, Great Christian Books, 1319 Newport Gap Pike, Wilmington DE 19804. (Home-school resources guide.)

Pride, Mary, *The Next Book of Home Learning*. Great Christian Books. (Home-school resources guide.)

Ray, Brian. "Home Centered Learning Annotated Bibliography." School of Education, Seattle Pacific University, Seattle WA 98119 (Bibliography.)

Reed, Donn. *The First Home School Catalogue.* Brook Farm Books, P.O. Box 66-HM, Bridgewater ME 04735. (Home-school resources guide.)

Roth, Robert A. "Emergency Certificates, Misassignment of Teachers, and Other 'Dirty Little Secrets'." *Phi Delta Kappan,* June 1986, p.725-727. (Truths about public education, especially teacher certification and course assignments, that provide ammunition for noncertified home educators.)

"Reading Beyond the Basals," Perfection Form Co., 1000 N. Second Ave., Logan IA 51546. (A series of booklets full of reading comprehension activities to accompany selected children's literature.)

Recyclopedia: Games, Science Equipment, and Crafts Made from Recycled Materials, 1976. Houghton-Mifflin. (Developed by the Boston Children's Museum; a fine guide.)

Rowland, Howard S. *No More School,* 1975. Dutton. (Story of a family's year of adventurous home schooling in Spain.)

Russell, William F. *Classics to Read Aloud to Your Children,* 1984. Crown, 225 Park Ave. S., New York NY 10003. (An anthology of excerpts from world classics.)

Sabin, William A. *The Gregg Reference Manual,* 1977. McGraw-Hill Book Co., 1221 Avenue of the Americas, New York NY 10020. (Comprehensive guide to the mechanics of English usage. Useful as a reference during writing and language lessons.)

Shackelford, Luanne and Susan White. *A Survivor's Guide to Home Schooling,* 1988. Good News Publishers. (Practical answers to Christian home-schoolers' questions.)

Smith, Frank. *Insult to Intelligence,* 1986, Arbor House, 105 Madison Ave., New York NY 10016. (On the negative effects of drilling, testing, and grading.)

Spalding, Romalda Bishop and Walter T. Spalding. *The Writing Road to Reading,* 1969. Quill, 105 Madison Ave., New York NY 10016. (An easy-to-use guide to teaching phonics, spelling, reading.)

Stribling, Mary Lou. *Art from Found Materials,* 1970. Crown, 1 Park Avenue, New York NY 10016. (A book full of inexpensive art projects.)

"Tips for Teaching the Marginal Learner," 1986. Appalachia Education Lab, P.O. Box 1348, Charleston WV 25325 (Keys to teaching marginal learners.)

Wade, Theodore E. *The Home School Manual*, 1986. Gazelle Publications, 5580 Stanley Dr., Auburn CA 95603 (Home-school how-to.)

Wallace, Nancy. *Better Than School; One Family's Declaration of Independence*, 1983. Lawson Publishing, New York. (A well-written account of a family's home-schooling experiences, with recommendations for other parents.)

Walsh, J. Martyn and Anna Kathleen Walsh. *Plain English Handbook; A Complete Guide to Good English,* 1972. McCormick-Mathers Publishing, Cincinnati Ohio. (Comprehensive quick-reference guide to the mechanics of English. Useful for writing and language lessons.)

Weaver, Roy, et. al. "Home Tutorials vs. Public Schools in Los Angeles." *Phi Delta Kappan*, December 1980, p. 254-255. (On home-tutorial results.)

"What Works: Research About Teaching and Learning," 1986. U.S. Department of Education, 1200 19th St. NW, Washington DC 20208. (Effective teaching and effective schools research results in easy-to-understand format for parents, teachers, and school administrators.)

Whitehead, John and Wendell Bird. *Home Education and Constitutional Liberties*, 1984. Goodnews Publishers. (Historical and legal arguments for home schooling.)

Williams, Jane. *How to Stock a Quality Home Library Inexpensively.* Bluestocking Press/Educational Spectrums, P.O. Box 1014, Placerville CA 95667. (On selecting, locating, and inexpensively securing books.)

Williams, Jane. *Young Thinkers Bookshelf: Books to Encourage Independent and Critical Thinking.* Bluestocking Press. (On book selection for a graduated reading program, indexed by subjects: literature, history, law, economics, communications, education, critical thinking — 300 books to stimulate creative and intuitive thought, reasoning skills, self-directed growth, and character development.)

Williams, Jane. *Who Reads What When: Literature Selections for Children Ages Three Through Thirteen.* Bluestocking Press. (Lists over 500 children's books, indexed by age, author, and title.)

Periodicals for Children

A number of excellent magazines are available for children today, especially in the nature science subject area. Perhaps your children would like to help you select those that are most appealing to them and that might be useful as supplements to their studies. While some of the listed periodicals are available on newsstands, others are not — you may want to secure a sample copy before entering a subscription.

Chicadee Magazine (56 The Esplanade, Suite 306, Toronto Ontario M5E 1A7, Canada) Invites hands-on approach to learning for ages 3 to 9, including stories, games, puzzles, crafts, personal experience and wildlife.

Child Life (Children's Better Health Institute, P.O. Box 10003, Des Moines IA 50340) Stories, photo features, puzzles, activities that help teach good health habits, history, adventure, humor, and mystery, for ages 7 to 9.

The Children's Album (Box 6086, Concord CA 94524) Children's writing techniques, children's literature, and writings by children, for ages 8-14.

Children's Digest (Children's Better Health Institute, P.O. Box 10003, Des Moines IA 50340) Suspenseful and humorous stories related to good health, articles on exercise, sports, nutrition, health, history, biography, safety, reviews, recipes, crafts, puzzles, for ages 8 to 10.

Children's Playmate Magazine (Children's Better Health Institute, P.O. Box 10003, Des Moines IA 50340) Science, cultures, humor, holidays, health, nutrition, safety, and exercise, for ages 5 to 7.

Clubhouse (Box 15, Berrien Springs MI 49103) Personal experiences, natural food recipes, emphasis on self-esteem, for ages 9-14.

Cobblestone (28 Main St., Peterborough NH 03458) Highly regarded magazine which emphasizes American history with firsthand accounts, lively biographies, poems, maps, games, puzzles, cartoons, songs, recipes, contests, for grades 4-9.

Creative Kids (P.O. Box 6448, Mobile AL 36660)   For and by gifted/talented children.

Cricket (P.O. Box 2670, Boulder CO 80322)   A magazine full of stories, poems, and activities by top notch writers and artists that encourage reading for elementary age children.

Current Health (3500 Western Ave., Highland Park IL 60035)   Health education, for grades 4-7.

The Dolphin Log (The Cousteau Society, 8440 Santa Monica Blvd., Los Angeles CA 90069)   An educational bimonthly magazine for children ages 7 to 15, including marine biology, ecology, the environment, natural history, and water-related stories and personal experiences. Family membership also includes a parent magazine.

Ebony Jr. (820 S. Michigan, Chicago IL 60605)   Inspiration, activities, articles with a focus on black children.

Faces, The Magazine About People (20 Grove St., Peterborough NH)   Fairy tales, legends, projects, puzzles, recipes, maps, photo essays and more that emphasize world cultures, civilization, geography, anthropology, for grades 4-9. Won the Parents' Choice Award in 1986 & 1987.

Highlights for Children (Parent & Child Resource Center, P.O. Box 269, Columbus OH 43272-0002)   History, science, sports, biography, crafts, poetry, stories, for ages 2-12.

Home School Gazette (P.O. Box 359, Burtonsville MD 10866)   A national newspaper published by and for home-educated children to encourage their writing. (Sponsors a Writing Christian Workshop for children who write at least at a fifth grade level and their parents.)

Humpty Dumpty (Child's Better Health Institute, P.O. Box 10003, Des Moines IA 50340)   Stories and poems, puzzles and other activities, that teach good health habits, for ages 4 to 6.

Jack and Jill (Children's Better Health Institute, P.O. Box 10003, Des Moines IA 50340)   Articles on health, safety, exercise and nutrition, adventure, humor, puzzles and craft projects, for ages 6 to 8.

Kid City (One Lincoln Plaza, New York NY 10023)   Adventure, fantasy, history, humor, mystery, westerns, for ages 6-10. Formerly *Electric Company Magazine*.

Muppet Magazine (300 Madison Ave., New York NY 10017)   Muppet stories, profiles of the muppet characters and people who work with them.

National Geographic World (National Geographic Society, Dept. 00385, 17th & M Streets NW, Washington DC 20036)   Nature, conservation, science, geography, history, sports, outdoor adventure, and children's activities, for ages 8-13.

National Wildlife (1412 Sixteenth St. NW, Washington DC 20036-2266) A nature magazine for older children and adults.

Nature Friend Magazine (P.O. Box 73, Goshen IN 46526) A nature/science magazine including stories and projects with a Creation perspective.

Odyssey (P.O. Box 92788, Milwaukee WI 53202) Astronomy and outer space, for ages 8-12.

OWL (56 The Esplanade, Suite 306, Toronto, Ontario M5E 1A7, Canada) How-to, personal experience, science, and nature, for ages 3-12.

Penny Power (Consumer's Union, Box 1906, Marion OH 43305) Consumer information for 8 to 12 year olds.

Plays: The Drama Magazine for Young People (Plays Inc., 120 Boylston St., Boston MA 02116) A magazine for third grade through junior high children and their parents who are looking for play production ideas and scripts.

Ranger Rick (1412 Sixteenth St. NW, Washington DC 20036) A reading, science, crafts, nature magazine for elementary level children.

Scienceland (501 Fifth Ave., New York NY 10164) Focus on science for ages 6-11.

Sesame Street Magazine (One Lincoln Plaza, New York NY 10023) Games, puzzles, stories, and parents' guide to learning skills, for ages 2-6.

Stone Soup: The Magazine by Children (Children's Art Foundation, P.O. Box 83, Santa Cruz CA 95063) A literary journal written by children, includes fiction, poetry, and artwork by mid-elementary to junior high school age children that can serve as models of creative writing for your children.

3-2-1 Contact (200 Watt St., P.O. Box 2933, Boulder CO 80322) Profiles, photo features, educational fun and games with an emphasis on science, for ages 8-14.

Turtle Magazine (Children's Better Health Institute, P.O. Box 10003, Des Moines IA 50340) Fantasy, humor, and health-related stories, for ages 2 to 5.

Weekly Reader (4343 Equity Drive, P. O. Box 16626, Columbus OH 43216) Children's newspaper of current events, features, science.

Young Author's Magazine (3015 Woodsvale Blvd., Lincoln NE 68502) How-to, profile, personal experience, adventure, fantasy, humor, mystery, poetry by young writers, for upper elementary through junior high children.

Your Big Backyard (1412 Sixteenth St. NW, Washington DC 20036) A reading, science, crafts, nature magazine for preschoolers and primary level children.

Wee Wisdom (Unity Village MO 64065) Nature, self-image, projects and activities to encourage an appreciation of life, for ages 13 & under.

Zoobooks (Box 85271, San Diego CA 92138) Science magazine for elementary level children.

Periodicals for Parent Educators

Some of the following periodicals are written specifically for home teachers. Others are written mainly for public school teachers, but are quite useable by home teachers able to adapt whole classroom activities to a single child or a few children. This is usually not difficult. Most of the teaching ideas presented in these periodicals are based upon current educational research and are often innovative and creative. By reading the annotations for each publication below, you can select those that may be most useful to you.

Arts & Activities (Suite 200, 591 Camino de la Reina, San Diego CA 92108) Learning activities for art education, materials and publications reviews, advertisers' directory, clip and save art prints.

Basic Education (Council for Basic Education, 725 Fifteenth St. NW, Washington DC 20005) Monthly journal provides updates on important education issues.

Childhood Education (Association for Childhood Education International, 11141 Georgia Ave., Suite 200, Wheaton MD 20902) An award-winning magazine with articles on innovative educational practices that can be used in home teaching plus educator's and children's book, film, and magazine reviews.

Childhood – The Waldorf Perspective (Rt. 2 Box 2675, Westford VT 05494) A newsletter related to Waldorf education, including practical teaching activities and resources.

Christian Parenting (P.O. Box 3850, Sisters OR 97759) Magazine whose articles cover parenting issues of all sorts – child care, the development of values and self-esteem in children, educating the young, discipline, and much more.

Classroom Computer Learning (2451 E. River Rd., Dayton OH 45439) Computer education teaching methods and information.

The Computing Teacher (ICCE, University of Oregon, 1787 Agate St., Eugene OR 97403) Computer education teaching methods.

Creative Learning Magazine (Box 37568, San Antonio TX 78237-0568) Learning activities K-12+ in various subject areas and reviews of products and publications of interest to home educators.

The Exceptional Parent (1170 Commonwealth Ave., 3rd Floor, Boston MA 02134) Magazine which covers issues of concern to parents of disabled children; practical guidance to those interested in the development of disabled people.

Gifted Children Monthly (P.O. Box 10149, Des Moines IA 50340) An award-winning monthly magazine for parents of gifted/talented children — strategies, product reviews, practical information, four page children's pullout section.

Gifted Child Quarterly (National Association for Gifted Children, Circle Pines MN 55014) A research-oriented magazine which includes practical ideas for applying research-based methods to teaching children.

The Gifted Child Today (P.O. Box 637, Holmes PA 19043) A magazine with activities for and information about gifted, creative, and talented learners.

Good Apple Newspaper (Box 299, Carthage IL 62321) Learning activities for grades 2-8 in various subject areas and including holidays.

Growing Without Schooling (729 Boylston St., Boston MA 02116) Bimonthly magazine including informative letters from readers, articles, directory of readers, legal information, and more.

Holistic Education Review (P.O. Box 1476, Greenfield MA 01302) Journal providing information on varied aspects of holistic learning, both theoretical and practical, including home schooling.

Home Business Advisor (NextStep Publications, P.O. Box 41108, Fayetteville NC 28309) A bimonthly newsletter aimed at helping parents achieve success in home-business endeavors while working at home around and with children.

Home Education Magazine (P.O. Box 1083, Tonasket WA 98855) Bimonthly magazine offering activity pages for children, book reviews, and helpful articles on methods of teaching at home and on home-school issues.

Home School Researcher (c/o Brian Ray, Science Ed. Dept., OSU, Corvallis OR 97331) A quarterly, interactive publication aimed at reviewing home-school research and sharing ideas, articles, etc., related to home-school research. (503) 754-4151 or 754-2511 or 838-1248

Home Schooling at Its Best (175 Gladys Ave., #7, Mountain View CA 94043) Periodical including teaching ideas and learning activities.

Instructor (P.O. Box 6099, Duluth MN 55806) A magazine covering teaching methods in various subject areas.

Journal of Reading (International Reading Association, 800 Barksdale Road, P.O. Box 8139, Newark DE 19714-8139) Journal including secondary reading instruction methods.

KidsArt News (912 Schilling Way, Mt. Shasta CA 96067) Ideas, activities, and information for art education for kids of all ages.

Learning (1111 Bethlehem Pike, Springhouse PA 19477) A magazine covering teaching tips, materials ads, learning activities.

Lollipops (Box 299, Carthage IL 62321-0299) Learning activities in varied subject areas for preschool and primary education.

Mother Earth News (Box 70, Hendersonville NC 28791) Popular magazine covering home crafts, how-to, home business, etc.

Mothering (P.O. Box 1690, Santa Fe NM 87504) A parenting magazine whose aim is to empower parents to make informed choices for the welfare of their children and which publishes articles on many aspects of parenting including home schooling.

National Coalition News (R.D. 1 Box 378, Glenmoore PA 19343) Newsletter of the National Coalition of Alternative Community Schools including information regarding the activities of the Coalition and regarding schooling alternatives and issues. Alternate address: National Coordinator, 417 Roslyn Rd., Roslyn Heights NY 11577.

New Families, a Journal of Transitions (Nextstep Publications, P.O. Box 41108, Fayetteville NC 28309) A quarterly magazine emphasizing parenting, family, work styles, and home business.

The Parent Educator and Family Report (Hewitt-Moore Child Development Center, P.O. Box 9, Washougal WA 98671) Nonsectarian Christian journal including legal updates, parent questions answered, news items, brief articles on teaching philosophies and teaching methods.

Parenting (P.O. Box 52424, Boulder CO 80321-2424) Magazine covering varied aspects of parenting — child health, travel, child care programs, nutrition, and much more.

Parents Magazine (P.O. Box 3055, Harlan IA 51593-2119) Magazine including many aspects of parenting, such as childbirth, infant care, mothers in multiple roles, child discipline, post-infant to age thirteen child care and child issues of all sorts. Sometimes includes articles useful to home educators.

The Reading Teacher (International Reading Association, 800 Barksdale Road, P.O. Box 8139, Newark DE 19714-8139) Journal including elementary reading teaching methods.

School Arts (Printers Building, 50 Portland St., Worcester MA 01608) Learning activities for art education; art materials; school/college summer program announcements; new art products news; separately, a booklet of criteria for purchasing school art supplies called "Selection, Testing and Specifications Guide."

School Shop (416 Longshore Drive, Box 8623, Ann Arbor MI 48107) Shop activities and projects that could be undertaken by individual home students working alone or with an adult tutor.

Shining Star (Box 299, Carthage IL 62321-1299) Reproducible activities and ideas for Christian home schoolers.

Shop Talk (5737 64th St. Lubbock TX 79424) Newsletter that includes home-school ideas and other parenting ideas through articles written by its parent readers.

The Teaching Home (P.O. Box 20219, Portland OR 97220-0219) A bimonthly magazine covering many Christian home-school topics, resource descriptions, good articles on teaching methods, and includes newsletter insets from several of the states — perhaps yours.

Home-School Curriculum Suppliers

Below is a sampling of suppliers of full curriculums. You'll want to read "Curriculum and Materials" in Section Three before ordering any curriculums. Then consider carefully the content of each subject area, potential teaching methods and student learning styles, and the philosophies behind any of the curriculums you might purchase. Remember, too, that it is quite possible, and in many cases beneficial, to design your own curriculum; i.e., to not purchase a commercial curriculum for *total* use. However, in designing your own curriculum a purchased one can effectively serve as a reference, or in some cases even a mainstay, as long as you remain in control of your overall curriculum. Or perhaps you'll decide to integrate ideas from several curriculums into your own. Please note that because home schoolers' needs vary so greatly, it is not possible to offer recommendations regarding the following curriculum suppliers, but many are among those heavily used by home schoolers. Also note that many of the home-school support organizations listed in Section Five offer assistance with curriculum development on an individual basis.

May I further recommend, as you consider curriculum, that if you have a precocious youngster or a high school home student, you contact colleges and universities in your area or state (and even out of state) regarding independent study courses offered by mail. Most state universities offer such courses and sometimes courses numerous enough to nearly fill out a high school home schooler's full curriculum. Just a few are listed below that were brought to my attention, but you are likely to find much more available. Also, in some cases, high school students are ready to attend regular college courses — junior colleges and community colleges often allow such enrollments. At times, too, younger students with special talents (in art or music, for example) may make special arrangements to attend courses at local colleges or participate in special groups (drama troupes or musicians' groups, for example). In proposing such possibilities, the best approach to a local college may be a personal one. Make an appointment to visit with an admissions administrator or with an instructor in the field of your child's interest.

Most of the other suppliers listed below should be contacted by mail with a request for information regarding their services, curriculum aids and prices.

241

ABeka Book Publications (Box 18000, Pensacola FL 32523-9160) Traditional approach, textbook oriented, Christian and patriotic, grades K-11. Curriculum guides and materials. Correspondence courses and courses on video available. (904) 478-8933

Abbott Loop Christian Center (2626 Abbott Rd., Anchorage AK 99507) Grades K-2 curriculums and materials. (907) 349-9641

Addison-Wesley (2725 Sand Hill Road, Menlo Park CA 94025) The *Math Their Way* beginning math curriculum and materials; teacher training.

Alpha Omega Publications (P.O. Box 3153, Tempe AZ 85281) Mastery learning and programmed learning approaches, Christian, grades K-12. Curriculums and materials and satellite programs for Christian schools are available. (800) 821-4443

Alta Vista College (Home School Curriculum, Box 222, Medina WA 98039) Skills mastery approach, unit-based, Christian, grades K-7 bi-level curriculums and materials.

American Christian Academy (P.O. Box 1776, Colleyville TX 76034) Self-instructional curriculums and materials, achievement test assistance and scoring, record keeping, consultations, diplomas. (214) 434-1776 or (817) 488-6565

American Heritage Christian Academy (9027 Calvine Rd., Sacramento CA 95829) Full curriculums, teacher training, achievement testing, group activities, teacher consultants. (916) 682-2382

American School (850 E. 58th, Chicago IL 66637) Grades K-12 correspondence courses in a wide array of subject areas. (312) 947-3300 or 3355

Associated Christian Schools (P.O. Box 27115, Indianapolis IN 46227) Preschool through grade 12 Christian curriculums and materials, teacher training videos, achievement test scoring and record keeping.

Association of Christian Schools International (Box 4097, Whittier CA 90607) Christian curriculums, emphasis on character development. Also *Bible Truths in Subjects* by Ruth Haycock.

Basic Education (A.C.E., P.O. Box 610589, D./F.W. Airport TX 75261-0589) Skill mastery approach, Christian curriculums, diagnostic placement tests, self instructional materials, grades K-12.

Bob Jones University Press (Greenville SC 29614) Traditional approach, textbook oriented, Christian, grades K-12. Curriculums, materials, teacher workshops, and achievement testing (Iowa Test).

Brigham Young University (Dept. of Independent Study, 206 Harman Continuing Ed. Bldg., Provo UT 83602) High school correspondence courses in an array of subject areas; also parenting courses.

Calvert School (105 Tuscany Rd., Baltimore MD 21210) Grades K-8 curriculums and materials, advisory teacher service, transcripts.

Cambridge Academy (1553 N.E. Arch Ave., Jensen Beach FL 33457) High school correspondence courses. (800) 327-4871

Center for Educational Guidance (P.O. Box 445, N. San Juan CA 95960) Holistic curriculums, cooperative game days, parenting/ teaching workshops. (916) 292-3623

Center for Independent Study Through Correspondence (University of Missouri, 400 Hitt St., Columbia MO 65211) Grades 9-12 corre-spondence courses.

Centralized Correspondence Study (P.O. Box GA, Juneau AK 99811) A wide array of elementary and secondary correspondence cours-es, free enrollment with materials-return (for Alaskans), regular advisory teacher assistance. CCS research studies are available from the Alaska Department of Education. (907) 465-2835

Christian Chapel Schools (1920 S. Brea Cyn Cut-off Rd., Walnut CA 91789) Curriculum and materials, home-school coordinator, achievement testing. (714) 498-9733

Christian Education Music Publishers (2285 W. 185th PL., Lansing IL 60438) Grades K-4 music curriculum.

Christian Liberty Academy Satellite School (502 W. Euclid Ave., Arlington Heights IL 60004) Grades K-12 correspondence cur-riculums and materials, record keeping, testing and copies of the Iowa Standardized Achievement Test.

Christian Light Education (P.O. Box 1126, Harrisonburg VA 22801-1126) Mennonite, self-instructional and personalized, grades K-12. Also, teacher training, achievement tests and diplomas. (703) 434-0750

Circle Christian School (3300 Edgewater Dr., Orlando FL 32804) Curriculum packages and other support.

Citizens High School (P.O. Box 80414, Atlanta GA 30366) High school correspondence courses. (404) 455-8358

Clonlara School (1289 Jewett, Ann Arbor MI 48104) Curriculums and materials, teacher assistance, achievement testing, tran-scripts, diplomas, teacher training. (313) 769-4515

Correspondence Study Office (University of Idaho Campus, Moscow ID 83843) Grades 9-12 correspondence courses in a wide array of subject areas. (208) 885-6641

Covenent Home Curriculum (3675 N. Calhoun Rd., Brookfield WI 53005) Grades K-12 correspondence curriculums and materials, Christian and secular options.

Davis Publishing (50 Portland St., Worcester MA 01608) Grades 1-6 art curriculums and materials.

Extension Independent Study Division, Correspondence for High School (Utah State University, UMC 50, Logan UT 84322) Grades 9-12 correspondence courses in a wide array of subject areas. (801) 750-2137 or 2132

Freedom Christian Academy (82 The Woods, Corinth TX 76205) Grades K-12 correspondence curriculums and materials.

Front Row Experience (540 Discovery Bay Blvd., Byron CA 94514) Curriculum guides for movement education, special education, educational games, and perceptual-motor development.

Glenn Distributors (6605 Bass Hwy., St. Cloud FL 32769) Grades K-12 curriculums and materials. (305) 957-3589

Hewitt-Moore Child Development Center (P.O. Box 9, Washougal WA 98671-0009) Readiness curriculum for ages 5-7, age 8 through grade 12 flexible academic curriculums, Christian and secular options, achievement tests.

High School Correspondence Courses (University of California Extension, 2223 Fulton St., Berkeley CA 94720) Grades 9-12 correspondence courses in a wide array of subject areas. (415) 642-8245

Home Education Services (728 S. Winnetka Ave., Dallas TX 75208) Essential elements of grade-level home-school curriculums for Texans; current research in education; consultations. (214) 941-6048

Home Educational Learning Program (333 75th St., Downers Grove IL 60516) Preschool through grade 9 correspondence curriculums, Christian, and a program for learning disabled students.

Home Schools United – Vegas Valley (P.O. Box 26811, Las Vegas NV 89126) Curriculum packages, consultations. (702) 870-9566

Home Study Alternative School (P.O. Box 10356, Newport Beach CA 92658) K-8 correspondence curriculums.

Home Study International (6940 Carroll Ave., Takoma Park, Washington DC 20912) Seventh Day Adventist, grades K-12 correspondence courses.

Independent Study Department (University of Oklahoma, 1700 Asp Ave., Rm. B-1, Norman OK 73037) Grades 9-12 correspondence courses in a wide array of subject areas. (405)325-1921, or in Oklahoma (800) 942-5702

Independent Study High School (269-PL NCCE, University of Nebraska, Continuing Ed. Ctr., Rm. 269, Lincoln NE 68583) Grades 9-12 correspondence courses in various subject areas. (402) 472-1926

Independent Study Program (Indiana University, Division of Extended Studies, Owen Hall 001, Bloomington IN 47405) High school correspondence courses in a wide array of subject areas. (812) 335-3693

International Institute (P.O. Box 99, Park Ridge IL 60068) Grades K-8 correspondence courses, parent advisory service.

Keys to Learning International (1411 Oak St., So. Pasadena CA 91030) Grades K-12 curriculums in all basic academic subjects. (818) 441-0020

KONOS (P.O. Box 1534, Richardson TX 75083) Multilevel elementary curriculum which emphasizes the development of Christian character.

Learning at Home (P.O. Box 270, Honaunau HI 96726) Curriculum guides, resource units, a catalog of materials. (808) 328-9669

Living Heritage Academy (P.O. Box 1438, Lewisville TX 75067-1438) Grades K-12 correspondence curriculums and materials.

Magic Meadow School (P.O. Box 29, N. San Juan CA 95960) Curriculums and materials, certified parent-educator advisors. (916) 292-3209

McGuffey Academy (1000 E. Huron, Milford MI 48042) Grades 1-8 correspondence curriculums.

Meyer Educational Center (916 Pineview Dr., Alexander City AL 35010) Curriculums involving such areas as organic gardening, wholesome living, natural foods, basic survival skills, with experiential sharing and exchange regionally and statewide among users of the curriculums.

The Montgomery Institute (P.O. Box 532, Boise ID 83701) A private enterprise umbrella school with Christian emphasis. Provides consultations and home-school program development, activity days, legislative and other information, quarterly informative magazine, bookstore, workshops. (208) 343-3420

Mott Media (1000 E. Huron St., Milford MI 43042) Nongraded, skills mastery approach, grades 1-8.

National Home Education Guild (515 NE 8th St., Grants Pass OR 97526) Individual K-12 curriculums. (503) 474-1501

Oak Meadow School (P.O. Box G, Ojai CA 93023) Grades K-12 curriculums, experienced teacher advisors who provide regular assistance, student progress evaluations, teacher training. (805) 646-4510. Midwest address: Rt. 1 Box 19M, Jamestown MO 65046

Our Lady of Victory School (P.O. Box 5181, Mission Hills CA 91345) Grades K-12 Christian curriculums and materials.(818) 899-1966

Phoenix Special Programs (3132 W. Carendon, Phoenix AZ 85017) Grades 9-12 correspondence courses, diploma. (602) 263-5601

Reading Instruction Support Programs (P.O. Box 105, Fulton MI 49052) Phonics-based reading programs, preschool through adult, at-home reading screening assessments, free consulting service for those using the programs.

Riggs Institute (4185 SW 102nd Ave., Beaverton OR 97005) *The Writing Road to Reading* multi-sensory, integrated beginning reading curriculum and materials; teacher training.

Rod and Staff Publishers (Crockett KY 41413) Traditional approach, Christian, grades 1-9 curriculums and materials.

Seton School Home Study (One Kidd Lane, Front Royal VA 22630-3332) Grades K-12 curriculums, correspondence courses and materials, integrated with lessons in Catholicism. Transcripts, achievement testing, consultations. (703) 636-9990

School of Home Learning (P.O. Box 92, Escondido CA 92025) Curriculum guides; record keeping.

Snohomish County Christian Home School Program (17931 - 64th Ave. West, Lynnwood WA 98037) Three possible home school curriculum and supervisory/support programs, extracurricular activities, field trips, library.

Southeast Academy (P.O. Box MM, Ball Park Ave., Saltville VA 24370) Grades 10-12 correspondence courses. (703) 496-7777

Summit Christian Academy (P.O. Box 802041, Dallas TX 75380) Grades 1-12 correspondence curriculums, teacher training, educational software.

Sunnyridge Alternative Learning Center (P.O. Box 713, Houghton MI 49931) Clonlara School curriculums and other services. (906) 334-2788

The Sycamore Tree (2179 Meyer Place, Costa Mesa CA 92627) Grades K-12 correspondence curriculums, Christian and secular options; standardized testing.

The Waldorf Institute (260 Hungry Hollow Rd., Spring Valley NY 10977) A network of Waldorf schools; an array of teacher training courses primarily for Waldorf education but also of interest to home educators. (914) 425-0055

Teaching Materials, Aids and Information Suppliers

Remember to design or select your curriculum and to decide how much control you want over your curriculum before you shop for materials with which to teach your curriculum. Textbooks and other learning materials *are not* curriculum. They *do not teach* curriculum. Your curriculum, as explained in Section Three, is your list of subject areas to be covered with accompanying rosters of learning goals in each subject area. Textbooks and other learning materials are aids to your children's learning and progression through the curriculum and they are aids to you as *you teach* the curriculum to your children. You, as teacher, control the curriculum and the textbooks and other materials; *they have no control over you* . . . unless, of course, you give them that control.

There are so many school materials and aids suppliers that listing them all here would be prohibitive. The following, therefore, is just a smattering of those available to you, but with these you should be able to locate suppliers who offer some of what you are looking for in learning or teaching materials and aids. Check with experienced home schoolers in your area, or even individual public school teachers at the grade levels you will teach, for suggestions and hands-on materials you can review. Visit a local computer store for educational software compatible with your computer, if you have one. Hundreds of educational computer programs are now available. Many large towns and cities also have school supply houses or stores which stock a multitude of items useful to teachers, parents, and parent teachers. Browse, too, through the children's section of a public library for titles and publishers of children's literature you may want to use. Return to Section Five in this book to find home-school organizations in your region that sponsor home-school curriculum and materials fairs that you might attend. Refer back, too, to question 9 in Section One for more materials ideas.

Lastly, remember that *you* can be an incredible resource of ideas for materials and aids, as well as for curriculums and settings for your children's home-school lessons. Also, I must emphasize again the importance of searching for materials that truly suit your style of teaching and philosophies and your children's styles and stages of learning. I also want to emphasize the importance of not relying too heavily on commercial materials rather than invented or environmental or human resources. As you begin teaching at home, you'll find yourself becoming more and more adept at creating your own materials based upon the learning needs and styles of your children and also at piecing together materials from more than one source.

[Note: When contacting the larger of the following sources, it may be beneficial to use a school name, even if yours is a one-family school, or a support group name indicating that several home schoolers will share catalogs and information. Suppliers will be happier to send free catalogs if they anticipate multiple sales.]

ABeka Book Publications (P.O. Box 18000, Pensacola FL 32532) Preschool through grade 12 Christian textbooks.

Addison-Wesley Publishing Co. (2725 Sand Hill Rd., Menlo Park CA 94025) The *Mathematics Their Way* materials, other manipulative math guides, other materials and textbooks, and software for several subject areas.

Alaska Nature Press (Box 632, Eagle River AK 99577) Nature books.

Alternative Education Sources (10506 Southshore Dr., Unionville IN 47468) Publications of interest to home schoolers.

American Christian History Institute (1093 Beechwood St., Camarillo CA 93010) Christian materials, principle approach, including Family Programs for Reading Aloud.

American Home Academy Materials (2770 S 1000 W, Perry UT 84302) Curriculum materials, including Brite music products, newsletter "Tender Tutor" for LDS members.

American Montessori Society (150 Fifth Ave., New York NY 10011) Teacher training and many publications related to child development and education.

American Textbook Committee (P.O. Box 8, Wadley AL 36276) Textbooks with a Christian perspective.

Ampersand Press (691 26th St., Oakland CA 94612) Game activities for science education.

Amsco School Publications (315 Hudson St., New York NY 10013) Textbooks, such as "Vocabulary for the High School Student," "Vocabulary for the College Bound" and others.

Animal Town Game Co. (P.O. Box 2002, Santa Barbara CA 93120) Cooperative and noncompetitive board games, puzzles, educational playthings, outdoor and group playthings, children's books, books on parenting and cooperation, rubber stamp sets, old time radio and nature tapes, science and nature kits.

Appalachian Mountain Club (5 Joy St., Boston MA 02108) Books about the outdoors, ecology, the environment, nature, recreation, photography, history.

ARCsoft Publishers (Box 132, Woodsboro MD 21798) Technical books including space science, personal computers, hobby electronics, especially for beginners.

Aristoplay Ltd. (334 E. Washington St., P.O. Box 7028, Ann Arbor MI 48107) Learning games.

Audio Forum (Rm. 1186, 96 Broad St., Guilford CT 06437) Audio cassette introductions to foreign languages (Spanish, French, German) for 5-10 year-olds, and other cassettes.

Bellerophon Books (36 Anacapa St., Santa Barbara CA 93101) Educational coloring books, cutout books, calendars, etc.

Bennett & McKnight (809 W. Detweiller Dr., Peoria IL 61615) Textbooks for home economics, industrial and technical education, career education, art, health, and vocational training — junior high through post-secondary.

Betterway Publications (White Hall VA 22987) Books about parenting, home-based businesses, home activities, and juvenile books.

Binford & Mort Publishing (1202 NW 17th Ave., Portland OR 97209) Books about Northwest biography, history, nature, recreation, reference, travel.

Binney & Smith (1107 Broadway, Rm. #1408, New York NY 10010) Art supplies and a booklet-guide to criteria for selecting and purchasing art supplies.

Blue Bird Publishing (1713 E. Broadway No. 306, Tempe AZ 85282) Publications of interest to home schoolers.

Bluestocking Press (P.O. Box 1014, Placerville CA 95667-1014) Materials for parents that promote reading, writing, & critical thinking in children.

Bob Jones University Press (Greenville SC 29614) Christian textbooks and a free home-school newsletter.

Bookmakers Guild, Inc. (Suite 202, 1430 Florida Ave., Longmont CO 80501) Books about children and families, child advocacy, behavior and education; children's literature.

Bookstuff (4B SW Monroe, Suite 139, Box 200, Lake Oswego OR 97034) Educational materials for thinking and problem solving.

Bosco Publications (475 North Ave., Box T, New Rochelle NY 10802) Books and textbooks for Christian education.

Bradshaw Publishers (Box 277, Bryn Mawr CA 92318) Biblical early readers for home-school use.

Buck Hill Associates (Box 28A, Out Church St., Saratoga NY 12866-2109) Replicas of historical posters, handbills, prints, broadsides, etc., for history education.

Builder Books (P.O. Box 7000-748, Redondo Beach CA 90277) Materials for various subject areas; books for parent educators and Christian character building.

Burt Harrison & Co. (P.O. Box 732, Weston MA 02193-0732) Materials for math & science education.

Byls Press (6247 N. Francisco Ave., Chicago IL 60659) How-to books for teachers; children's books about baking and Jewish holidays.

Caedmon Tapes (1995 Broadway, New York NY 10023) Recordings of children's literature.

California State Dept. of Education (Publication Sales, Box 271, Sacramento CA 95802-0271) Catalog of publications and curriculum frameworks such as the "History-Social Studies Framework."

Career Publishing, Inc. (Box 5486, Orange CA 92613-5486) High school textbooks.

Carolina Biological Supply Co. (2700 York Rd., Burlington NC 27215) Science supplies and nonfiction books for high school students.

Carstens Publications (Hobby Book Division, Box 700, Newton NJ 07860) Hobby books on model railroading, toy trains, model aviation.

Chaselle, Inc. (9645 Gerwig Lane, Columbia MD 21046) Toys and teaching materials and aids for infants through elementary and special education.

Childcraft Education Corporation (20 Kilmer Rd., Edison NJ 08818) Learning games & toys for infants and early childhood and special education; early childhood educational assessments.

Children's Book and Music Store (P.O. Box 1130, Santa Monica CA 90406) Records and tapes of children's literature and other books; children's books and musical instruments.

Children's Recordings (P.O. Box 1343, Eugene OR 97440) Story tapes.

Chinaberry Book Service (3160 Ivy St., San Diego CA 92104) Books of interest to parents; children's literature; videos; audio cassettes; toys; unusual books — all listed in a well-annotated catalog.

Christian Life Workshops (182 SE Kane Road, Gresham OR 97080) Workshops for parents on home-centered education, covering academics and family ministry from a biblical viewpoint.

Christian Teaching Materials Co. (P.O. Box 647, Santa Ynez CA 93460) A storeful of discounted, used textbooks, workbooks, and teacher's guides.

Cliffs Notes, Inc. (Box 80728, Lincoln NE 68501) Self-help study aids for junior high and up, teaching portfolios for literature lessons, textbooks.

Communication Skill Builders (Box 42050, Tucson AZ 85733) Materials for special education, early childhood education, speech-language education and therapy, and assessment materials.

Compute! Books (Box 5406, Greensboro NC 27403) Books about computers and computer programs and for computer education.

Consumer Information Center-G (P.O. Box 100, Pueblo CO 81002) "Consumer Information Catalog" of consumer education booklets, including several for children.

Consumer Reports Books (#1301, 110 E. 42nd St., New York NY 10017) How-to books for children.

Council for Basic Education ((725 Fifteenth Street NW, Washington DC 20005) A monthly journal, *Basic Education*, including updates on issues in education, books and reports including several relating to subject area teaching methods. Also, a speakers bureau, information, referrals, consultations.

George C. Crane Company (P.O. Box 426, Indianopolis, IN 46206) Materials for geography.

Creation's Child (1150 N W Alder Creek Drive, Corvallis OR 97330) Primary level materials.

Creative Learning Association (RR #4 Box 330, Charleston IL 61920) Computer literacy instructional kits.

Creative Publications (P.O. Box 10328, Palo Alto CA 94303) Math materials.

Cuisenaire Company of America (12 Church Street, New Rochelle NY 10805) Supplies for math education.

Davenport Publishers (26313 Purissima Rd., Los Altos Hills CA 94022) Children's nonfiction, children's literature, textbooks.

David C. Cook Publishers (850 N. Grove Ave., Elgin IL 60120) Christian materials.

Davis Publications (50 Portland St., Worcester MA 01608) K-6 art program.

Dennison (9601 Newton Ave. S., Minneapolis MN 55431) Early childhood teaching aids.

Discover: The World of Science (GTE School Program, 10 North Main St., Yardley PA 19067) Free teaching materials to accompany the PBS - TV series "Discover: The World of Science." Also, the series allows off-air taping rights to viewers so they can tape each segment in the series to collect their own science video library.

Discovery Crew (P.O. Box 113, Fiskdale MA 01518) A science education club which sends out a monthly boxful of science items and instructions for experiments, inquiry, and exploration

Eakin Publications (Box 23066, Austin TX 78735) Historical books for children.

Edmund Scientific (101 E. Gloucester Pike, Barrington NJ 08007) Supplies for science education.

Education Associates (Box 8021, Athens GA 30603) Books of interest to parent educators.

Educational Development Corporation (P.O. Box 470663, Tulsa OK 74147) Books for various subject areas.

Education Voucher Institute (26211 Central Park Blvd., Suite 324, Southfield MI 48076) A research center and information clearinghouse which makes available various publications related to education issues.

Educational Alternatives Bulletin Board Service: Log on 24 hours a day by dialing 408-353-2394 [300/1200 baud] for conferences related to educational issues, including home schooling and curriculum.

Educators Publishing Service (75 Moulton St., Cambridge MA 02238-9101) Preschool through grade 12 curriculum materials and textbooks, including those for the learning disabled.

Enslow Publishers (Bloy St. & Ramsey Ave., Box 777, Hillside NJ 07205) Books on science and social issues for children.

Entelek (Box 1303 Portsmouth NH 03801) Computer books and software of interest and use to home educators.

The Essential Whole Earth Catalog (Whole Earth Access, 2990 Seventh St., Berkeley CA 94710) Book and organization recommendations, learning resource people and groups.

ETC Publications (Drawer ETC, Palm Springs CA 92263) Textbooks; books on gifted education.

Evangelistic and Faith Enterprises (Rt. 2, Poplar Creek Rd., Oliver Springs TN 37840) Testing, record keeping, consultations.

Families on the Go (1259 El Camino Real #147, Menlo Park CA 94025) Books on places to travel and things to see with children from toddlers through teens; children's books; outdoor activity books.

The Family Educator (P.O. Box 309, Templeton CA 93465) Publications of interest to parent teachers, intensive phonics and arithmetic materials, principle approach materials.

Family Pastimes (RR 4, Perth, Ontario, Canada, K7H 3C6) Cooperative games.

Family Resource Coalition (230 N. Michigan Ave., Suite 1625, Chicago IL 60601) Activities, conferences, monitoring and lobbying policy makers with the purpose of promoting the development of prevention-oriented, community-based programs to strengthen families.

Fleet Press Corp. (160 Fifth Ave., New York NY 10010) Juvenile books on history, arts, religion, sports, and biographies; stresses social studies and minority subjects; for ages 8-15.

Foreign Languages Through Song & Story (P.O. Box 293, Coeur d'Alene ID 83814) Materials for foreign language instruction.

Frank Schaffer Publications (1028 Via Mirabel, Dept. 415, Palos Verdes Estate CA 90274) A variety of teaching aids.

"Free Education Guide," by Michelle Sokoloff (502 Woodside Ave., Narberth PA 19072) A directory of available free books and materials.

Garden Way Publishing (Schoolhouse Rd., Pownal VT 05261) How-to books on gardening, cooking, animals, country living, country business.

Gazelle Publications (5580 Stanley Drive, Auburn CA 95603) Publications of interest to and for use by home educators.

Gentle Wind (Box 3103, Albany NY 12203) Story tapes.

Geode Educational Options (P.O. Box 106, West Chester PA 19381) Materials which facilitate ethical, responsible, ecological parenting and teaching and materials that stimulate the thinking and creativity of children. (215) 692-0413.

Gifted Child Today Inc. (314-350 Weinacker Ave., P.O. Box 6448, Mobile AL 36660-0448) Curriculum materials and aids for gifted, creative, and talented learners.

Gifted Education Press (10201 Yuma Ct., Box 1586, Manassas VA 22110) Books about how to educate gifted children, including teaching procedures, methods, and curriculum.

Ginn & Co. (P.O. Box 573, Lexington MA 02173) Textbooks.

Globe Book Company (50 West 23rd St., New York NY10010) Textbooks.

Good Apple, Inc. (Box 299, Carthage IL 62321) Teaching materials for various subject areas, preschool through junior high, including religious education, books, tapes, software, and more.

Greenhaven Press (577 Shoreview Park Rd., St. Paul MN 55126) Juvenile books, reference books, textbooks — animals, business and economics, history, nature, philosophy, politics, psychology, religion, sociology. for grades 3-8.

Gryphon House (3706 Otis St., Box 275, Mount Rainier MD 20712) How-to books and creative educational activities for home teachers of preschoolers and kindergartners.

Hammond Inc. (515 Valley St., Maplewood NJ 07040) Map skills materials.

Harcourt Brace Jovanovich (1250 Sixth Ave., San Diego CA 92101) Textbooks.

Harvest House (1075 Arrowsmith, Eugene OR 97402) Juvenile books, reference books, textbooks.

Hearth and Home Ministries (P.O. Box 835105, Richardson TX 75083) Publications of interest to home-school families. (214) 231-9838.

Hearthsong (2211 Blucher Valley Rd., Sebastopol CA 95472) Wholesale art supplies, toys and books.

Holt, Rhinehart and Winston (383 Madison Ave., New York NY 10017) Textbooks.

Home Educators Computer Users Group – Bulletin Board Service: Log on between 3 pm and 5 am, Monday-Friday, and 24-hours daily on weekends and holidays, by dialing 301-937-2303 [300/1200 baud] for legal news and resource and support group lists.

Home School Supplies (3446 N. Avenida de la Colina, Tucson AZ 85749) Materials, both Christian and secular, in various curricular areas.

Home School Supply House (3254 E. Mitchell, Petoskey MI 49770) Textbooks, science kits, art supplies, children's literature.

Homeschooling Marketplace (Rt. 2 Box 11, Fontanelle IA 50846-9702) An advertising flyer of home-school resources; a directory of home-school newsletters.

Homestead Publishing (Box 193, Moose WY 83102) Natural history and nature books for children.

Honey Tree Educational Services (Rd. 10, Woodville Rd., Mansfield OH 44903) Materials for home education.

Hoover Educational Equipment (P.O. Box 1009, Kansas City MO 64141) General teaching supplies.

Houghton Mifflin (Two Park St., Boston MA 02107) Textbooks.

Humanics Limited (Suite 201, 1389 Peachtree St. NE, Atlanta GA 30309) Resource books for teachers.

Incentive Publications (3835 Cleghorn Ave., Nashville TN 37215) Resource books for teachers.

Institute for Creation Research (P.O. Box 2666, El Cajon CA 92021-0666) Materials and workshops on science education.

International Reading Association (800 Barksdale Rd., P.O. Box 8139, Newark DE 19711) Resource books and booklets for K-12 reading.

Interstate Printers (19 N. Jackson St., Box 50, Danville IL 61834-0050) High school vocational education textbooks.

Jalmar Press (45 Hitching Post Dr., Bldg. 2, Rolling Hill Estates CA 90274-4297) Self-esteem materials for parenting and teaching; peacemaking skills activities for parenting and teaching; self-concept and values materials.

Jamestown Publishers (Box 9168, Providence RI 02940) Textbooks and teaching booklets for improving reading, literature, and study skills, K-12.

JerryCo., Inc. (601 Linden Place, Evanston IL 60202) Surplus educational and other supplies.

John Holt's Book and Music Store (2269 Massachusetts Avenue, Cambridge MA 02140) Books of interest to parent educators and texts, materials and publications for use in home schools.

Joyful Learning (Box 1294 RD 2, Douts Hill RD., Holtwood PA 17532) A catalog of over 350 educational enrichment materials; assistance in locating materials appropriate to individual situations.

Just for Kids (324 Raritan Ave., Highland Park NJ 08904) Toy, game, and learning products for elementary-age children.

Kar-Ben Copies (6800 Tildenwood Ln., Rockville MD 10852) Jewish children's literature and nonfiction.

Katzenmeyer's (3010 E. Williamette, Littleton CO 80121) Discounted books and curricula.

Key Curriculum Press (P.O. Box 2304, Berkeley CA 94702) Materials for math education; computer software.

Keys to Learning International (1411 Oak St., So. Pasadena CA 91030) Materials, workshops, newsletter, field trips.

Lakeshore Curriculum Materials (P.O. Box 6261, Carson CA 90749) Infant, preschool, elementary, and special education curriculum materials and supplies.

Larson Publications (4936 Rt. 414, Burdett NY 14818) Books and audio tapes of interest to home schoolers.

Learning Publications (5351 Gulf Dr., Holmes Beach FL 33510) Reference books for teachers, books to help parents of children with reading problems and special needs, teachers' art activity books.

Learning Things, Inc. (P.O. Box 436, Arlington MA 02174) Math, science, and other learning aids.

Learning Together Directory (P.O. Box 60, Montvale VA 24122) Used books, instruments, computers, etc.

Lee's Books for Young Readers (813 West Ave., Box 111, O'Neil Professional Bldg., Wellington TX 79095) Nonfiction historical books for junior high reluctant readers.

Library and Educational Services (8784 Valley View Drive, P.O. Box 146, Berrien Springs MI 49103) Wholesale books for Christian education.

Lippincott (E. Washington Square, Philadelphia PA 19105) Phonics and other subject area textbooks.

Longman, Inc. (95 Church St., White Plains NY 10601) Textbooks.

McGraw-Hill Book Co. (1221 Ave. of the Americas, New York NY 10020) Textbooks and other curriculum materials; achievement tests.

Macmillan (866 Third Ave., New York NY 10022) Textbooks.

Michael Olaf (5817 College Ave. {Rockridge}, Oakland CA 94618) Books, musical instruments, cooperative games, and other learning aids.

The Mind's Eye (P.O. Box 6727, San Francisco CA 94101) Children's literature on cassette tapes.

Modern Curriculum Press (13900 Prospect Rd., Cleveland OH 44136) Textbooks.

Morrow & Co. (105 Madison Ave., New York NY 10016) Children's books, textbooks.

Mother's Bookshelf (P.O. Box 70, Hendersonville NC 28791) How-to and self-help books.

Multiplication Made Easy (20380 Excelsior Blvd., Excelsior MN 55331) Apple computer software.

Music for Little People (P.O. Box 1460, Redway CA 95560) Cassettes, videos, musical instruments for music education.

Nasco (901 Janesville Ave., Ft. Atkinson WI 53538) Educational materials for science, home economics, arts and crafts, math, elementary and special education, agriculture.

National Center for Constitutional Studies (P.O. Box 37110, Washington DC 20013) Educational materials related to the United States Constitution, for all grade levels.

National Geographic Society (17th & M Streets NW, Washington DC 20036) Educational magazines and other publications, maps and globes.

National Home Study Council (1601 18th St. NW, Washington DC 20009) Professional development program for home-study educators, magazine, publications.

National Wildlife Federation (1412 16th St. NW, Washington DC 20036) *Ranger Rick, Your Big Backyard, National Wildlife* nature magazines for children, a Gardening with Wildlife Kit, and teaching manuals for all levels on nature/science subjects — ask for *NatureScope* manuals catalog.

National Women's History Project (P.O. Box 3716, Santa Rosa CA 95402-3716) Curriculums and learning materials for teaching about women in American history. Multicultural.

Norris Science Labs and Kits (4561 Sacks Drive, Las Vegas NV 89122) Materials for science education.

Nystrom Atlases (3333 Elston Ave., Chicago IL 60618) Atlases.

Open Court Publishing Co. (P.O. Box 599, Peru IL 61354-0599) Reading and mathematics textbooks and aids.

Palmer Co. (1720 W. Irving Park Rd., Schaumberg IL 60193) Materials for handwriting education.

Parenting Press, Inc. (7744 31st Ave. NE, Suite 726 A, Seattle WA 98115) Children's books that deal with problem solving, decision-making, safety, self-esteem, and cooperative living.

Perfection Form Co. (1000 No. Second Ave., Logan IA 51546) Teaching materials including "Reading Beyond the Basals" teaching guides for use with children's literature.

Prentice Hall (School Division of Simon & Schuster, Englewood Cliffs NJ 07632) Textbooks.

Presents for the Promising (P.O. Box 134, Sewel NJ 08080) Books of interest to parents of gifted/talented children; teaching aids; books and games for gifted/talented children.

Priority Parenting Publications (P.O. Box 1793, Warsaw IN 46580) Publishes "Priority Parenting," a newsletter for alternative parents who believe in *natural* child rearing, and other publications covering topics related to parenting but that may be considered out of the mainstream, such as home schooling.

Reading Reform Foundation (949 Market St., Suite 436, Tacoma WA 98402) A national, nonprofit organization which encourages the teaching of intensive phonics in reading instruction. Provides information, materials, workshops, speakers, courses, referrals, consulting, and a newsletter all related to reading instruction for parents and other teachers.

Resources for the Gifted (P.O. Box 15050, Phoenix, AZ 85060) Materials for gifted education.

Revels, Inc. (Box 290, Cambridge MA 02238) Children's records and books.

The Riggs Institute (4185 SW 102nd Ave., Beaverton OR 97005) *Writing Road to Reading* and other materials.

Rubberstampede (P.O. Box 1105, Berkeley CA 94701) Assorted rubber stamp products for children, kits with stationery, alphabet sets, ink pads in several colors.

S & S Arts & Crafts (Colchester CT 06415) Supplies for arts and crafts education.

Scholastic, Inc. (P.O. Box 7501, 2931 E. McCarty St., Jefferson City MO 65102) Textbooks; filmstrips for social studies.

School Zone Publishing Co. (P.O. Box 692, Grand Haven MI 49417) A parent-teacher catalog; materials and aids.

Scott, Foresman & Co. (1900 E. Lake Ave., Glenview IL 60025) Textbooks; educational software.

Shekinah Curriculum Cellar (967 Junipero Dr., Costa Mesa CA 92626) Materials and aids, including Christian.

Silver Burdett & Ginn (4343 Equity Drive, P.O. Box 2649, Columbus OH 43216) Textbooks.

Social Studies School Service (P.O. Box 802, Culver City CA 90232) Materials on history, home economics, geography, government.

Story-Stone (Another Place, Rt. 123, Greenville NH 03048) Story tapes.

Sycamore Tree (2179 Meyer Pl, Costa Mesa CA 92627) Instructional materials for various subject areas, including Christian; newsletter, testing, record keeping, legal insurance.

Symbiosis Books (8 Midhill Drive, Mill Valley CA 94941) Curriculum packages, aids and publications.

Textbooks for Parents (Box 209, Kendrick ID 83537) Textbooks and teacher's guides from a variety of publishers for K-12 home-teaching, curriculum advice and assistance by mail or phone. (208)883-0991. Alternate address: 405 N. Jefferson, Moscow ID 83843.

Thinkseeds (P.O. Box 777, Rockport ME 04856) Books, audio and video tapes.

Thomas Geale Publishers (Drawer C.P. 223, 1142 Manhattan Ave., Manhattan Beach CA 90266) K-12 thinking skills workbooks.

Timberdoodle (E. 1610 Spencer Lake Rd., Shelton WA 98584) Hands-on learning materials that encourage critical thinking.

TOPS Learning Systems (10970 So. Mulino Rd., Canby OR 97013) Task cards and activity sheets for science education.

Wilcox & Follett Book Co. (1000 W. Washington Blvd., Chicago IL 60607) Textbooks and workbooks — used and new, current and older editions.

World Book - Childcraft International. (6 Merchandize Mart Plaza, Chicago IL 60654) Learning sets and materials in various subject areas.

Young Astronauts Council (P.O. Box 65432, Washington DC 20036) Youth chapters throughout the nation which engage in science activities.

The Young Naturalist Foundation (56 The Esplanade, Suite 306, Toronto, Ontario M5E 1A7, Canada) Environmental magazines *Chicadee* and *OWL*, books, computer games, annual awards program.

Zaner-Bloser (P.O. Box 16764, Columbus OH 43216) Handwriting workbooks.

✳✳✳

Appendix **A**

Teaching Methods/ Approaches

Teaching Methods/Approaches

American home schools, religious and other private schools, and public schools incorporate a wide variety of teaching methods or approaches, some more commonly used than others. You may need at least a cursory understanding of these methods during discussions with school officials and with other home schoolers, throughout your search for and analysis of curriculums and materials, and during your reading of home-schooling literature. Thus the aim here is definition and familiarization.

The methods listed below and others can be blended for combined use in many ways. Also, one approach may be used for one subject and another approach for another subject, and different subjects may be taught with differing combinations of methods. Teachers (like you) are free to create their own methods and styles of teaching any given subject. In most instances, I have briefly noted means by which home teachers could implement each approach.

Teachers select teaching methods according to student learning styles, ages, needs; the form and content of the subject to be taught; the teacher's own teaching style; the availability of suitable materials and resources; and other considerations. Home educators have the double advantage of close observation of individual student learning styles and the flexibility to apply when appropriate any of the possible teaching methods.

Following the descriptions of seventeen approaches that may be used in any curricular area are fourteen methods particular to the teaching of reading.

General Instruction Methods/Approaches

1. activity-centered learning In activity-centered learning children engage in manipulative, experiential, physically active learning activities. In public school classrooms learning centers may be set up or special equipment used for such activities. At home you can more easily take children to the real setting — such as a forest, a pond, a garden, a tool shed, a kitchen — for activity-centered lessons. These lessons don't always involve an entire setting; they may simply involve materials or items for activity, such as pattern blocks and measuring implements for activity-centered math lessons.

2. learning center approach In the same manner that highways, trails, lakes, and rivers constructed in a sandbox by an aspiring 5-year-old trucker make a playing (and learning) center, learning centers in school can be used for experiential, exploratory, activity-centered learning. A learning center is a space designed to stimulate learning through various activities that are made possible in the center. The child selects the activities in which he wishes to participate. In a public or private school classroom, for example, a nature learning center might include such items as an aquarium, a terrarium, crosscuts of small logs and branches, a nature filmstrip on a small screen for individual use, nature books for children, a large diagram of the structure of a tree with magnetic labels for the parts, a forest-scene puzzle, a live rabbit, a nature-related worksheet, books on cassette tape available for listening with earphones, and so on. Usually learning centers aren't solo approaches to teaching a subject; centers will be supplementary to other more direct methods. At home school you can also construct learning centers. However, as with activity-centered learning above, at home school *real* settings can easily and probably more effectively be used as learning centers.

3. mastery learning With this approach instruction involves the identification (through testing) of those parts of an instructional unit that a student did not learn, reteaching this material through peer-tutoring or programmed learning or some other means not usually the same as the initial teaching, and finally evaluating learning through testing that pits the learner against criteria of mastery rather than against her fellow students. The home teacher may design or purchase ready-made mastery learning materials.

4. programmed learning With programmed learning the student functions in great part on his own, materials in hand. The materials include questions the student answers and a correction column or an answer card which he then checks to determine whether or not his responses are correct. The student is thus given immediate corrective or affirmative feedback. If he does well, he may go on to the next lesson. If he does poorly, he repeats the lesson or completes a reteaching lesson. In effect, the textbook is the teacher and lessons primarily involve literal recall and rote memorization. Several text series are available which use the programmed learning approach exclusively. Such a set of materials would be essential were a home teacher planning to use this approach.

5. computer-assisted instruction (CAI) Instruction is presented to students with the aid of a personal computer. Computer-assisted instruction may involve visual presentations, interactive exercises, creativity activities, and even sophisticated simulations of real-life situations such as operating a plane's flight instruments. CAI is usually supplementary to instruction by a teacher. Obviously, a home teacher would need to have the necessary computer equipment on hand, a knowledge of how to use that equipment, and access to educational software.

6. competency-based instruction With this approach learning is measured through demonstrations of a student's skills or knowledge, as opposed to being measured by the amount of time spent exposed to instruction. Having completed a unit of study within an allotted period of time would not constitute real completion unless the needed skills had been gained. Likewise, having completed a year of third grade would not necessarily qualify a student for classification as a fourth grader, unless competency of expected third grade skills had been demonstrated. This approach is not commonly applied in our public schools or even most private schools, but a home teacher could easily base her instruction upon student-demonstrated competencies.

7. direct instruction Direct instruction is formally said to occur when the teacher states the learner objective, gives small bits of instruction, models the skills involved, and then asks for student response . . . then more instruction and more response, and so on throughout the lesson. Research supports such direct instruction, which, incidently, can be practiced by the teacher in any subject area and with any materials other than programmed materials. Some teaching materials, typically for language arts and reading, identify their teaching approach as "direct instruction." With these materials unison response is usually requested so that no one student leads or prompts the response. In this way, theoretically, each student must remain alert to the instruction and the teacher can quickly determine if one student has missed an item. Then reteaching can be immediately applied.

The term *direct instruction* is also sometimes used to refer simply to lessons in which there is much student-teacher interaction.

8. traditional An approach described as "traditional" would include the basics in subject matter and be text-based and teacher-directed rather than child-directed, activity-centered, or innovative. Traditional materials are available to home teachers.

9. unit study approach With this approach lessons are grouped into broad units of study, each followed by tests or other assessments to determine skills and knowledge gained throughout the entire unit. Through this method students are able, for example, to view happenings or concepts in survey form, in chronological form; i.e., time-based units, or in large subcategories of a given subject. For instance, history units might be segmented by centuries or decades or major historical events. This is a commonly used approach and involves the use of other approaches or teaching methods as well. A home teacher may either locate materials arranged in units of study or design her own units of study by drawing from various sources and including various resources and activities.

10. child-directed learning (aka child-centered learning) Lessons that are child-directed proceed in directions established by the child as his next step, his next interest, his next challenge, his next enthusiasm. Lesson formats may be somewhat designed by the teacher but in an unimposing fashion and with the student's input. Lesson objectives are based upon the child's current keenest interests or needs within a curricular area. The child-directed learning method is typically most used with preschool and primary grade children. This approach is particularly possible for home schoolers, since the home teacher doesn't instruct large numbers of students with widely varying interests. Purchased as well as self-made materials can be used — as necessitated by the child-established goals of the lessons.

11. integrated subject areas The teacher who uses the integrated subject approach will draw from several curricular areas at once to teach any unit of study. For example, a history unit on the American Civil War might include Civil War poetry and song, military statistics, dioramas of the housing of Civil War soldiers, the literature of slavery, the economic impact of the war, the writing by students of letters between fictitious cousins living on opposite sides of the Mason-Dixon line, the enactment of a Civil War drama, the singing of spirituals, a video of "Red Badge of Courage," as well as the reading of the Civil War section of the history text. Thus the curricular areas of literature, mathematics, architecture, social history, economics, creative writing, drama, music, and visual arts are blended or integrated in order to teach the *history* lesson.

The theory behind the integrated approach is that in order to fully understand any one segment of study, such as the Civil War, a student needs to view the whole scene, understand the full scope of influencing factors, develop a sense for the ambiance of the entire situation, recognize how many variables fitted together to create the situation. The integrated approach also allows for input involving both creative and logical thinking and all of the physical senses, thus enhancing the possibility that students with varying learning styles will learn. The integrated approach to teaching is research supported and is easily adaptable to home teaching. With a little practice, the home teacher can learn to design lessons in an integrated fashion.

12. diagnostic/prescriptive learning With this approach a child is given a pretest to determine his deficiencies and strengths before a particular unit of study, then he is taught whatever he appears to need in order to acquire the deficient skills and finally he is given a post-test. In other words, instruction is designed (prescribed) according to the results of the pretest (diagnosis). The student does not spend time working on skills he has already mastered. Thus instruction is individualized to meet a student's particular needs. A parent could construct pre- and post-tests for any upcoming home-school lesson if she chose to use the diagnostic/prescriptive method. Also, many commercial materials are designed with this approach built in.

13. individualized instruction When a teacher individualizes his instruction, he determines the learning needs of each student and designs instruction to meet those specific needs. Students with similar needs may be grouped for instruction. Thus individualized instruction does not require one-on-one teaching. At home, individualized instruction can be accomplished much more easily than in a full classroom setting. As you begin to home school, you will find yourself increasingly tuned in to your children's learning needs and at the same time more and more able to design instruction to meet their individual needs. Individualizing instruction to meet student needs is a research-supported approach.

14. manipulative learning Instruction that allows for manipulative learning includes much handling, exploring, and manipulating of real objects by students. Although research supported, manipulative learning is underused in our public schools partly because of the number of pupils in typical classes and the unavailability in the classroom of many real objects, but can easily become an integral part of home learning. Manipulative learning is useful, for example, in early math instruction, for experiments in science instruction, and for developing experiences upon which the writing and reading of stories can be based. This approach is especially suited for younger learners because their foremost means of learning is manipulation.

15. principle approach The principle approach usually involves lessons which are based upon biblical precepts and perspectives.

Study and activities involve research, reasoning, relating, and record-ing (writing) of biblical principles and truths as applied to lesson top-ics. The principle approach lends itself to an integrated subject area approach as well, for the learner's research may include a blend of correlated information and resources, including as its core, of course, the Bible. The Christian home schooler may choose this as her pri-mary method of instruction, particularly with study areas such as history, science, personal development, government, international relations, and so on.

16. thematic lessons   Lessons or units of study may be centered around a significant concept, abstraction, or theme. An integrated subject area approach may be taken with respect to the theme. For example, were a thematic unit centered on love, the unit might include love poetry, biographies of persons whose lives were based upon the extension of loving acts of brotherhood towards others, love as the river of Christian expression and motivation, histories involv-ing significant events stemming from love/hate motives, stories exploring family relationships, the writing of personal essays on the subject of love, a stage play with a love theme, special recognition of those people in a child's life whom he loves, and so on. The home teacher can handily create study units centering on such themes and involving varying activities and resources.

17. the writing process   Composition assignments in public schools have traditionally been oriented towards the end product, the final form of the composition. Students were shown what a paragraph, essay, poem, short story, or other form was and then were asked to write one. The process a student used was not taught. Today the pro-cess of writing has become as important as the product in writing instruction. When the writing process is taught, learners begin with the thinking that must occur before one can write — in effect, brain-storming. During this stage ideas may fly in many directions related to the central topic, but are given form shortly afterwards by the identification of the writer's audience and his purpose for telling that audience what he wants to tell them. Then composing rough writings takes place and may involve free-writing — uncensored and nonstop writing of one's spontaneous thoughts about a topic. Next the stu-dent revises. Rough work is read, oftentimes aloud to other students for feedback, and then it is reread, perhaps several times. With each reading the student may ask for help from listeners who may offer straightforward reactions to what the student has written — what pleases, what is clear, what is awkward or confusing, what is thor-ough, what needs further detail, what is out of order, what needs to be more concrete, and so on. Following these reactions, the writer returns to his writing, pencil in hand, to consider the reactions and to revise as he wishes. Once revision has been fairly well completed so that a final copy is close at hand, editing occurs. Editing involves checking and improving the mechanical aspects of writing — punctuation, spelling, grammar, layout, neatness, and so on. Then the student is ready, if required, to write a final copy for submission to the teacher who as soon as possible provides feedback. Research indicates that teaching which includes the writing process (in various subject areas) improves learners' writing skills.

Home educators and home learners can become writing partners in the writing process by helping each other think — cooperative brainstorming, if you will — and by being listeners who offer feedback to each other's writings. Use of the writing process can and should become integral to every subject area in which a learner writes.

Reading Instruction Methods/Approaches

A reading instruction program includes several components. Learning to read begins, for example, with unwritten language. Thus the first component in a child's reading development is oral — first listening, then speaking. When a teacher first begins to formally teach reading to a youngster, oral language activities of various sorts precede and later are intermixed with activities involving written letters, words, and sentences. Second, written symbols — letters — are presented for identification and decoding. Letter identification, letter-sound associations (phonics), sounds affected by letter positions in words, blended letter sounds, word-part families of sounds, and whole-word reading (sight reading) — all are forms of decoding and may be elements of beginning reading instruction.

While oral language experiences constitute the first component of a child's reading program, and decoding activities the second, reading comprehension; i.e., understanding, is the focus of the third component. Oral language activities often aim to stimulate comprehension of oral words, sentences, and compositions, and some aid comprehension of written material. However, all of the above symbol-related activities only teach the decoding of letters and words; none teaches reading comprehension. Decoding alone is not reading — in full. Nor does comprehension alone enable the reading of written symbols. Decoding facilitates comprehension. Comprehension, in turn, makes decoding worthwhile and meaningful. Therefore, beginning reading instruction must involve both decoding and comprehension. As the learner advances in reading ability, decoding lessons are no longer needed, but comprehension activities remain valuable.

A fourth component of reading instruction is fluency, which involves the speed and flow of a child's reading. Skillful decoding and good comprehension enhance the development of reading fluency.

Controversy exists in the United States regarding the best methods of teaching beginning reading. Three approaches, in particular, are currently at the center of conflicting views: the sight word approach (which critics call "the look-say method"), intensive phonics instruction, and the whole-language approach which has most recently appeared on the scene. The best and most effective resolution of the conflict regarding these three methods is simply to recognize that none of the three need be used exclusive of the others. While phonics instruction is research supported and should be included as part of any beginning reading program, phonics by itself does not constitute an entire reading program. Oral language experiences, comprehension activities, and fluency development should also be included. Likewise, any use of the sight word approach should be in combination with other methods — including phonics.

Used alone, the sight word approach is slow and restrictive. Finally, while the whole-language approach places much emphasis on comprehension and the wholeness of language versus language parts, it is, nevertheless, inherently a combined approach. Any description of its components will show you that word attack, vocabulary development, fluency, comprehension, story schema, language experience, and so on, are all involved — and sight word reading as well as phonics instruction can be integrated into a whole-language reading program, or vise versa.

In other words, polarized views towards these three or any other reading instruction method are unnecessary. If you feel intensive phonics is the best early reading instruction method, fine. However, that conviction need not leave you fearful or disdainful of other methods. Your phonics lessons will teach the decoding (unlocking symbols) component, but you can select other approaches to teach comprehension and fluency. Study them all and develop a blend of methods that works well for you and your children.

One consideration that may influence your selection of methods is your children's individual learning styles. For example, if you have a child who does not learn well aurally (through sound), phonics instruction may be more difficult for him than for other children. Then you can look for alternative methods to supplement phonics instruction. Perhaps that child is a strong visual learner, able to mentally "photograph" word configurations. For him, sight word instruction may be a helpful side dish to his phonics lessons.

As you read the following explanations of reading instruction methods, therefore, try to think in terms of possible combinations and of methods most suited to your children's styles of learning and stages in reading development. Recognize, too, that nearly all seventeen of the general instruction methods may apply to reading instruction. A reading program, for example, may be a direct instruction program. Activity-centered exercises or a learning center may help build background knowledge for readings. Unit study in reading could be segmented by forms of literature — poetry, short stories, novels, essays — or by themes. Diagnostic/prescriptive or mastery learning methods may be applied to reading instruction. Reading selections and activities could be based upon the principle approach. Computer activities can assist you with reading instruction. Likewise, many of the reading methods below could facilitate reading done in connection with any subject area, not just during reading instruction. For example, activities involving language experience, word attack, comprehension, vocabulary, sustained silent reading, and whole-language could be valuable to reading required in any content area — social studies, science, home economics, health, and others. So look for ways to combine approaches.

1. oral language methods Listening and talking are prerequisites to reading and writing. Therefore, at the primary level reading instruction includes oral language activities, such as listening to directions that require a physical response, listening to and discussing children's books read aloud, storytelling, listening to puppet shows, conversing about topics related to readings, performing skits or plays, talking on the telephone or CB radio, choral reading, recognizing and reciting rhymed words or lines, oral use of key vocabulary in upcoming readings, sharing personal anecdotes, listening to taped stories, responding to informal questions, listening to and reciting poetry, and many other oral language activities.

While oral language activities are vital at the primary level, they only partially diminish in importance as children become more advanced readers. At the intermediate level and beyond, storytelling, play performances, choral readings, background discussions for upcoming readings, and vocabulary practice are particularly beneficial to students' reading achievement. At the secondary level, in all subject areas, much conversation involving topics about which students soon will be reading and oral practice with vocabulary which will appear in upcoming readings are valuable to most students and often crucial to the poorer readers.

Despite their importance, oral language methods are not often built into commercial learning materials, especially for intermediate and older children. However, beginning with the suggested activities above, you can design and conduct even casually many oral language experiences for your children.

2. sight word approach With this approach an instructor teaches single whole words until quick sight recognition is achieved by the student. The words taught are those that appear in the *readers* (story texts) that are used in the classroom. Typically the teacher introduces each word by writing it in view of the student, reading it aloud, and then having the student read it aloud and write it himself. Independent activities follow which involve responses to and applications of the learned word. Through repeated exposure, the student memorizes the word and then practices reading it in the context of a story. Eventually the student builds a *sight vocabulary* (a body of words he recognizes instantly).

The sight word approach may be used particularly as a supplement for learners who do not easily learn to read using another approach such as phonics, for learners who are especially oriented to visual learning, or as one of a combination of methods. Sight-reading materials can be purchased by the home teacher, or she can learn the method itself and select words to include in graduated levels of difficulty and/or that can be applied in the actual reading of selected children's literature. There are also available basic lists of sight words for sequential levels of learning.

3. phonics The teacher teaches the letter sounds one-by-one and then teaches how they are blended to form words. Students learn to *sound out* words (read by letter sounds). Typically students are first taught beginning consonant sounds, then ending consonant sounds, then vowel sounds, several combined-letter sounds, and the rules for blending sounds. As they learn the letter sounds they are given practice in blending the sounds to read simple one-syllable words, then brief sentences, then two-syllable words and slightly longer sentences, and so on.

The more work a student does with letter-sounding to read words, the closer he gets to instant recognition of whole words; i.e., sight recognition. So eventually he develops a sight vocabulary for which he no longer needs to use the phonics method he has learned. To read unfamiliar words, however, he can continue to use the phonics method. A home teacher wishing to use the phonics approach would be wise to purchase phonics-based reading materials in order to determine a sound sequence of instruction and to ensure the inclusion of all phonic elements. Many such materials are available. Materials which integrate other methods with the phonics method also exist.

Research supports the use of the phonics method with beginning readers. It has its best effect when it is one part of an overall reading program and is not taught as a separate subject. Phonics instruction should be completed with reasonable rapidity — by the end of the child's first year of reading instruction, if possible, or his second.

4. linguistics Like phonics, linguistics uses letter sounds. However, with the linguistics approach the teacher teaches groups of letter sounds that frequently appear together to form *word families* (sets of words in which the same sequence of sounds appears, such as *-end* in lend, send, mend; or *-og* in dog, log, frog). Students learn to instantly recognize the group-sound and to heed the initial letter in order to read new words.

The ability to rhyme is an important prerequisite to linguistic learning; thus rhyming is often taught first — orally, with no print in sight. The linguistic method is frequently integrated into a phonics approach for the teaching of reading. As with the sight method and the phonics method, eventually the student develops a sight vocabulary of tens, then hundreds, and then thousands of words. Unfamiliar words can still be attacked linguistically. The purchase of specifically linguistic materials would be wise for the home educator wishing to use this method.

5. language experience approach When this approach is used, the child's own language becomes the basis for instruction. He dictates to a teacher or aide, or talks into a tape recorder, or learns to type his own words into a computer. He will later see his words, phrases, sentences, and stories in print (provided by the teacher or aide) and learn to read them. He may also learn to read stories, rhymes and songs that were previously auditorily familiar to him. The theory behind the language experience approach is that a learner learns best by beginning with what he himself experiences and knows. He learns to read his own expressions about his own experiences and his own knowledge before learning to read about the experiences and knowledge of others in the words of others.

While watching his words being translated into symbols, he learns the link between spoken and written language. He may be given the experience of *writing* the words himself by tracing with colored pencil or crayon over the teacher's writing. When his composition is read back to him, the spoken/written link is reinforced, comprehension is again engendered, and the child may do his first reading of his own discourse.

His own language, then, becomes a vehicle for instruction and is typically not corrected in writing or reading unless meaning is hampered. In other words, reading errors are accepted unless the meaning of the text is altered by the error. If, for example, a child has been reading about a boy named Bill but when the child sees the word *Bill* on the page, she says *boy*, no correction would be offered by the teacher because the meaning of the passage had not been changed. In fact, it is apparent that the meaning is clearly understood by the child. If, on the other hand, the child says *bag* instead of *Bill*, the meaning of the passage would be changed and the child would need correction. It is apparent in this latter case that the child does not comprehend the meaning of the passage or he would not *read* a word that doesn't make sense in the passage.

This approach is used mostly with primary students. Public school classroom management and organization often make this approach difficult to include, but such instruction could easily become a daily occurrence at home school and requires no special training or even special materials on the part of the home instructor — just a clear understanding of the process and the many various applications of it to lesson activities. Also, it blends well with other approaches as part of an overall reading program.

6. word attack in context   Some approaches to teaching reading primarily involve sounding out symbols — letters and punctuation — on a page, such as phonics. Such decoding comprises a reader's basic processes for *word attack* (means of figuring out unfamiliar words). However, there are additional means having to do with the *context* (sentence or composition) within which an unfamiliar word appears. These means involve reading comprehension; i.e., an understanding of the meaning of the words and sentences on a page.

The *Bill-boy-bag* illustration above is one example. The child must comprehend the passage in which the word *Bill* appears in order to decode that word accurately or with a logical substitution such as *boy.* Through word attack instruction the teacher encourages the child to heed clues that occur in the passage or context. Use of these *context clues* depends upon the reader's comprehension of the passage and can be used to figure out unfamiliar words. Perhaps, for example, the sentence in which the word Bill appeared included references to a boy's basketball game and masculine pronouns such as *his* and *him.* Obviously, a girl would not be named and a bag would not be involved in the meaning of that sentence. The context clues would limit the reader's choices for decoding the word *Bill.* Materials are available which include the teaching of such word attack techniques to youngsters, but the home teacher who simply learns about the techniques could help a child learn to use them with any reading that he does.

7. comprehension activities The goal of reading comprehension activities is the child's understanding of the meaning of a written passage. Unfortunately, many public schools tend to emphasize decoding activities while neglecting comprehension activities. At home school you needn't make that error if you keep in mind that the ultimate goal of **all** reading is comprehension. Virtually no reading lessons should occur without comprehension activities. Otherwise the beginner may believe that decoding symbols equals *reading, in toto,* whereas in actuality decoding is merely one reading task, a route to comprehension. Reading, in the whole, must result in understanding . . . *meaning* . . . comprehension.

When a child is first learning to read, comprehension activities are oral. Oral comprehension is the natural prerequisite to the comprehension of written material, as noted in number *1* above. Oral comprehension activities should be one component of a reading comprehension program.

Oral storytelling and story reading, for example, can encourage students' recognition of what is called "story schema." Story schema are the parts of a story that we can expect will be present, such as a setting, an event from which conflict evolves, a sequence of events that build suspense and develop the plot, a climactic event, and an ending that unwinds any leftover complications in the story and usually leaves the reader with a sense of closure. Recognition and expectation of these common story parts aids comprehension.

Once the learner has been introduced to the written word and begins to recognize the connection between spoken (read aloud) and written words, comprehension of written material begins. At this point the home teacher can introduce comprehension activities for use with written materials. The context clue activities noted above are examples. The teacher can also teach comprehension by working on vocabulary in preparation for a reading; exploring the youngster's prior knowledge of the content of an upcoming reading selection;

providing non-reading experiences to expand that prior knowledge; working towards understanding abstractions and key concepts that will appear in a reading; focusing on differences between literal and figurative meaning; encouraging critical thinking and comprehension before, during, and after a reading; involving the child in interpretive activities which stem from a reading; conversing about the topic of a reading, and so on. Another effective comprehension activity is called "prediction." Based upon what has already happened in a reading, the learner anticipates what will happen next. Comprehension is emphasized because prediction is impossible without comprehension of what occurred in the story before the learner is asked to predict upcoming events.

Few reading materials include a wide enough array of comprehension activities, but through familiarity with methods such as those noted here, the home teacher can ensure the inclusion of these activities in reading instruction.

8. vocabulary development Vocabulary development is an important factor in reading comprehension. Vocabulary instruction may stem either from lists of words that are related to each other in meaning — unusual color words, nature words, words describing character traits, for example — or from lists of key words from upcoming readings. While both help expand a child's overall vocabulary, the latter is vital to his immediate need to comprehend what he reads. Prereading activities should almost always include vocabulary instruction, or at the least an informal, oral exploration of the child's familiarity with key words in the reading. This will allow the teacher to determine whether or not vocabulary instruction is needed.

With primary level children, vocabulary instruction may be entirely oral. With intermediate and older children, it should include listening, speaking, reading, and writing activities with an emphasis on vocabulary word *use*. As a result of such activities, a student should eventually internalize the words — own them, in effect.

Perhaps the best benefit of home-taught vocabulary lessons is the ease with which you and your children can orally practice the words. At home oral practice can begin informally, before actual vocabulary lessons, and continue endlessly in everyday conversation to ensure internalization.

9. sustained silent reading Much attention has recently been paid to the naturalness of silent reading in addition to the traditional reading aloud that has been done for years in schools. As a result, many schools now include periods of sustained silent reading. The period of sustained time is typically fifteen to thirty minutes. Surprisingly, even the youngest of children whose attention span would ordinarily average seven minutes can "read" silently for fifteen minutes, especially if allowed more than one book for each session.

Students benefit from the sessions in several ways: First, they experience *real* reading, rather than a reading lesson during this time. Second, reading for pleasure or for recreation is encouraged. Third, students are able to self-select the reading materials that interest them most. Fourth, a daily reading habit is engendered. Fifth, since everyone present reads during the SSR time, the teacher and any aides model reading behavior. Finally, because the SSR time is typically followed by a brief and informal sharing time during which students and teacher discuss what they have read, the focus remains with comprehension. Later, reading lesson activities may make use of the materials that are read during SSR time. Sustained silent reading time is not a reading lesson, *per se*, but is instead one segment of a child's overall reading instruction and practice. SSR can easily and informally become a part of a home-schooled child's reading education. It never by itself comprises a reading program but is used in combination with other approaches.

10. children's literature With an approach whose core materials are children's literature, decoding and comprehension are taught in connection with library books for children — storybooks primarily but also nonfiction. Some emphasis may be given to the qualities and elements of literature, such as characterization, plot, and conflict and to the building of a literary background in students. Also, of course, the learners would be developing a knowledge and appreciation of the literature of our culture and perhaps of other cultures as well. Unfortunately, many school reading programs neglect the use of children's literature or use it only for supplementary, spare-time reading. At home school children's literature could be utilized even to the extent of designing a literature-based reading program.

11. whole-language approach In great part child-directed, the whole-language approach involves children in experiment and experience with all sorts of written materials. This approach allows natural discovery of patterns and meanings and shapes and sounds of written language. Comprehension is emphasized. Task-by-task approaches to reading, such as phonics, are deemphasized. Included in a whole-language reading program might be combinations of the following: predictable stories (repeated language patterns or story lines allow for anticipation and prediction), much story reading and shared reading, sustained silent reading, language experience, reading writings that are found around us — signs, grocery containers, ads, menus, etc., reading writings that help us do things — recipes, directions, etc.

Proponents of intensive phonics instruction may elect to use several of the whole-language comprehension activities as complements to the phonics approach.

12. content area reading methods   Most educators recognize that reading doesn't stop with reading lessons, but extends into all aspects of a student's school day and beyond. For this reason teachers will sometimes "teach" reading comprehension during *content area classes* (history, biology, home economics, government, and many other classes aside from reading class or language-related classes). Comprehension activities such as those noted in *8* above are used.

Content area reading instruction may be crucial to a student's understanding of the material he is asked to read, particularly if the student is a poor reader. Yet such instruction is not often given in public school content area classes. At home school where the parents and children can engage in experiential activities and critical thinking activities most freely, the home teacher has the opportunity to provide much instruction that will enable her children to comprehend fully their content area readings.

13. fluency training   When students work on fluency in reading they are attempting to read efficiently, smoothly, and with relative speed. Training in fluency will involve silent reading and out loud or timed reading which enables the teacher to assess fluency. Such training will include activities that encourage efficient eye movement, regular practice activities, and may be computer-assisted.

14. There is an additional teaching method for reading instruction that is not listed above and which doesn't actually have a professional term applied to it. Strangely, it is often a neglected approach to reading instruction. However, it is a method that should *always* be used, whether in public, private, religious, alternative, or home school, and should be used in combination with any of the other methods. This method is simply ***reading*** — reading to your child, reading with your child, listening with your child to taped readings with book in hand, listening to your child read, shared reading with other children, encouraging your child to read independently, modeling independent reading — *every* day. Research tells us that the amount of time a child spends reading is directly reflected in his ability to comprehend what he reads, the size of his vocabulary, his reading fluency, and his achievement in reading. Nothing will help your child learn to read better nor more profoundly generate a marvelous, lifelong love for all kinds of literature than loads of daily reading.

❊❋

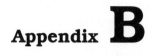
Effective Teaching

1. Engaged Time
2. Focus on Learner Outcomes
3. Teacher-Student Interaction
4. Individual Learner Levels
5. Teacher Expectation
6. Positive Feelings and Congenial Communications
7. Realia
8. Intrinsic Motivation
9. Conversation
10. Direct Instruction
11. Application, Analysis, Synthesis, Evaluation

Effective Teaching

"Effective teaching practices" has become a catch phrase for the results of a body of educational research conducted in recent years by various persons, groups, and institutions. These results are finally providing public school teachers and administrators with solid hooks upon which to hang "teaching effectiveness" tags. Although the results are only slowly being heeded by school personnel and in many instances are difficult to implement in the full classroom setting, the identified effective teaching practices are valid and reliable. Furthermore, although these studies were conducted on classrooms of children, I believe many of the resulting recommended teaching practices lend themselves more surely to home schooling than to public schooling.

Effective teaching research addresses the issues of teaching style and efficiency, teaching processes and dynamics, learning atmospheres, interpersonal relationships between teacher and student(s), and instructional management and organization — rather than methods of or approaches to teaching a subject. While I will not attempt here to cover the entire gamut of what are now called "effective teaching practices," I would like to present a few that you may find applicable to your home-school situation. You may also use this information to interject statements that reflect knowledge of effective teaching research into your paperwork and discussions as you seek approval, if necessary, for your home school or undergo a visitation by officials or accumulate records to demonstrate the quality of your home school. Further, of course, should public school officials speak of effectiveness research results, you will have gained bits of knowledge here that will enable you to understand their comments. What then does effective teaching research tell us?

1. While a teacher's management practices typically apply to a full classroom and school setting, there are components of instructional management that apply to home-school settings. Research on classroom management has demonstrated that in the public school setting precious little time is actually spent on instruction — an average of three to four hours out of a typical six- to seven-hour school day. Also, of that three or four hours the time during which any one student is "engaged" may be as low as one or two hours. This in itself is both startling and revealing. The most important factor derived from this information is that **a consistent relationship exists between how much students learn and the actual amount of time students are engaged in learning**. In other words, the teacher who manages the instructional day so that student engaged-time is at its maximum is the most effective teacher. This teacher's students learn more.

Because public school teachers have to spend time on routine matters such as taking roll and recording lunch money received, on transitional movement from one activity or one location in the building to another, on discipline and assistance for one student while others wait, and so on, they can increase student engaged-time only to a limited degree. At home school you'll have almost none of such routine, small student numbers nearly eliminate waiting, and transitional movement can easily become learning time. In addition, you have an entire day for learning rather than an allotted time period. This enables you to stretch far beyond the typical one to two or three hours of engaged student time, with either formal lessons or informal learning situations, or a blend. You can accomplish *engaged-time* in a single day during perhaps a one-hour sit-down lesson, a one-hour manipulative or experiential period, another sit-down lesson, a casual on-site exploration of a real setting, a session of cooking lunch together in the kitchen (math, health, etc.), a third sit-down lesson, an independent research activity, a joint experiment (science), a music lesson at the neighbor's house, a conversation during snack time (history, current events, children's literature, farming practices), a trip to the library, gardening together . . . on and on. Your days with your children can become the fullest of all possible learning days — simply, happily, effectively spilling over with engaged-time.

You will soon discover that time-related efficiency is a key factor. In other words, to be effective actual sit-down lessons mustn't be interrupted by Cousin Julie slipping in for coffee and a chat. An on-site or in-the-field learning session may be fun and casual but should remain focused on the process of gaining experience, skills and knowledge. Time to walk or ride to a piano lesson can be, if you make it, learning time. You might, for instance, use it to discuss the feelings of characters in a story read recently or to encourage your child to retell the story in sequence — both comprehension activities. You'll learn to smoothly move from activity to activity and to manage as much of each day's time as possible for engaged, although at times very informal, learning.

Because the effective management of time can be so freely achieved at home school, without institutional limitations and impositions, the potential for learning at home is extraordinary. As you design or contemplate your children's home-learning days, remember this first criteria for effective teaching — the effective management of (use of) time, which translates to the "maximizing of student *engaged* learning time."

2. One aspect of effective time management in teaching involves knowing what it is that the student is trying to learn or achieve. In public schools clearly-stated, specific learner objectives supposedly guide the direction of each lesson and unit of study. As a home teacher, you may be expected to record specific lesson objectives for submittal to officials, or you may be asked to keep a record available. You may be allowed to record general goals instead of specific objectives. Or, if your state allows more freedom to home schoolers, no written objectives or goals may be required.

In any of these cases, the research regarding the importance of **centering lessons on the desired learner outcomes** is applicable. It is directly applicable for formal lessons — there is little gained by performing an odd assortment of academic activities aimed in no consistent direction. Well, one thing may be gained: confusion. And another: a lack of forward growth. Generally, most of what humans learn they learn sequentially, whether in school or in life. The acquiring of human language serves as an example. As infants we first simply listen to the cadences, pitches, and tones of human sounds. Then we begin to attach emotions and eventually meaning to certain human sounds. Next we attempt to emulate some of the sounds. Eventually we use the sounds as whole sounds with meaning — words. Further along we notice that people spout strings of sound — phrases and sentences, and we begin to understand those strings. In time we too string together word sounds with meaning. Thus, the learning of language progresses and actually never ends all of our lives. The point here is that an obvious sequence of learning occurs. A consistent direction is followed, in this case, naturally.

As in this example, children are often quite able to establish clear and consistent direction for their learning by themselves. The teacher then becomes a facilitator. But facilitation will be best carried out if the teacher-facilitator helps students focus on the final outcome of the learning and on the sequence of skills that they are trying to learn in order to reach the outcome. Without thinking about it formally, we do help the toddler focus on the outcome of his language-learning efforts. We frequently repeat words to him, we tell him to "say daddy" and "say momma," we urge him to respond when we speak, and we talk and talk to him even though we have no idea what he understands, if anything. Helping a student focus on outcomes is similarly important during less natural and more formal learning, even when learning approaches are used that are holistic in nature rather than task-by-task oriented.

This is likewise true if the current learning taking place is experiential, like the building of a shed or the maintenance of a small business or farm; learning outcomes can be and should be identified by the home teacher. This will enable the teacher and learner to concentrate on steps and skills and knowledge and experiences that lead towards the outcome. It's just a matter of saying, "Hmmm. Johnny and Janey seem very interested in growing and selling trees. OK, that means they are going to try to establish and run a tree nursery business. That's the goal, the outcome. Now what *fields of study* and *sequence of steps* are involved in reaching that goal? What sorts of knowledge and skills must they gain in order to establish their nursery business? And how can I, as home teacher, facilitate their gaining that knowledge and those skills?" While the skills don't necessarily need to be taught or learned one-by-one, acknowledging your children's need to learn them will provide you with guidelines for helping them reach their goal. You will probably find that working out the details on paper at least in outline form will help you maintain the focus. Johnny and Janey will no doubt want to help you work out the details, maybe even work them out without you! This is just the sort of planning that any business person would carry out before beginning a business venture. However, in the case of you and your children, having less background knowledge will cause you to begin at a more basic step than the experienced business person.

As the project (unit of study) progresses, the goal serves as a guide. You and your children may discover that additions, deletions, and alterations may need to be made as your children learn and move towards their goal. You may find your children eager to jump right into the middle of a project — a naturally holistic approach — and that's fine, but as facilitator you can informally help them recognize where to begin, with what skills, how to backtrack when mistakes are made because basic skills weren't learned first, how to move ahead when skills have been mastered. All "lessons," all activities, all attempts to proceed will continue to be centered on reaching the identified learning outcome, a nursery business. Reliable educational research indicates that learning fashioned in such a way will be the most effective learning.

In addition, because the home teacher is so thoroughly involved in all aspects of the home learner's studies, the home teacher will be cognizant of current goals in all subject areas towards which her students are working. This awareness enables the home teacher to relate literally anything that occurs in the life of the learner to a learning goal. Thus, not only his formal and informal lessons, but nearly all of a home learner's life experiences can be directed, often quite subtly, at learning outcomes.

3. Throughout the progression of a learning project or other unit of study or single lesson, **the effective teacher is the highly interactive one.** Research studies show that the teacher who is physically and verbally interactive with his students during the learning process enhances his students' learning. He is not overpowering, but is a lively assistant to the learners — exchanging information, generating excitement, monitoring progress, drilling, questioning to stimulate thinking, praising, providing input and feedback, sharing, working alongside, modeling, guiding, focusing and refocusing. Through his direct, active involvement he keeps the learning pace brisk and the learning atmosphere exciting. Nowhere could this happen more assuredly that at home school. With a one-to-one or one-to-few student-teacher ratio and the energy and devotion of a parent teacher, this research-based effectiveness criteria — teacher interaction — can be well met at home school.

4. The effective teacher establishes **learning goals and objectives appropriate to the individual learner's level.** In other words, having assessed the student's abilities, formally or informally, and continuously monitored progress, the teacher focuses and helps the student focus on the next sequential steps, not on steps for which he has insufficient background or skill. The key is to challenge but not to frustrate. The frequently frustrated learner is likely to become a nonlearner. The challenged but successful learner will more likely become a lover of learning. A learner should consistently experience success at least 75 percent of the time during learning sessions in which the teacher plays an active part. A learner should consistently experience nearly 100 percent success during independent work. In other words, if a child is having a difficult and unsuccessful (less than 75 percent) learning experience with a certain set of activities, he is not equipped to handle those activities. Goals and objectives should be set at a more appropriate level for that child. However, *the expectation that he can and will eventually be successful at the higher level should be maintained.* Also, if a child is achieving 100 percent during interactive learning sessions with the home teacher, that child probably needs goals and objectives adjusted to a higher level.

Keep in mind, too, that sometimes high goals look deceptively difficult. The shed building project is an example. A couple of bright, well-schooled, high school home students who have never constructed any building may not be overwhelmed by the shed building project — it may not be too high a goal — if the students have the skills needed to approach the steps involved in completing the project. If they have the investigative skills necessary, for instance, to complete the initial planning steps, they will be able to successfully proceed, learning skills pretty much sequentially, until they are able to actually build the shed.

Since a home teacher guides nearly every learning experience of her children, she should be more closely in tune with each of her children's mastery levels in any one subject area than a public school teacher would be. Such close monitoring of progress should enable her to effectively and consistently establish learning goals and objectives that are well suited to her learner's skill levels. Experience as a home teacher will soon enable you to recognize your children's levels and to meet the effective teaching criteria of establishing appropriate goals and objectives for your children's lessons.

5. Expectation, as mentioned above, also plays a role in effective teaching. Studies have documented that **teacher expectation can lend powerful stimulation to student learning**. In effect, low expectation reaps low achievement and high expectation reaps high achievement, regardless of *known* student abilities. Whether at home school or public school, effective teachers set appropriate goals for their students and then consistently convey an optimistic, confident expectation for student success. This is easier done at home school where full-classroom management doesn't interfere with a teacher's acceptance of a child and of his ability. A bright child who is a discipline problem in a full classroom, for example, may be viewed as incapable of good performance by the teacher, which results in lowered academic expectation or an unwillingness to feel optimistic with regards to that child's academic performance. Similarly, a slower learner who has received negative feedback for his slowness may eventually exhibit self-deprecation and disinterest. These behaviors, in turn, cue the teacher to lower her expectation — unjustifiably. The "average" student, as a third example, may even be denied opportunities to participate in special interest classes and events or to enroll in college preparatory courses because she isn't *expected* to succeed. Public school teachers have a tendency to rely upon a child's past history in public school to determine the child's ability. Studies show that this reliance is erroneous. One such study, for example, demonstrated that when a teacher was informed that a group of previously low-performing students was a group of bright students, the teacher's expectations were set high and, lo and behold, the students' performance was high for the first time in their school lives.

Public school teachers often let grade and test records and comments from previous teachers also tell them what expectation levels they should address to each of their students. In contrast, the home teacher is likely to approach the whole notion of teaching his children with much enthusiastic expectation for their achievement.

6. Along with optimistic expectation, **effective teachers display positive feelings and engage in congenial communications with children**. In the effective teacher's dealings with children there is an absence of negative behavior. No belittling or berating or needling or hassling or embarrassing of children occurs. Children are trusted, supported and respected. Research has consistently revealed a negative relationship between student learning gains and any teacher behaviors that are derogatory to students. Effective teachers heed that research. A loving parent is much more likely to feel congenial towards her children as they learn than anyone else. Even if you are sometimes frustrated with snags in your children's progress, you are no more frustrated than a public school teacher would be, and probably less so considering your deep, personal desire to see your own children learn. Who more than a caring parent would consistently treat her young learner with trust, support, and respect?

7. Effective teaching includes realia. Manipulatives, demonstrations, experiments, exploration, field trips, resource persons — all sorts of sensory, experiential activities — can be continuously integral to learning. This is particularly important in science instruction in which experimentation clarifies what is being learned, but the use of realia is also highly effective in other subject areas. Through his own experimentation and exploration a child learns to trust himself as a capable learner, learns to question and innovate, learns with a free flow of enthusiasm, and discovers the benefits of industriousness. The foremost learning mode of young children, in particular, is manipulation, which suggests that much of any young child's learning should involve realia. The inclusion of realia is one of the greatest benefits of home schooling because realia is often so close at hand and because time can be so easily taken to open the home-school door and bring in items and people from the outside world or walk out into that world to learn.

8. Students learn best and maintain a love for learning when they are motivated intrinsically. Research tells us that long-term intrinsic motivation is not engendered through extrinsic rewards. In attempts to mold and control student behavior, public school teachers frequently offer tangible, extrinsic rewards (parties, snacks, free time, stickers, etc.). Such extrinsic rewards may result in desirable short-term behaviors. For example, whenever public school teacher Mr. Ross wants students to complete an assignment quickly, he offers bags of popcorn as a reward, and the students respond with fast work. However, as a sideline effect of this reward situation students will gradually become motivated to work fast only when popcorn or some other extrinsic reward is offered. Eventually, extrinsically rewarded students select easier learning tasks, utilize random guessing rather than logic in problem-solving activities, produce more stereotyped and less creative work, and are less likely to return to a task they once found interesting.

Research shows that students will be most motivated when they are consistently allowed to follow their own curiosities and enthusiasms into their learning world and to *feel for themselves* the excitement and joy and pride in learning. Your role is to encourage their excitement, joy, and pride. In addition, at home school you can ensure that extrinsic rewards for learning are simply not offered, so that your learners are allowed to become intrinsically, rather than extrinsically, motivated.

9. A learner's ability to successfully read, reason and understand are enhanced through much conversation. I once heard a principal counteract a school visitor's complaint about the noise in one classroom with this reply: "Ah, but such a wonderful noise . . . . the noise of learning." If such noise is in actuality conversation or discussion related to the subject matter, then indeed learning is enhanced by that noise. We know, for example, that reading comprehension is increased when students and teacher discuss background knowledge or issues and difficult word meanings before a reading, interrupt the reading to express reactions and to predict upcoming events, and after the reading reflect together upon interpretations and applications of what was read. For poor readers, in fact, reading-related discussions may be crucial to their comprehension. The positive effects of such conversations apply to all situations and subject area studies that require reading, reasoning and understanding.

In public schools noise is often toned down to maintain a quiet or studious atmosphere, and, of course, at times this is necessary. But it is not always academically productive. At home school conversation can not only be allowed, but stimulated and guided and participated in by the parent teacher who wants to let it become a learning tool. Research tells us that abundant conversation can, in fact, be a valuable and even vital learning tool.

10. Direct instruction increases student learning. Direct instruction occurs when a teacher explains to students exactly what they are expected to learn and when during instruction the teacher demonstrates or models the steps that lead toward achievement of the learning task. In other words, students need to know the goal, focus or direction of a sequence of learning steps before they attempt those steps. Also, demonstration and modeling enable students to more easily visualize their own potential and peak task performance. It seems apparent that home school offers a natural setting for demonstration and modeling and an opportunity to gear these elements to the individual student's next performance level or goal.

11. While memorization is an important learning tool because memorized information facilitates the learning of further information, **student achievement is improved when teachers design questions and lesson activities that encourage students to apply, analyze, synthesize, and evaluate** old and new information. Questions don't necessarily need answers and activities don't necessarily need to end in right vs. wrong finality in order to stimulate higher level thinking processes. It is the design of the questions and activities that stimulates thinking. While public school teachers are usually aware of the importance of such stimulation, they often find applying such questions and activities difficult for various reasons. At home, where you can be comfortable with predictions, estimates, wrong answers, varied ideas, contrasting reactions, experimentation, and innovation, you can freely encourage your children to use application, analysis, synthesis, and evaluation. You can also help your youngsters develop the ability to follow their thinking all the way through complex issues, projects, topics, happenings, and to produce involved and thorough responses and results. These abilities are also important to improved learning.

Become familiar with the above teaching practices. They represent the heart of effective practices research and offer you eleven keys to home-teaching success. Indeed, judging by our review of these results of effective teaching research to which our public schools now subscribe, and wisely so, home-school teaching has the potential for winning the gold medal in the effectiveness competition. Where indeed could these teaching effectiveness criteria be better met than at home school?

✻✻

Appendix **C**

The Lesson

Step 1	**Anticipatory Set**
Step 2	**Instruction**
Step 3	**Guided Practice**
Step 4	**Closure**
Step 5	**Independent Practice**

The Lesson

To familiarize you with the structure of what many educators consider a good lesson, I include below what is known as the "5-step lesson format," sometimes referred to as the "7-step format" or the "Madeline Hunter format." From this lesson format a home teacher can derive an acceptable design for written, daily or weekly lesson plans, as demonstrated in the "Lesson Planning" portion of Section Three. An understanding of the following 5-step lesson format should help you to write plans if you must that are acceptable to officials, or to write just sketchy plans but be able to discuss how they fit into 5-step lessons, or to recognize what public school officials are talking about should they refer to the 5-step plan or just to lesson plans in general. As we look at the 5-step format now, remember that you are not locked into using it for lessons or for lesson planning, unless required, of course, but that it does offer a viable design for good lessons.

We will again rely on the turtle lesson which was given in Section Three so you can relate the explanations below to the actual plans shown on pages 128 and 129.

5-Step Lesson Plan

Step 1 — Anticipatory Set (Serves as an introduction.)

> <u>The teacher engages the students' attention or participation</u> through an attention-getting activity aimed at arousing student interest in the subject of the lesson. Possibly the students themselves will become enthused in an area for study, thus creating a spontaneous anticipatory set.
>
> > Example: To draw attention and arouse interest, the teacher would take the children to watch a turtle in its natural habitat and elicit, as well as offer, numerous open-ended questions. The questions might be recorded for later reference.

The teacher states aloud the learning objective(s) of this lesson.

> Example: "Students, after learning about turtles, you'll be able to identify all of the parts of a turtle's body and tell how those parts are useful to him. You'll also be able to explain the turtle's life cycle and needs, food, dangers, reptilian characteristics, and habitat."

Then, she links the objective to the activities that will follow. She may have planned these activities herself or in cooperation with her children.

> Example: "To find out about turtle bodies and body functions we will read books, check encyclopedias, watch and listen to a demonstration by a biologist who knows a lot about turtles. We'll also examine turtles ourselves, paint a mural of a turtle in his habitat, and keep track of what we're learning on a large chart we will make."

Step 2 — Instruction

Information is provided from a combination of sources — by the teacher, a textbook, an expert, a close examination of the subject (turtle, in this case), a photograph, an experiment, etc.; or information is searched for and found in subject-specific books, dictionary, encyclopedias, children's educational magazines, textbooks, etc.

The teacher may model and assist book-research techniques, firsthand examination of the subject or photograph, listening, questioning, perhaps note taking during expert's presentation, subject-specific story reading if books are storybooks (primary level), and even textbook reading with note taking.

Throughout these instructional activities the teacher frequently asks questions or requests that certain tasks be performed that allow her to determine whether or not students are understanding the information. (Some call this "checking for understanding.") Also, the teacher and students regularly review what they've learned and try to identify what still needs to be learned.

Step 3 — Guided Practice

The teacher engages the students in <u>an activity through which they practice using the knowledge and skills they've gained</u>. She continues to provide information (for clarification now), to assist, and to check for understanding. She may summarize or elicit student summaries of the learned information.

Step 4 — Closure

The teacher engages students in <u>an assessment activity</u>, an activity through which she can determine how much of the learned information can be applied by individual students functioning on their own.

Those students who have difficulty here are given more instruction. Then they will be given another closure or assessment activity. Then they will go to Step 5.

Those who successfully completed the closure activity go immediately to Step 5.

Step 5 — Independent Practice

The <u>students engage in individual projects or activities</u>.

The teacher monitors, with little or no assistance, checking for students' demonstration of the learned information.

To finish this activity the teacher might orally ask for comments related to the procedures students followed in order to apply the learned information and complete the projects.

Typically such a lesson, which may, incidentally, take a few days to complete, is only one part of a unit of study which may take a few weeks to complete. In the case of the turtle, it might be a unit on reptiles, or perhaps in primary grades a unit on animals that carry their homes with them. Also, it is likely that at some later date a test will be given that will include the knowledge gained from this lesson as well as other lessons in the unit.

While lessons may be organized in other ways as well as with the 5-step format, and while some home schoolers may not believe lesson plans are necessary at all, many home teachers do find lesson plans useful or do need a plan design that will be acceptable to public school officials. You may be one of the latter two, and if so, you may want to rely on the above 5-step lesson format as you write your lesson plans.

✳✳

Glossary

Terms that make talking about education sound like gibberish are really few compared to the body of terms related to many other occupational fields, such as medicine or law. Nevertheless, the use of those terms arouses distress in many parents because education terms relate to an ongoing aspect of a child's daily life that parents are continually trying to understand. As a home-school parent you are likely to hear from school personnel or read in education-related documents many of the same terms that public school parents hear and read, and find the terms just as baffling. The glossary of terms below will help you understand the more commonly used of these education terms.

Several of the terms presented are specifically home-education terms, such as *activity day* and *assurances*. Most, however, refer to the field of education in a broader sense. Subject areas are included, such as *business education* and *language arts* so that those who are responsible for writing home-school curriculums will recognize which courses fall within each subject area category.

ability level The maximum level at which a child is believed able to perform successfully, due to intelligence and previous learning. (see also *expectation*)

absence (from home school) The nonparticipation by a child in any learning activity related to the child's home-school curriculum due to illness or other circumstances. This should not be confused with simply being away from one's actual home or normal instructional setting on an excursion which involves learning activities.

academic progress The movement by a child through a sequence of learning objectives in a curriculum as demonstrated by mastery of the skills and concepts involved.

accountability Teachers' ability to prove through testing that their students have mastered all or most of the material outlined in a curriculum. A term used by parents, educators and legislators to express a desire for greater and more concrete knowledge of what teachers are or are not accomplishing.

accreditation The official recognition of a school or college by an accrediting agency, such as the Northwest Association of Schools and Colleges or the National Council for Accreditation of Teacher Education. Such accreditation may or may not denote quality in the program or product, but is, nevertheless, considered essential by many educators.

achievement Mastery of learned skills and knowledge.

achievement test (see *standardized achievement test)*

ACT American College Testing Service — the college-entrance exam offered by this service, which tests a student's general knowledge and skills in English, math, social studies and natural science.

activity-centered learning (see Appendix A)

activity day The involvement of a home-school student in a recreational and/or learning experience outside of the usual home-school setting, often in consort with other home-schooling students. (see also *field trip)*

administrator A person who administers a school or school district, or has particular administrative responsibilities within either, such as a superintendent, a principal, or vice principal.

affidavit A written statement made to an authorized official which has the status of having been made under oath.

age-appropriate curriculum Learning objectives that a student will typically master at a particular age based upon normal intellectual, emotional and physiological development. Example: Children normally do not fully understand the concept of cause and effect until they are beyond the ages of primary students; likewise with the development of sufficient hand-eye coordination to write within narrow lines. What constitutes "normal" in the case of age-appropriate curriculum may not be normal for your child or dozens of other children, but, nevertheless, age-appropriateness is often expected in home-school curriculums.

alternative education Schooling options other than public schools. Those schools identified by such labels as *private, community, Christian, parochial, alternative,* and *home school.*

alternative school A school established by a private group or individual as an alternative to public education. A private school which typically embraces an educational philosophy and instructional methods that differ from those of public education, and which usually maintains low or non-existent tuition charges.

annual calendar A record of the days that a home school will be in session during a given academic year; includes beginning date, vacation days, and closing date as well as in-session days.

annual evaluation A compilation of the data available on what a student has learned during a given home-school year. Such information may take the form of standardized achievement test results, other written work, teacher observations, grades for work finished during the term, completed projects, observations by others.

In *special education*, this term refers to a formal assessment of a special education student's progress toward completing the objectives of a specific individual education plan (IEP).

anticipatory set (see Appendix C)

appeal process Steps available to a parent whose proposal for a home-school program has been denied initial approval. If the original proposal went to a school superintendent, an appeal process may involve the presentation of the proposal to the local school board or committee; if the denial came from the school board, an appeal may be possible to the state superintendent of instruction or the governing body of the state department of education. Finally, courts may be involved. The procedures for an appeal process vary by state.

art education Instruction in and practice with colors, depth perception, shapes, size relationships, picture composition, art mediums, art appreciation and history, and so on.

assessment of progress (see *progress assessment*)

assurances Typically a signed agreement which states that a home-schooling parent is complying with all state requirements for home schools.

attendance register/record A dated grid on which are denoted the days during which a school is in session and the days of attendance and absence of each enrolled student.

baccalaureate degree (see *bachelor's degree*)

bachelor's degree A degree awarded by a college or university to students who have completed a specific course (roster) of study, typically involving four years of academic work.

basic education (basic skills) Core courses or subjects taught in a school, such as reading, language, math, social studies, and science; and basic or common skills within those core subjects, such as addition, subtraction, division, and multiplication in math.

burden of proof The responsibility of a home-schooling parent to maintain and/or provide those records and documents necessary to demonstrate compliance with a given state's statutes and regulations dealing with home schooling.

business education Traditionally instruction in the skills associated with office work such as typing, shorthand, business English, office machines, bookkeeping, accounting, marketing, computers in business, and additional business-related courses. Business education courses may come under the umbrella of "vocational education." At home school experiential entrepreneurship may be the vehicle for business education.

calendar (see *annual calendar*)

career education Instruction about the world of work that typically includes job categories, training requirements, salaries and working conditions, career paths, and the choices involved in career decision-making.

case law Legal decisions rendered in courts at various levels of our judiciary system that may set precedents for findings in similar, subsequent cases. Case law resulting from home-school litigation may affect home-schooling procedures within the state where the legal proceedings took place.

certificate of exemption A document which declares a child's official exemption from compulsory attendance in a public school.

certification The formal licensing of an individual to teach or perform other professional duties assigned to school personnel. Certification may be for various periods of time, and is usually granted with endorsements in specific areas; e.g., elementary, high school science, K-12 counselor, principal, etc.

certified consultant A state-certified teacher who assists a home-schooling parent in performing various aspects of the home-schooling process, such as planning a curriculum and conducting an annual student evaluation. A certified consultant may or may not be required by a state's home-school statutes and regulations.

Chapter 1 A federally funded compensatory program for disadvantaged children designed to help them improve their academic performance; a remedial reading or remedial math program to which low-achieving students are assigned. Chapter 1 regulations require local school districts to offer similar services to any private schools located within school district boundaries.

child-directed learning (see Appendix A)

child study team (CST) A group consisting of a child's teacher(s), principal, parent(s) and one or more special education personnel (teacher, school psychologist, etc.) who jointly make decisions about the instructional program of an exceptional child in a manner specifically prescribed by federal law. (see also *IEP* and *Public Law 94-142*)

children's literature (see Appendix A)

chronological age A child's *actual* age in years and months.

citizenship Part of a school's curriculum, sometimes of an unwritten, informal curriculum, and involving the inculcation of particular values in children. Examples include learning to be considerate of other children, to play cooperatively, to respect adults, to contribute to group efforts, to develop a sense of one's role in American society, and so on.

class schedule A listing of times during the instructional day during which given subjects will be taught; e.g., 9:00 - 10:00 reading, 10:00 – 10:30 arithmetic.

closure (see Appendix C)

competency testing The testing of students to see if they have achieved minimal skill levels. Sometimes used to screen students for graduation diplomas. (see also *teacher competency test.*)

competency-based instruction (see Appendix A)

compliance The condition of having met any and all requirements for state or local school board approval of your home-school plan. Also, continuing to meet those requirements throughout your home-school year.

compulsory education The legal requirement in all states that children of certain ages be enrolled in an approved school program.

computer literacy The ability to understand basic computer terminology and to utilize a computer in performing rudimentary tasks, such as word processing.

computer-assisted instruction (see Appendix A)

consultant (see *certified consultant*)

consumer education Instruction in the skills and knowledge necessary to be an informed consumer in our economic system. Examples include critical analysis of advertising, understanding consumer credit, and savings and investment alternatives.

content area reading methods (see Appendix A)

core curriculum The basic subjects, including reading, language and math, and in most cases also science and social studies.

correspondence study A learning situation in which teacher and student are physically separated, with an exchange of written interactions (lessons, completed assignments) typically sent through the mail. The student mostly works independently, but in the case of home schoolers may have his at-home teacher assist him. Correspondence study is in a process of change with the advent of video instruction, electronic mail systems, and instruction via live teleconferencing and videoconferencing.

course syllabus (see *syllabus*)

creative writing Writing instruction involving various forms of written composition, such as language experience stories, expository compositions, short stories, poems, and many others. (see also Appendix A)

criterion-referenced test (CRT) An achievement test with outcomes described only in terms of the number of correct responses each student makes. CRT's enable an instructor to determine whether a student has adequately mastered a given set of skills. CRT's do not provide for comparisons of your child's achievement with others taking the same test.

CST (see *child study team*)

curriculum A description of the content of an instructional program stating what a student is to be taught. Usually in roster or outline form, including broad learning goals and specific learning objectives, and often prefaced by educational philosophies. There can actually be several different curricula at work in an educational setting, ranging from the official curriculum described above, to the classroom curriculum which includes what the teacher actually teaches, to the hidden curriculum which includes lessons taught unconsciously through the actions of teachers and the structure of the learning environment itself.

curriculum fair A conference or other gathering where curriculum and instructional materials are displayed, instructional equipment is demonstrated, and other teaching aids and ideas are presented.

curriculum guide A book or notebook, often prepared by a school district, department of education or publishing company, which contains outlines of learning objectives that are to be taught in one or more subject areas. (see also *curriculum*)

curriculum mastery The development by a student of a high degree of competence in the skills contained in a given curriculum and of an understanding of the relationships among information in that curriculum that transcends rote learning of facts.

department of education The branch of state government that licenses teachers, dispurses state funds to school districts, administers federal education programs within a state, and oversees the implementation of state laws governing education.

diagnostic/prescriptive teaching (see Appendix A)

diploma Formal recognition by an educational institution that a student has completed a particular course of study. Such recognition takes two forms: the actual paper document and, more importantly, an official record of program completion in the form of a transcript available in the school's files.

direct instruction (see Appendix A; see also Appendix B)

documentation A written record generally considered as proof to an authority. In the case of home schooling, such items as an attendance register, curriculum outlines, and test results that may constitute proof that a parent is meeting state statutes regulating home instruction.

education journals Periodical publications that address issues in education as their primary subject matter. Some education journals are scholarly publications for professionals (e.g.: *Harvard Education Review, Reading Research Quarterly, School Psychology*), while others contain information that is of interest to both education professionals and parents in differing degrees (e.g.: *Phi Delta Kappan, The Reading Teacher, Instructor*). Many of the latter offer activities and ideas directly applicable to one's home teaching.

educationally-deprived child A child who has had fewer than the "normal" pre-school or out-of-school learning experiences and as a result is not as prepared for public school as other children. Socioeconomic class and culture often are factors behind this educational concept.

emergency certificate A temporary license to teach granted to an individual who does not meet the requirements in a given state for a regular certificate. An emergency certificate is usually granted for a limited time period, such as one year.

emotionally-disturbed child A child whose state of emotional health requires special instruction or other services to enable him to achieve an acceptable level of academic progress.

engaged-time (see *on-task time*; see also Appendix B)

enrollee Any student who is regularly attending a given school. In the case of home schooling, your children become enrollees of your home school (or, in some instances, your private school).

equivalent instruction A term included in several states' home schooling statutes to indicate that a home-school curriculum must be closely correlated with the public school curriculum in the respective states. However, the exact meaning of *equivalent instruction* in any one state may be subject to interpretive review during home-school litigation occurring in that state.

ESL English as a second language. Instruction in the English language for students whose first or primary language is not English.

evaluation of students Testing or other observational data-gathering that enables a teacher or other school personnel to determine a child's ability or achievement level. (see also *annual evaluation*)

exceptional child A child who is either gifted or handicapped to the extent that modifications of the school's regular instructional program are necessary for the child to develop educationally to maximum potential.

exemption An officially granted waiver from compulsory attendance in a public school.

expectation The level of academic or other achievement you convey to your child as acceptable or praiseworthy; the level of achievement conveyed as acceptable or praiseworthy to individual students by a teacher. In either case, a likely unintentionally imposed cap on levels of formal learning. (see also Appendix B)

extracurricular School activities offered in addition to instruction in the regular curriculum. (e.g., production of a play, sports activities)

extrinsic reward A reward that is external to an activity but which is provided for engaging in that activity. The reward may be contingent upon the length or quality of the performance. (e.g., a child receives a grade of "A" on a math test; a child receives a smiley sticker for following the rules)

field trip A brief trip, usually a few hours, during which students leave their home-school building to learn in another setting. (see also *activity day*)

fine arts education Instruction in courses such as music, painting, creative writing, dance, art or music or literature appreciation, and so on.

functional illiteracy (see *illiteracy*)

GED The General Education Development exam taken by unenrolled high school aged students or adults who hope to earn a sufficient score to be awarded a high school equivalency diploma by a state department of education.

gifted and talented student A student whose learning ability in one or more academic areas is sufficiently exceptional to require special instruction, or whose talent in a particular field is determined to be such that special training is warranted. Each state and/or school district utilizes its own criteria for defining this term, such as a minimum score on a specific I.Q. test and demonstrated academic achievement in the top three percent of students.

grade equivalent score (GE) (see "Annual Evaluation" in Section Three.)

grade placement End-of-the-year placement of a student in his next year's grade level.

guided practice (see Appendix C)

handicapped child A child who requires special educational services to enable him to reach his educational potential as determined by a child-study team (CST). Further, a child who meets one of several definitions of the handicapped (e.g., mentally retarded, emotionally disturbed, learning disabled).

health education (see *safety/health education*)

home economics Courses involving homemaker skills and sometimes parenting skills, such as cooking, sewing, nutrition awareness, child growth and development and interior home design.

home school plan A statement or notice or declaration of intent or some other form of home-school program proposal or design which explains and describes one's at-home education program. The plan will include any combination of segments required by the laws and procedures of the individual home schooler's state. (See also *statement of intent*)

home-bound student A student who is unable for health reasons to attend public school and so is taught at home either by a parent or by a certified educator.

humanities Courses such as classical literature, languages, fine arts, philosophy, and others which are not considered as *the sciences*.

IEP (see *individual education program*)

individual education program A formal, annual statement of a special education student's instructional goals, objectives, and the activities planned to achieve these objectives. The IEP is formulated by a child study team, requires parental approval (with rare exception), and contains means for evaluation of the plan's success. (see also *CST* and *Public Law 94-142*)

illiterate, illiteracy Inability to read or write. Various descriptors suggest degrees of illiteracy. *Functional illiteracy*, for example, indicates that a person is unable to function safely, productively, and with his own welfare assured, because of his inability to read and write.

independent practice (see Appendix C)

independent work Work completed alone, or mostly alone, by a student. (e.g., workbook pages completed by a student at her own desk with little or no assistance). (see also *independent practice* in Appendix C)

individualized instruction (see Appendix A)

industrial arts Courses such as woodworking, auto mechanics and metal work.

instructional level The level at which a student is able to understand new material being presented.

instructional time In-class time during which students actually receive instruction.

integrated subject areas (see Appendix A)

intelligence A student's capacity for learning, understanding, reasoning or thinking critically. A student's score on an I.Q. test.

intermediate Grades four, five, and six.

intrinsic reward A reward that is inherent in engaging in an activity itself. (e.g., A child feels *pleasure* from successfully solving a riddle. A child feels *satisfaction* for having successfully completed a science experiment. A child feels *pride* in having won a race.) (see also Appendix B)

junior high Grades seven and eight, and sometimes nine.

language arts Spelling, grammar, creative writing and related areas. Literature and reading are also subcategories of language arts, but are sometimes listed separately.

language experience approach (see Appendix A)

learning center (see Appendix A)

learning community All the human resources that a child can utilize in becoming educated, including parents, grandparents, siblings, neighbors, community elders, organization leaders, and peers.

learning disability A malady ascribed to children placed in special education who are not academically successful in school, do not meet the definitions of other special education categories, and whose learning problems are ostensibly not attributable to differences in language or culture.

learning goals The desired, broad outcomes of a child's lessons. Usually specific knowledge and skills are needed in order for a child to achieve his learning goals.(see also Appendix B)

learning objectives Specific skills taught to a student which he needs to master as a step towards a broader learning goal. It is generally thought that each lesson taught should be geared towards one or more identifiable learning objectives.

learning time (see *instructional time*)

lesson plan A teacher's written design for a lesson; usually includes one or more learning objectives. Typically teachers write, in advance, lesson plans in each subject for an entire school week. (see also Appendix C)

linguistics (see Appendix A)

literate, literacy Able to read and write at least at a functional level.

litigation Addressing an unsettled issue in the court system through a legal proceeding.

log A written, dated record of events.

manipulative learning (see Appendix A)

mastery learning (see Appendix A)

mathematics Courses which involve the recognition and manipulation of numbers, from counting through division, fractions, and such secondary courses as algebra, geometry, trigonometry, and pre-calculus.

mental age The age of a child stated in terms of his mental capacity, and determined by comparing his knowledge and abilities with the age at which the average child has the same knowledge and abilities. Thus a child with a chronological age of 8.5 might have a mental age of 7.0 or 9.3 or some other mental age.

mentally retarded Children whose general intellectual functioning is in the lowest 2.5 percent of their age group as measured by an I.Q. test and who have been unable to learn expected academic and social skills. It is further necessary that these deficits are not due to cultural or linguistic differences.

middle school Typically a school which includes only grades four, five, and six.

monitor A person who serves as a noninstructional overseer of the activities of students, such as a teacher's aide or parent volunteer in a public school classroom.

motivation system Means by which a teacher or a school staff attempts to control students' behavior, including learning behavior. In public schools extrinsic reinforcers are typically used, such as smiley stickers (the new gold stars), parties and special events, grades, threats, loss of privileges, and suspension. Research indicates that intrinsic rewards (felt within the child and inherent within the activity) are more effective motivators for the development of long-term patterns of behavior. (see also Appendix B)

music education Instruction involving music for pleasure, recognition of musical instruments, harmony, note-reading, music appreciation and history, and so on.

National Teacher Exam A standardized test of basic English and mathematical skills and of knowledge of the field of education used by some states in the process of teacher certification.

networking The sharing of information about home schooling through informal written or spoken contact among individuals or groups. Newsletters, support group meetings, one-on-one exchanges, consultations, referrals, shared resources or resource information, and joint activity days and field trips are a few networking activities.

nonpublic education All education programs which do not receive local, state or federal government funds.

normal curve equivalent (NCE) (see "Annual Evaluation" in Section Three.)

normed test A standardized test for which there are available past-performance averages which enable a child's test scores to be compared to those of other children who took the same test.

notice of test selection A statement made by a home-schooling parent to a local school district or state department of education naming the specific standardized achievement test that will be utilized as part of one or more students' annual evaluation process.

occupational education (see *vocational education*)

official curriculum Written learning goals and objectives, usually listed by subject area, recommended or mandated by a school district's board of education for teaching in its district.

official policy Written policies officially adopted by a district school board.

on-task time In-school time during which a student is actually engaged in learning activities. The amount of engaged or on-task time varies considerably in different classrooms, and studies show a direct relationship between the amount of on-task time and the amount of learning that takes place. (see also Appendix B)

Our Nation at Risk The report prepared by the National Commission on Excellence in Education and presented to the American people in 1983. The report heavily criticized the condition of public education in the United States and fueled the ongoing criticism of public education that had been occurring in the public media.

parent rights Legally mandated rights that parents have with respect to the public schools, such as the right to review their children's school records or to have a child evaluated for special education services. Sometimes used in reference to other than legally mandated rights by various parent advocacy groups.

parent-principal conference A formal meeting between a school's principal and a child's parent(s) for the purpose of resolving a problem that exists in the child's educational program which the parent is unable to resolve at a lower level of the educational hierarchy. In the case of home schooling, a parent-principal conference may involve such matters as a child's participation in some extra-curricular activity or making use of a school resource like the library.

parent-teacher conference A meeting between one or both parents and a child's teacher. Typically an initial parent-teacher conference is scheduled by school personnel at the end of the first quarter of the school year (and sometimes subsequent quarters) for the purpose of presenting an overview of a child's instructional program and indicating the child's progress therein.

parochial school A school operated by a religious organization.

percentile score (see "Annual Evaluation" in Section Three.)

permanent file A complete record of a child's educational progress maintained throughout a child's school years. This file includes yearly grades in all courses, attendance records, and achievement test scores. A copy of a child's permanent file is normally transferred with the child from school to school.

phonics (see Appendix A)

physical education Courses in which students learn about and practice physical exercises, recreational games and sports, teamwork, and sportsmanship.

physical therapist School or other professional personnel who treat children's physical maladies or deficiencies through special exercises.

placement test A form of achievement test administered to a child in order to help make a decision about which grade level, reading program, or other instructional setting will best suit his educational needs.

policy manual A notebook containing a school district's official policies. (see also *official policy*)

portfolio A file folder containing examples of a student's work and also perhaps of written assessments.

prescriptive teaching (see *diagnostic/prescriptive teaching*)

primary Grades kindergarten, one, two, and three.

principal A school's chief administrative officer who is responsible for the overall operation of the school. This responsibility includes the supervision of all personnel, budget and physical plant management, instructional leadership, and community relations.

principle approach (see Appendix A)

private school A school established and operated by a private group which typically espouses a common educational philosophy and/or value system. A Christian school is one example. In some states, a single-family home school may be considered a private school.

programmed learning (see Appendix A)

progress assessment An evaluation of a student's progress in a particular educational subject, program or setting. Such an assessment may include formal testing, review of past work, observations and/or interviews, and other means of assessment.

Public Law 94-142 The Education for All Handicapped Children Act passed by Congress in 1975. This legislation was designed to ensure that handicapped students throughout the nation received appropriate educational services. It provided large sums of money to states to accomplish this, while requiring states to prove that they were doing so.

quarter One-fourth of a school year. The typical time when schools report to parents the educational progress their children are making in an instructional program. In a few states home schoolers are expected to submit quarterly progress reports.

raw score (see "Annual Evaluation" in Section Three.)

readiness A young child's ability to successfully deal with kindergarten and first grade academics and socialization, or any child's ability and inclination to successfully learn to read or to learn other skills at a particular age.

reading Instruction involving learning activities in phonics and other means of word attack, comprehension, literature, fluency, and so on. (see also Appendix A)

reading comprehension (see Appendix A)

reading fluency (see Appendix A)

register (see *attendance register/record*)

religious conflict exemption An official exemption from compulsory attendance in a public school granted to a child for religious reasons.

remedial reading Special instruction in reading provided to children who are decidedly below average in reading ability for their age or grade placement. Remedial reading is necessitated by the graded-classroom approach to instruction. Research shows that short term reading gains attributed to remedial reading instruction often wash out over several month's time. Research also indicates that the best remediation may simply be great amounts of reading and listening to stories and other types of writing being read by others.

report card An individual report provided by a school to both its students and their parents in an effort to indicate the degree of academic and social success being achieved by the student in question. The grades and other indicators of such achievement can only be correctly interpreted by understanding the criteria a given teacher uses in completing the report card.

resource room A classroom where a *special education* teacher provides supplemental instruction primarily to *learning disabled* and other handicapped children. A student's visits to the resource room may be for instruction in one or more subjects (typically reading and math) and often vary in prescribed length from twenty minutes to two hours.

retention Requiring a student to repeat a year of schooling at the same grade level due to the student's lack of academic progress and hence lack of preparation for the next grade. Colloquially termed "flunking."

rote learning Learning by memorization.

safety/health education Instruction including such topics as personal hygiene, nutrition, traffic awareness, bicycle safety, and poison awareness.

SAT Scholastic Aptitude Test A verbal and mathematical aptitude test given to pre-college students to determine their potential for college success.

satellite school A school which enrolls home students as satellite students. Satellite school services may be minimal and primarily provide a legal option for otherwise illegal home schoolers or cover for home schoolers who want to avoid standardized achievement tests. On the other hand, the services may be many and perhaps include correspondence courses, record-keeping services, consultations, materials, and other services.

school board Elected, non-paid officials who are responsible for the overall operation of a school district. May also be referred to as a board of directors or board of trustees. A school board's main responsibilities include the establishment of general policies, the hiring of a district superintendent, and budgetary decisions. School district employees then implement school board policies in the day-to-day operation of the schools within the district.

school counselor A certified school employee with special training who provides professional counseling services to students. Such services can range from giving students guidance regarding vocational choices to assisting them with both short-term and long-term emotional problems.

school officials Local and state school board members, state department of education administrative personnel, local school district

311

superintendents, assistant superintendents, principals, vice principals. Some states also have county level school officials, such as a county superintendent.

school psychologist A certified educational specialist with concentrated training in the field of psychology. The individual most responsible for a student's evaluation for special education through the use of I.Q. and other tests.

school suppliers Companies that sell textbooks and workbooks, record forms, subject specific equipment and materials, and other school products. These companies vary in size and may support one or more curricular areas. Some cater exclusively to the needs of home-schooling parents.

school year The period of time between the first and last days of a designated block of instructional time. During this time period a student supposedly learns the outlined content of a particular curriculum. For example, third grade reading, third grade math, etc., are covered during the third grade school year. Each state has designated a minimum number of days that comprises a full school year.

sciences Biology, physics, chemistry, astronomy, geology, earth science and other common science courses at levels of difficulty appropriate to the ages/grades of the students being taught.

scope and sequence chart A chart accompanying a curriculum or a textbook series which shows the sequence of learning goals and skills that are covered in the curriculum or series.

secondary (high school) Grades nine, ten, eleven, and twelve. In some school districts grades seven and eight are also designated as *secondary.*

semester One-half of a school year. In high school, some courses of study last just one semester.

sequential curriculum (or sustained curriculum) A curriculum listing learning goals and objectives in order of increasing difficulty.

sight word approach (see Appendix A)

slow learner A student whose academic progress is slower than that of his peers. Such a designation may be appropriate in only one subject, such as arithmetic, or in all subjects. A student may make slow progress for a number of reasons besides ability, reasons such as language barriers, lack of background information, inexperience, or poor prior instruction.

social behavior A student's interactions with his peers and with school personnel in the normal routine of a school day. In the case of home-schooled children, peers would include other children with whom a child interacted, and school personnel would include the general adult community that comprises the child's extended learning community.

social progress The development of age-appropriate individual and group interaction skills.

social promotion The passing of a student from one grade to another even though the student has not mastered the year's curriculum. This action is frequently taken due to a student's chronological age and sometimes size, limited probability of academic success through retention, or the potential emotional damage resulting from retention.

social studies Courses involving history, government, sociology, world cultures, current events, citizenship, and so on.

socialization Development of social characteristics such as cooperation, participation, a sense of brotherhood, and interpersonal behavior.

special education A program in each public school of legally-mandated educational services for students who are defined as learning handicapped, mentally-retarded, emotionally disturbed, learning disabled, etc. Special education also includes special services for gifted and talented students when such services are provided. (see also *Public Law 94-142*)

special services Education-related services provided to children in addition to the regular curricular and extra-curricular instructional program. These services are often designed to enable a student to participate successfully in the regular program, always encompass what is otherwise referred to as special education, and may include additional services such as counseling, physical therapy, and speech therapy.

speech therapist School or other professional personnel who treat children with speech defects or provide other special education programs for them.

standard error of measurement (see "Annual Evaluation" in Section Three.)

standardized achievement test A test which measures academic achievement, is given under the same conditions in each testing (hence is *standardized*), and which has *norms* which enable a student's test results to be compared with those of other children.

state commissioner of education The executive officer of a state's department of education responsible to a state board of education. May be referred to as state superintendent of schools.

state board of education A group of citizens usually appointed by a governor which provides policy direction for a state's commissioner of education (or similar administrator) and hence a state's department of education in implementing the educational program of a state government.

state department of education The division of state government which administers public education in a given state. Responsibilities typically include the licensing (certification) of all professional education personnel, managing the state's funding of school districts, serving as a flow-through agency for federal funds, establishing recommended state curricula, and providing technical assistance to school boards and district personnel.

statement of intent Also called *declaration of intent, notice of intent,* and *home-school proposal,*. A statement of intent is in effect an enrollment document, enrollment, that is, in a home school. It also often includes a home-school program plan and other requirements. Statement of intent and home-school proposal formats and contents vary from state to state.

student placement Placement of a student in a particular classroom, with a particular teacher, or at a given grade level.

student rights Legal and other rights guaranteed to all students by the Constitution and federal statutes, by state laws governing public education, and sometimes by school district policies.

success/failure ratio The percent of problems or questions which a student completes successfully while engaging in guided practice or independent work. If lessons are at appropriate levels, a student will experience at least 75% success during guided practice and close to 100% success during independent work.

superintendent The executive officer of a school district, responsible for the administration of the district's entire education program. The superintendent is hired by and responsible to the district school board.

support group A group of parents who home school their own children or are otherwise involved in the home-schooling movement and who provide encouragement and assistance to each other and to newcomers interested in learning more about home schooling. (see also *networking*)

sustained silent reading (see Appendix A)

syllabus A description of a course of instruction that includes a statement of the course goals, learning objectives, the general topics covered, materials to be utilized, teacher expectations with respect to assignments, grading procedures, assignment due dates and test dates, and time periods for various other instructional activities.

teacher competency test A standardized test administered to a teacher or potential teacher to determine whether or not the individual in question possesses skills and knowledge thought essential to successful teaching. Many present teacher competency tests are nothing more than basic skills tests at approximately an 8th to 10th grade level.(see also *National Teacher Exam*)

teacher expectation (see Appendix B)

teacher qualifications The requirements in a particular state for the issuance by the state's department of education of a certificate (or license) to teach in a public school. Teacher qualifications usually include at a minimum the possession of a bachelor's degree and the completion of a teacher training program at a college or university. Teacher qualifications for home schoolers vary greatly and in most states do not mandate teacher certification.

teacher-student interaction (see Appendix B)

teacher's manual/guide A book that accompanies student textbooks and which tells the teacher how to teach the material in the textbook, and sometimes includes supplementary activities.

test format The manner in which the questions on a test are presented. Examples: essay questions, multiple choice, true or false, select the one answer that is not correct, etc. The manner in which a student indicates an answer is also part of the test format. For example, completing an answer may involve circling a number or letter, checking a box, filling in a space. Students familiar with a test's format prior to taking the test tend to achieve higher scores than students with equal knowledge of the test's content but who are unfamiliar with the test format.

test management guide A handbook test publishers make available to schools who use their tests. Includes information regarding testing environments, test readiness activities, test item formats, and outlines of test content.

testing service An organization or individual authorized to administer certain tests. Some states require home schoolers to have their children take an annual achievement test and to have this test administered by an authorized party such as someone from a testing service.

textbook series A series of books in one subject area, one text for each ability level or grade level, published by a single publishing company. Students progress from text to text as they move from grade to grade.

thematic lessons (see Appendix A)

traditional instruction (see Appendix A)

transcript A record of classes completed, credits earned, grades achieved and diplomas or degrees awarded to an individual by an educational institution such as a high school or college.

transition time The time required in a classroom to move from one learning activity to another. A part of noninstructional time.

umbrella school (see *satellite school*)

unit study (see Appendix A)

unofficial policy Customary practices established informally by school personnel and carried on as tradition.

vocational education Courses intended to prepare students to enter vocations. Often include business courses and industrial arts courses.

waived regulation The exempting of an individual or individuals from the requirements of a regulation. For instance, in the case of home schoolers, sometimes teacher certification requirements can be waived.

whole-language approach (see Appendix A)

WISC The Wechsler Intelligence Scale for Children. The most commonly used intelligence test in public schools.

word attack (see Appendix A)

writing process (see Appendix A)

Index of Checklists,
Worksheets and Samples

State Index

General Index